UNFINISHED
CONVERSATIONS

PAUL SULLIVAN

UNFINISHED CONVERSATIONS

MAYAS AND FOREIGNERS BETWEEN TWO WARS

UNIVERSITY OF CALIFORNIA PRESS
Berkeley and Los Angeles

University of California Press

Berkeley and Los Angeles, California

First Paperback Printing 1991

Copyright © 1989 by Paul Sullivan

Maps copyright © 1989 by Anita Karl

Owing to limitations of space, acknowledgments of permission to reprint
previously unpublished material will be found on page 269.

Library of Congress Cataloging-in-Publication Data

Sullivan, Paul R.

Unfinished conversations : Mayas and foreigners between two wars /
Paul Sullivan. – 1st pbk. print.

    p.   cm.

Reprint. Originally published: New York : Knopf, 1989.

Includes bibliographical references and index.

ISBN 0-520-07244-8

1. Mayas – Government relations.   2. Mayas – Politics and
government.   3. Yucatán (Mexico : State) – History – Caste War,
1847–1855.   4. Visitors, Foreign – Yucatán Peninsula.
5. Anthropologists – Yucatán Peninsula.   6. Indians of Mexico –
Mexico – Quintana Roo (State) – Politics and government.   I. Title.

[F1435.3.P7S85 1991]   90-22458

303.48′2′089974 – dc20   CIP

1 2 3 4 5 6 7 8 9

Contents

Illustrations

Acknowledgments

THE FIELD RESEARCH upon which this book is partly based, conducted between 1978 and 1986, was supported by a Fulbright-Hays Grant for Study Abroad; a National Science Foundation Graduate Fellowship; a grant from the Joint Committee on Latin America of the Social Sciences Research Council and the American Council of Learned Societies, with funds provided by the National Endowment for the Humanities, the Ford Foundation, and the Andrew W. Mellon Foundation; and by a Tinker Foundation Postdoctoral Fellowship awarded by the Mesoamerican Ecology Institute of Tulane University. A Mellon Postdoctoral Fellowship granted by the Center for the Humanities at Cornell University supported the writing of early drafts of this book.

My debts to individuals are many. Alfonso Villa Rojas, who conducted the earliest and finest ethnographic research in the area about which I write, kindly lent his good offices with old friends in the region so that my wife and I could find a modicum of acceptance in the village I had chosen to study. He also permitted my extensive use of his unpublished diaries, field notes, and letters. Other Mexican colleagues, including Arturo Warman, Roberto Melville, Mireya Rubio, and Patricia Torres, lent logistical and intellectual support at trying moments in the research. Among American colleagues, I owe thanks foremost to Sidney Mintz and Christine Gray for their crucial support and criticism, and to Victoria Bricker, who generously lent me her copies of the British Foreign Office documents cited in this work.

Finally, this book is dedicated to my late wife, June Marchi, who shared with me many of the adventures and more than her share of the hardships of fieldwork.

A Note on Names and Foreign Words

Here is some help with the pronunciation of a few of the names of people and places commonly mentioned in this book.

People		Places	
Villa	ve-yah	Xcacal	sh-ka-kal
Cituk	key-took	Tuzik	to-seek
Zuluub	sue-lube	Tulum	to-loom
Itza	its-ah	Chichen Itza	chee-chen-its-ah
May	my		

For transcribing spoken Yucatec Maya several orthographies have been or are currently in use. For the few Maya words in this book you will need to know the meaning of these symbols:

¢ or tz = the sound in English of "ts"

¢̣ or dz = the same as above, but more emphatically pronounced

ṭ, ḳ, etc. = like English "t" and "k," only more emphatically pronounced

' preceding a vowel = a glottal stop, an "explosive release" of the vowel

č, š = ch, sh

´, ` = rising-falling or low-trailing tone, respectively, on the vowel over which such tone symbols appear

Introduction

THIS BOOK recounts a long conversation between Maya Indians of Quintana Roo, Mexico, and a train of Mexican, European, and North American lumbermen, merchants, military officers, diplomats, spies, teachers, explorers, adventurers, tourists, historians, linguists, archeologists, and anthropologists, myself included. Sometimes lost kings and deities chime in with their say, as well.

The first exchanges in this long conversation were uttered more than a century ago during a savage and apparently interminable war between rebel Mayas and the Hispanic rulers of the Yucatan Peninsula. Whether the future would bring peace or continued war, prosperity or more desperate poverty, freedom or a return to slavery, and what part deities and foreigners would have in answering those questions—such common themes unite three lifetimes of encounters between Mayas and foreigners into a collective dialogue. In each encounter, less grand, more tangible topics were often the matter at hand—money, merchandise, labor, weapons, information—and the recurrence of these topics, too, links half-forgotten meetings of predecessors to words uttered only yesterday.

Since the urgent wartime beginnings of this long conversation, peace has come to Mexico, and Mayas of Quintana Roo for many years have enjoyed freedom and some measure of security. But times are getting tough again in that nation so burdened by debt, inflation, unemployment, poverty, corruption, and enduring political anachronisms. Times are getting very hard for people like the Mayas, so far removed from the places, social classes, and political organizations that rule their lives. As rumors of war waft in from neighboring nations of Central America, these Mayas now wonder how long it will be before war again erupts upon their increasingly difficult lives. For that reason, it seems to some of them, this long conversation with foreigners is still relevant and should go forward.

We foreigners—whether Americans, Europeans, or Mexicans who are not Mayas—would do well to pay attention to what has been and is being said. This is especially so for those of us concerned about the fate of the peoples of Central America and troubled by North America's so often misguided, even malevolent, involvements in that region of the world. As an epilogue to one war, this long conversation reveals how a Central American people reconstituted new lives, a new past, and a new future out of the ruins of great suffering and defeat. We may discern here as well the prologue to yet another war: the murmurings of discontent and hope, the imagining of homicide, the changing thoughts about who is friend and who is enemy. The future will emerge from such fertile ambiguities of public opinion, before the starkly clarifying dawn of renewed battle.

Eavesdropping upon this long conversation, we will learn how at least one Central American people views us, what expectations, fears, and hopes they harbor about us, and how they respond to our presence and influence in their lives. These Maya views are expressed in the terms of an Indian language and the logic of a culture quite different from our own. Such an Indian perspective is usually left hidden or obscured when we speak among ourselves in generalities about Central America and our relations with its peoples. Straining to hear and understand these indigenous views requires us to appreciate the difficulties of cross-cultural communication, and this appreciation can enlighten our encounters not only with the Mayas and other culturally different peoples of Central America, but with peoples everywhere.

Finally, a close reading of the history of this long conversation may usefully remind us of how action initiated with even the best of intentions can be refracted, deformed, or perverted when tested by the realities of political violence, mutual ignorance, and fear that impinge upon so many of our foreign encounters. For reasons such as these, I have thought this story worth telling.

I ARRIVED in a small community of Yucatec Maya–speaking people in Quintana Roo, Mexico, in 1978 to begin two years of anthropological field research. I had not been in the village of Tuzik three days when, while I was sitting with a man on the stoop of a village store, he asked in Maya if I thought the Epoch of Slavery would return and if war would come again. Village rumor and the radio both spoke of revolution in Nicaragua, and some people had heard of fighting in Guatemala, too. I did not know enough Yucatec Maya to reply at any length and simply answered, "I don't know. What do *you* say?" "Who knows?" was his similarly dull response, and we changed the topic. Yet after a year or so in that village, and once I had learned to speak Yucatec Maya with some fluency, I found myself ever more often engaged in conversations about slavery and freedom, peace and war, the distant past and the imminent future. It was a conversation, I came to learn, that had begun long before my time, and I was expected to participate, if only for a little while.

The part of the Yucatan Peninsula where Tuzik lies belongs to Mexico, but for most of the centuries since the Spanish conquest of the Mayas, the Caribbean coast of the peninsula has been a tenuous possession at best. The lack of good roads running back to the ultimate seat of authority in the distant highlands, periodic attacks by Caribbean pirates, recurrent revolts of Maya Indians, the hazards of the tropical forests, and the absence of the gold and silver that elsewhere attracted the attentions of Hispanic élites—all these factors dictated that what is today Quintana Roo would remain a sparsely inhabited and lightly administered frontier of Latin America. In fact, all along the western rim of the Caribbean Sea, through much of Central America, runs an aged fault line of obsolete empires, a seam in the social, cultural, economic, and political fabric of the Western Hemisphere.[1] In the formative period of hemispheric geopolitics the conflicting mercantile, territorial, and strategic interests of young world powers and new Latin American nations strained against one another in war, commerce, and colonization along that fault line dividing the Hispanic-ruled mainland to the west from the coastal and maritime Anglophone domains to the east. The nineteenth-century War of the Castes, one of the most prolonged and successful of New World Indian rebellions, erupted along it in Yucatan in 1847. Thanks to the overly harsh response of an ill-governed state and to the armaments supplied to Indians by neighboring British Honduras, a fledgling conspiracy of several prominent Maya men seeking to influence gubernatorial politics in Yucatan exploded into a peninsula-wide race war lasting over half a century and consuming tens of thousands of lives.

Contemporary Mayas in central Quintana Roo are descendants of

[1]Notes will be found in a group beginning on page 223.

one hundred thousand rebels and fugitives of that tragic war. They hold the War of the Castes—or simply the "Revolution," as they call it—to have been part of their True God's plan for history. It made life what it is today, and the wholesale slaughter of those receding times exemplifies, many believe, what must be done to renew the world in the Final Days of the Era of Man. From villages scattered throughout vast forests extending inland from the Caribbean Sea and surrounding ancient ruins at Chichen Itza, Coba, and Tulum, Maya Indians spy change in the world about them and mark the passing of each year as another collective step toward an imminent End and a new Beginning. For in the year 2000 "and a little," as Mayas say, this world will end and another will dawn, one much better than the present. A few Mayas may survive the apocalypse, depending on just how the end comes. If it comes in war—a holy war of Maya Indians against their ungodly enemies—then some Mayas will live on as seed for the new beginning. Failing apocalyptic war, however, True God will take it upon Himself to destroy us all, renew the face of the earth, and people it with creatures of another, improved design. He has done that several times before, and so He will again if Mayas tarry much longer in releasing themselves from the foreign yoke which they have borne since the Spanish conquest four and a half centuries ago.

For this decaying world to be cured of its ills and things to be set right again—with corn growing in abundance as it once did, men paid a decent wage, cheap goods and fine foreign manufactures offered in local markets, honest government mindful of the needs of its citizens, men and women treating each other properly, children speaking respectfully to their parents, adults heeding their leaders and worshiping their gods, prayer efficacious in the treatment of afflictions or the summoning of vital rains—human blood must first flow copiously, many say. Mayas will shed the blood of foreigners and allow their own to be shed, until the blood of all nationalities and races mingles in ankle-deep lagoons covering the central plazas of their towns and villages.

Apocalyptic war may be necessary for the survival of the human race. No Maya man or woman can say for sure, though they say their ancestors so prophesied. Very old women and men say that when they were children their parents and grandparents spoke of the End as though it were then imminent. Those childhood years seem eons ago, and the elderly know they will die before such prophecies are fulfilled. But they have relayed divine words to the next generation and can soon leave this world confident that *their* children and grandchildren will finally see the End. As for these younger Mayas, many suppose that an end of sorts is approaching, and that for better or for worse it will be they who usher out the old era and herald the arrival of the new.

Western scholars studying ancient Maya hieroglyphics and colonial-era Maya manuscripts long ago learned that Mayas took the past to be harbinger of future times and events. But that this ancient habit of mind still continues, though much transformed, is little known, and I have written this book in part to report on it and to reflect upon the manner in which a people's vision of the past and future is shaped and reshaped to suit the changing human projects of the present. In any event, one cannot write about encounters between Mayas and foreigners without writing about prophecy, too. Foreigners have long been central topics of Maya prophecy, and prophecy a topic of Maya conversations with us foreigners, who figure so prominently among the forces and contingencies that have repeatedly altered the conditions of Maya lives. There is something about these people who suddenly appear in order to talk with Mayas. They come from very distant lands and speak very different languages; they have evidently lived strange lives and seen many fantastic things. Time and again the appearance of people like ourselves has moved Maya men or women to speak of things of the distant past and imminent future. Seldom merely idle recollecting, such talk has often been crafted to move us to play a positive role in Maya history. Foreign visitors in turn have encouraged such talk and the hope for foreign assistance, sometimes unwittingly, sometimes quite consciously, in order to break open the coffers of Mayas' historical knowledge, cultural esoterica, and prized antiquities. Our conversations have had their effects—often not those that either quite intended, but others engendered by the confrontation of their motives and ours and the sharing of our different visions of past and future times.

I WENT to Quintana Roo to conduct research for my Ph.D. dissertation in anthropology, intending to investigate the social, cultural, and political adaptations that rebel Mayas had made to many decades of peace. Over the previous year in graduate school, as I considered where to conduct the fieldwork required of aspiring professional anthropologists at that stage of their career, the Mayas and Mexico did not come first to mind. Rather, I first decided to study the changing lot of once-servile agrarian laborers in Iran, until the outbreak of the Iranian Revolution prompted me to look elsewhere. Next, the Atlantic coast of Nicaragua seemed like the place to go. I would study the recent history and current circumstances of the Miskito Indians, living on a peculiar node of international commerce and political rivalries. But a Guatemalan classmate kindly disabused me of that notion and of my woeful ignorance of a dictator named Somoza, who more discerning eyes than mine could see was headed for a violent fall.

In the meantime I undertook a few weeks of summer fieldwork in western Belize, in a riverine settlement of Yucatec Maya and Mopan Maya Indians, non-Indian Guatemalans and Mexicans, and Afro-Americans. In that scenically beautiful region of a despairingly poor country, people spoke with me quite readily. Some even thought my labor a worthy one, attempting as I was to document through genealogies and oral histories the founding and rapid growth of that former logging camp. With their help the work went well, though villagers were acutely worried about the next few weeks of their lives, as Great Britain and Guatemala appeared headed toward war over the long-festering issue of Belizean sovereignty. The Maya woman in whose house I ate fretted that people like her know nothing of war, and if the Guatemalans came she would not know what to do. Flee, stay, fight, surrender? Her grandparents knew war, she mused aloud. They *made* war themselves. But those living now would not know what to do. As the hostile parties talked in Washington during the final hours of a Guatemalan ultimatum, British troops and tanks took up positions in the village and most residents fled to their cornfields in surrounding forests or to towns well out of harm's way.

Many of the Maya residents of that village, like the Maya woman I just mentioned, knew themselves to be descendants of refugees from a nineteenth-century war to the north. I left Belize at the end of the summer with the idea of conducting my dissertation research in the heartland of that past war and with the still vaguely conceived intention of learning what people up there remembered of war and what lives they had fashioned since its passing. By the start of my fieldwork a year later the project had received a more definite design, informed by recent social-science theorizing about a world economic system and its myriad local effects. A comprehensive ethnography of the region was also available, written by a Mexican anthropologist who had studied in the 1930s. Using that earlier work as a historical baseline (and helped by local introductions from that previous student of Maya society), I would study changes in the social organization and intervillage relations of once-rebel Mayas, as well as changes in the ways they made their livings, their governance, and their understandings of their place in the world and in history. Such study of the Mayas of Quintana Roo would, I hoped, provide a detailed description of how "exotic" peoples are incorporated into a web of direct and indirect global connections linking almost all of us in political and economic interdependency. Though that was my intention, once in the field I was insistently directed by Maya interlocutors into subject matters seemingly peripheral to the focus of that study—into religion, prophecy, and language itself. Such is the fate of much anthropological field research: fashioned in the beginning by dialogues and debates with colleagues, refashioned by dialogues with the "objects" of study, who turn, inevitably, into active subjects as we, uninvited, intrude upon conversations and events that constitute their lives.

Persistent Western curiosity about things Maya dates back to the mid-nineteenth century, when the well-known travel writer John L. Stephens was dispatched to Central America as a confidential agent of President Martin Van Buren. Stephens was charged with locating a government in Central America, any government, with which the United States could deal for diplomatic and mercantile purposes. Though he found none in that region, then afflicted by endless civil wars, he did return with eloquent reports of an "American Egypt" in the lowlands of the Yucatan Peninsula—great temples and palaces abandoned to the forest no one knew how many centuries before. His were not the first modern reports of a lost civilization in the Americas, but they were the most striking, accurate, extensive, and well illustrated.

Furthermore, where others of his contemporaries had guessed the architects of those ruins to have been antediluvian, or Phoenicians, Egyptians, Carthaginians, Greeks, or Jews, Stephens returned to what the first Spaniards there had known—that those ruins were the work of Maya Indians themselves, the ancient ancestors of contemporary denizens of the lands through which he traveled. From the publication of Stephens's *Incidents of Travel in Central America, Chiapas, and Yucatan* in 1841 until the present day, Mayas and the relics of their high culture have fascinated Western audiences, both scholarly and lay. Several generations of professional lives have been consumed in the continuing endeavor of locating, mapping, photographing, and reconstructing abandoned centers, deciphering hieroglyphic texts, tracing the rise of classic Maya culture, and explaining the causes of its sudden collapse ten centuries ago.

Living Maya Indians have come under equally intense scrutiny. The thirty-odd Maya languages—spoken by millions in the highlands of Guatemala and southern Mexico, hundreds of thousands in the lowlands of the Yucatan Peninsula partitioned by Guatemala, Belize, and Mexico—represent the most vital family of enduring Indian languages and cultures.

The scholarly work of ethnographers and linguists from the 1920s on have made the modern Mayas among the most studied "exotic" folk in the world.

Anthropologists have lived among the Maya for reasons of science. We have aspired to contribute to a unified Science of Man through systematic and insightful recording of the life ways of these people so different from ourselves. The results of that research, conjoined with the findings of similar studies of other peoples of the world would, it has long been hoped, result in scientifically valid conclusions about the cultural history of our species.

Most anthropologists spend the better part of their scholarly lives attending to scientific questions less ultimate though still quite grand — the interconnectedness and dynamics of social institutions; the nature of symbols, language, ritual, religion, gender; the sources and processes of social and cultural change; the ecological bases of particular realms of society and culture, to mention just a few. As a still more immediate motive, anthropologists acquire their professional credentials and their first academic employment by yet more narrowly defined field projects among foreign peoples, and many of us go on to develop scholarly reputations from the repeated study and documentation of the life ways of at most one or two particular peoples of the world. Anthropologists have made their strange journeys to the Maya for all such reasons of science and career.

We act upon those scientific motives through fieldwork, a mode of data gathering embraced as *the* defining feature of what we, as ethnographers, do. Fieldwork entails residence for a year or two among the people under study, firsthand observation of their activities, repeated conversations and interviews with them, and endless recording of a wide range of data in written, tape-recorded, and photographic mediums. Our conduct in fieldwork is predicated upon multiple scientific motives — motives that distinguish what we do from espionage, market analysis and product promotion, smuggling, whimsical adventure, tourism and recreation, the search for gold or oil or slaves, reconnaissance of possible sites for airstrips, military bases, or hotels, flight from persecution or prosecution, political or religious proselytism, social service, provocation, subversion, or conquest. (Many of these possibilities occurred to my Maya hosts when they speculated on what had *really* brought me among them.) Apart from realizing this scientific intention underlying ethnography, fieldwork itself is not a practical action for effecting personal gains or collective goods. It is, in fact, a peculiarly detached variety of human interaction, the ethnographer remaining uninvolved and dispassionate before the significant local struggles in which wealth, power, and life chances are generated, distributed, and destroyed. Such uninvolvement is happily consistent with the scientific motive and the value placed upon objectivity in the methodical seeker of truth.

Yet from time to time, especially during the Vietnam War, anthropologists have collectively questioned that alleged detachment of our discipline. Anthropological practice was, after all, made possible by the expansion of European power over the indigenous peoples of the Americas, Africa, Asia, the Middle East, and Oceania. That ethnographers had people to study was a consequence of empire, as anthropologists typically arrived upon the scene to study "primitives" made accessible and problematic in the wake of European conquest and colonial administration, trade, and Christian evangelizing. The typical objects of ethnographic research before the Second World War were recently dead and dying languages and cultures, "natives" to be administered, rebels suppressed and repacified, occupants of reservations or of the last remaining nooks and crannies of subject lands to which other white men had yet to go for want of ready access or the promise of profit. After World War II anticolonial wars and modern social revolutions restricted our access to large parts of the globe but added new categories of non-Europeans to the roster of human diversity with which anthropology should concern itself—peasants, agricultural wage laborers, the urban poor, miners, factory workers, and other dangerous classes of what came to be called the Third World.[2]

In the conduct of research some anthropologists have lent their services and insights directly to the cause of government administration and counterinsurgency. Others have more openly and appropriately worked for programs of agricultural and community development, public health, education, and so on. Yet the anthropologist conducting field research more typically remains above the fray of empire, neo-colonial politics, and international development, reasserting the distant, ultimate, collective good of human enlightenment. Toward this goal disinterested science aims while simply suggesting, often for the benefit of our sponsors, that others might find some practical uses for the data generated by our studies.

Such has been the scientific intention in its seemingly purest form, though many anthropologists now accept that it, too, has a conservative political character. In focusing upon the tribe, the peasant community, the urban *barrio,* and other well-bounded, small-scale human arenas, our discipline cultivated and defended a peculiar blind spot in its vision of the world beyond Europe and the United States. We long tended to study and write about the colonized but not about colonialism, about the new Third World recruits to an expanding capitalist system but not about capitalism or imperialism, about the impact of the West but not about the systematic connections between the West and the Rest. We wrote about social change but not about the forces and patterns of change that are manifest only on a geographic and temporal scale greater than that encompassed by the standard practices of ethnographic research and writing.[3]

The result of such willful blindness to the significant historical processes of modern world making, we by now realize, has been a great deal of misconceiving of the nature of social and cultural change, mislabeling of the types of humankind we studied, omission of significant data (which we had often, in fact, recorded) from our published reports on the lives of other people, miseducating of our students and the public. Despite anthropologists' customary championing of the victims of conquest, administrative mistreatment, economic exploitation, and political domination, many opportunities have been lost to criticize effectively the role of our own societies in that ongoing victimization.

The practice of ethnography is not so disinterested and uninvolved in the social, economic, and political struggles of our times. Just how interested and involved it can be is most palpable in our personal experiences, for the very ways we go about realizing our scientific purposes through fieldwork require cultivating worldly engagements with the subjects of our study and involving ourselves, sometimes quite significantly, in their lives. To begin with, the conduct of fieldwork requires an entrée among the people to be studied: getting the things and relationships we need to sustain our lives among them—shelter, food, transportation, medical assistance, protection, and companionship; and gaining access to ever more interior domains of people's lives. It requires securing cooperation in our data-gathering efforts through acts of sale and exchange, conviviality, sharing in the labors of everyday life, and repeatedly explaining the reasons for our presence in the hope that some of our hosts will find them harmless and worthy of their help.

Such cultivated engagement is reciprocal, though we seldom know why our hosts do consent to have us live among them—always snooping around, asking ever more peculiar and intimate questions. Curiosity; fear of the repercussions of refusal; the esteem and status that may accrue from close association with a foreigner; personal pecuniary gain or advantage over neighbors, competitors, and enemies; and in some rare cases, a shared interest in the explicit description and analysis of their own life ways—we can well suppose these to be among their motives. How we might like to believe the romantic musings of one of Joseph Conrad's fictional characters, an Englishman running guns to the "natives" of then Spanish-ruled Mindanao:

> There are those who say that a native will not speak to a white man. Error. No man will speak to his master; but to a wanderer and a friend, to him who does not come to teach or to rule, to him who asks for nothing and accepts all things, words are spoken by the campfires, in the shared solitude of the sea, in riverside villages, in resting-places surrounded by forests — words are spoken that take no account of race or colour. One heart speaks — another one listens; and the earth, the sea, the sky, the passing wind and the stirring leaf, hear also the futile tale of the burden of life.[4]

Yet surely no word may pass from one heart to another that is not conveyed for motives, by means, and in settings suffused with the social difference of interlocutors, however much that difference and its significance may be transformed in the very course of such encounters.

Our reciprocal involvements in each other's lives can cause a mutual subversion of scientist and subject. For our part, we have taken up residence among the other; have labored, eaten, played, celebrated, prayed with them; have tried to be useful by procuring aid for the sick, burying the dead, giving lifts to market, helping in production, drafting letters and petitions, and in sundry other ways; have learned, perhaps, to speak their language well, to joke and swap stories and be worthy audiences for native raconteurs; have courted and cajoled and encouraged them to think of us favorably and assist us in our efforts. By these means (known as participant observation, rapport building, and the acquisition of linguistic and cultural competencies, in the jargon of our profession) we bring about the at least temporary suspension of our subjects' traditional restraints upon close and complex social intercourse with our kind, and produce an ambiguity of statuses, relationships, and feelings within which our scientific labor then proceeds. For their part, through their acts of cooperation, self-presentation and self-explanation, their cajoling and their criticisms of us and our endeavors, they can substantially alter our radical single-mindeness of scientific purpose and so create and negotiate involvements tangential to, if not actually inconsistent with that foreign purpose.

The ideal comportment of the ethnographer before subjects of study is utopian in conception, and so one with utopian goals of the Science of Man: truth deployed in the search for Truth, good deeds done in the service of Good, openness and communion with the other as we labor for ultimate Openness, Communication, and Mutual Understanding among all people. More specifically, members of the American Anthropological Association have enjoined their colleagues above all else: Do no damage — either to those whom we study or to the reputation of our professional community. With that there follows: Do not exploit. Do not violate confidences and promises of anonymity. Do not deceive. Explain the purposes of your presence and your research, as well as the possible consequences for the people whom you study. No surreptitious or covert research, and no secret reports to sponsors, especially those whose purposes are other than scientific (such as the State Department, the Army, the CIA, the Drug Enforcement Agency). Cooperate with host-country colleagues in planning and executing your research.[5] (The many of us who receive funds from the federal government are similarly enjoined by federal laws on the protection of human subjects in scientific research.)

Yet the inevitable drift from scientific detachment to engagement and involvement in the course of fieldwork draws the scientist back to humanity, for better and for worse, making evident the internal contradictions of our scientific intentions, endowing our work with an extra modicum of the humane, while reducing the cherished distance of our purposes and actions from those of other foreigners and from the amoral pragmatism so pervasive in our time.

Moral and ethical issues cannot be charted so specifically that one need only open a book of manners to know exactly what to do. Anthropologists expect each other to exercise honest and informed judgment in the infinitely varied circumstances of their dealings in the field. But we need also remember that the character of our action in foreign lands is only in part born of our good intentions. The exchange of words and deeds between ourselves and others is inevitably charged by the political and economic inequalities that structure the world we all live in.

In the history of North American and European dealings with the Mayas of Quintana Roo, the contradictions in purpose, the undermining of traditional fears and restraints on intercourse, and their multiple consequences for lives and for knowledge are apparent in every possible complexity. That is much more evident now, from the safe and omniscient vantage point adopted in much of this book, than it was to many of the people I write about. Some of the actions recounted here, undertaken for purposes of research, most of us today would find unacceptable, and some readers may be pleased to think ill of those of whom I write. I do not, and it is my hope that the reader will not, think ill at least of those anthropologists and archeologists of half a century ago from whose personal and professional writings I have constructed a major portion of this account. For the ethical shortcomings revealed in this history are in many instances, I believe, only somewhat exaggerated examples of still-common misadventures in foreign lands.

THE SEVERAL lifetimes' worth of encounters between rebel Mayas and Hispanic Mexicans, Germans, Swedes, Frenchmen, Englishmen, and Americans described in this book wander far beyond the familiar brief, face-to-face exchanges of meaningful words and gestures that we normally have in mind when referring to a "conversation" between people. My calling the history of these episodic encounters a "long conversation" is a literary convenience, though not a whimsical one. I have invoked the metaphor of "conversation" because dialogue was such a central and unlikely event in each encounter between Maya and foreigner.[6] More than that, I have found the metaphor of a continuous dialogue already inscribed in some of the very events I write about. For at times Maya and foreign interlocutors—aware of continuities of settings, topics, conversational means, and motives of their many interactions—fashioned and interpreted words and deeds as responses to those of predecessors.

Commonplace conversations begin when two people approach each other, exchange greetings or other openers, and commence to speak. They proceed with one person having his say, then another in turn responding, then the other again, and so on for anywhere from a few seconds to a few hours. The end eventually comes with conventional closings, an exchange of parting farewells or insults, and separation. Ordinary conversations involve people who know they are conversing, who know who they are and in what relation they stand to one another, where they are in significant time and space, what they are talking about, why they are talking about that, and, when it is over, what has been said. We may at times lack the answers to some of these questions— if a total stranger stops us on a street and begins to speak to us, if we are amnesiac or stoned or suffer severe short-term memory lapse, if the person to whom we speak has multiple personalities, if we have grievously misunderstood one another, or if our words and relationships are ambiguous, or under many other imaginable circumstances. But, in our better moments and more successful conversations, we do not doubt that these questions do have accurate answers that we can, perhaps will, come to know in the course of the conversation, or by listening to a recording of it, by studying a transcript of it, or with the expert help of detectives, psychiatrists, social scientists, and others trained to advise us of the motives, means, conditions, and consequences of interactions between people.

In my metaphorical long conversation, we must be less confident that there *are* answers. Each encounter between Maya and foreigner was an extraordinary experiment in cross-cultural communication. Many a Maya and foreigner had never met individuals of the other kind. They did not speak each other's language very well (if at all); were guided by very different motives; had different ideas about speaking and writing and the kinds of beings who can use language; had different senses of place, time, causality, and different knowledge of what had gone on before. They could not share one set of answers to questions about their dialogues. Each side, in fact, would have quite different questions to ask about what had and was transpiring between them.

On top of that, time can corrupt our ability to speak accurately about what we have done, despite our belief that objectivity is enhanced by the waning of a moment's passion and interest. Imagine a conversation that lasts much, much too long—so long, that is, that even as interlocutors converse, refusing to let go of some evidently engrossing topic, they age perceptibly. Some die, and suitable onlookers step in to pick up the thread. As time passes, the pronunciation, syntax, and vocabulary of the speakers drift away from those of their predecessors, whose remembered utterances now seem subtly out of date, their references to the world obscure. The place where the speakers meet and the landscape about them are modified by human hand or natural forces, and to them attach new sentiments and meanings for the things that have happened there during this long conversation. The households and families of these interlocutors are of course transformed by the inexorable cycles of birth, maturation, marriage, and death, but so too change the very rhythms of those cycles, reflecting the new opportunities and misfortunes of particular times and places. This conversation goes on so long, in fact, that all significant features of personal and collective identity shift—all the standard experiences and doings of an ordinary life, all the shared communicative means of our avid conversationalists, and the wider world context that shapes the motives for their speaking and the meaning and effect of what is said. So much may have changed— except the fact that they still seem to be talking to one another—that it will be difficult for them to judge accurately whether they are still talking about the same thing and for the same reasons as when they or their predecessors commenced, or whether what was intended at the outset has in fact been achieved. There are no fixed landmarks in the mind, culture, or society by which to reckon whence and how far they have come to the present moment.

At each moment in this long conversation those addressing one another may well think that they are the same kind of people as their predecessors, engaged in the same pursuits. Yet from our distant perspective we can appreciate how much has changed in the course of that absurdly long conversation. While the interlocutors bridged their personal, social, and cultural differences in dialogue, another equally profound divide opened, separating each of the participants from what they and their predecessors had once been.

Such is the long conversation about which I have written this book, and which threads its way through the lives of the participants. This long conversation is a braid of human emotions, world views, motives, linguistic means, settings of encounter and dialogue, and the changing conditions of life and livelihood. Each strand of this braided history is potentially distinct, and we could unravel each one to examine its nature along any short segment we choose. Linguistics and anthropology are skilled at such ahistorical, or micro-historical, studies of language activity, and much has been learned about the contesting of power, the constructing of social relations, and the assertion of alternative views of the world immanent in the ways we address one another. Yet understanding language as a creative and transforming effort in society and history also requires study of longer life histories and social histories of language activity.

In writing this book I adopted a historical perspective on language activity, pulling out what individual strands I could for closer examination, before twisting them back together to constitute the story I tell. Though I was a participant in a small part of what I recount, I look back upon this history from a vantage point not accorded to any of my interlocutors— presumably a higher lookout—accessible through my scholarly training, the written records of past encounters, and the contributions made by a great many different Maya individuals who deigned to speak with me. Yet reflection upon my claim to a privileged perspective may leave the reader with the justifiable suspicion that this book is not truly above or outside that long conversation it describes. In its peculiar way it is but another utterance in the ongoing exchange between Mayas and foreigners, one that is, I hope, appropriate and benignly effective at this moment in our shared history.

UNFINISHED
CONVERSATIONS

I

SPEAKING WITH
THE ENEMY

THE WAR OF THE CASTES began in 1847 with an uprising of Maya
Indians against the government and white settlers in the isolated villages
and towns of eastern Yucatan. In the first few months of the war, rebel
Maya bands under many leaders ebbed and flowed across the peninsula
of Yucatan, sacking villages, estates, and towns that lay in their north-
westerly path. They massacred, enslaved, or put to flight the entire
non-Indian population of the land, even as they drew support and
recruits from at least part of the Maya population of each newly
liberated province. For a while it seemed that white Yucatecan society
and its discrimination on the basis of race (*casta* or caste) might vanish
from the peninsula, as by mid-1848 only the largest cities, Merida and
Campeche, and a narrow route to the sea had not yet fallen under rebel
Maya control. The Maya offensive disintegrated, however, just short of
Merida, the capital of Yucatan. The rebels began to retreat.

By the end of 1848, after months of counteroffensive against the
rebel armies, all the formerly settled parts of the peninsula were once
again under at least nominal government control. Many of those who
had fought alongside or supported the rebels remained behind as their
villages and towns were recaptured, while up to one hundred thousand
rebels and their families retreated to the almost uninhabited forests of
the east and south. From the forest strongholds that these refugees
quickly raised around their capital, Santa Cruz, rebel Mayas resisted
reconquest for over half a century, periodically raiding the towns of
Yucatan while searching for a peace that would guarantee their hard-
won autonomy.

3

During the early years of the twentieth century the Mexican army was still hunting rebel Maya Indians in the forests of Quintana Roo—raiding villages, burning cornfields, ambushing travelers on woodland trails. And sometimes Maya rebels would still retaliate in kind. Mayas today recall that time as the "epoch of slavery," a time of fear and persecution, abject poverty, and great injustice. They say that in those terrible years one among them, Florentino Cituk, undertook night-long vigils praying to Our Lord True God in the main church of the sacred village called Chun Pom. He prayed as such poor men would to their poor man's god, seven times shuffling seven painful meters on his knees up to the altar of that god, who, seeing the man so holy and humble, blessed him with the knowledge of "night writing"—prophecy. As the great fifteenth-century Maya prophets were said to have foretold the first coming of Spanish conquerors to their land, so the visionary Cituk foresaw the imminent dawn of a new era:

> Today stone to stone we walk, on hidden roads we walk.
> But there will be, says He, says True God,
> there will be the opening of all roads.
> We will eat together with the foreigner.
> We will eat together with our enemy.
> We will converse with him.

Florentino Cituk perished during the latter of two epidemics, smallpox and influenza, that devastated the Mayas of Quintana Roo in the second decade of this century. Referred to by Mayas today as the "Great Fire" that swept their land, those epidemics marked a watershed in Maya history, cutting the remaining rebel population in half (from ten down to five thousand, it seems, though no one can say exactly), extinguishing whole villages, and depriving the survivors in many others of the leadership of the elderly, who succumbed more surely than their children and grandchildren. Cituk died, then, while fugitive Mayas still walked through the forest stepping from stone to stone so as to leave no footprints in the soft soil of the forest floor; before trails were allowed to widen and become easy to follow; and before Mayas ceased to slay and be slain by those they called the ¢ùul, a term for foreigners in general and for Spanish-speaking overlords and soldiers, the enemy, in particular.[1]

Florentino Cituk was not the first rebel Maya to have received divine revelations or to have acted as a human voice for True God. Since at least the second year of their war, after rebel armies once on the verge of victory had been driven back into the recesses of coastal forests, rebel

Mayas communed with their deity and received what they thereafter called the "Divine Commandments" (*santo 'almahtàan*). In 1850 at the site that would become the rebel town of Noh Cah Santa Cruz Balam Nah (literally translated as "Great Town of the Holy Cross Jaguar House") a Christ impersonator, Juan de la Cruz, delivered a message of divine sorrow, anger, love, and commitment:

> *My very beloved,*
> *Ye Christian villagers,*
> *Now is the hour;*
> *There have arrived*
> *The day*
> *The hour*
> *For me to show you*
> *A sign*
> *Upon the land of all my engendered people*
> *In the world;*
> *To the end that*
> *It might be read to be heard by all the Commanders,*
> *And to be heard by all the Captains,*
> *And by all the Lieutenants,*
> *And by all the Sergeants,*
> *And to be heard by all my engendered people*
> *In the World;*
> *To the end that*
> *They might know it,*
> *All my children.*[2]

He spilled His blood for them, this god first reminded his Maya audience, when He created them and the world in which they live. It was time to make His commandments known.

> *Whoever is not believing in my commandments*
> *Will have drunk a draught of suffering*
> *Without end.*
> *Whoever will obey my commandments*
> *Will also win the fullness of my Grace.*
> *They will also win my love.*[3]

If His Indian children then suffered the ravages of white men's attacks, it was because they had not obeyed His commandments. If they

5

suffered poverty and hunger, it was divine punishment for their failures and their sins. Therefore the time for war had come again. His children should have no fear of battle, however, as He went in the vanguard of the troops, and so long as He did, no harm would befall His soldiers. Battle instructions were given in that revelation for an attack to be launched, presumably forthwith, against advanced enemy outposts. Even as the divinity claimed command of the Maya war, He admonished human commanders for harsh and unjust punishments they had meted out to their common people, for not having followed His orders, and for not having remunerated the personal services of subordinates.

The Maya rebels were reassured:

> *Because my Father has already told me,*
> *O ye children,*
> *That the Whites will never win,*
> *The enemies.*[4]

But half a century later the war still dragged on, and by the time Florentino Cituk spoke in the words of True God, it must have seemed to Mayas that the enemy, the foreigner, would soon be upon them.

Rebel Mayas in their forest sanctuaries had never been completely isolated from foreigners. During the War of the Castes they traded with the merchants of British Honduras for munitions and other supplies. At times they slipped into Yucatecan towns under enemy control to make purchases and gather intelligence. On rare occasions they received diplomatic missions come to rebel territory to negotiate the release of captive non-Indians, or for other reasons still. Such peaceful contacts were occasional counterpoints to the raids and counterraids that rebels and their enemies continually launched against each other. However, the decline and cessation of active hostilities during the first two decades of this century eventually brought what Cituk is now said to have prophesied—more frequent and peaceful intercourse between rebel Mayas and a variety of foreigners. Among the latter were an increasing number of explorers interested in the geography, natural history, and cultural history of the Yucatan Peninsula.

The earliest of such contacts were fleeting affairs, and rebel Mayas remained unknown and unknowable within a forest outsiders warned each other was "a place of desolation and death," "inhabited only by birds, wild beasts and Maya Indians more fearsome than the wild beasts themselves" and, all told, "an excellent place to keep away from."[5] In part it was the forest itself that repelled would-be visitors to central Quintana

Roo—a vast, heterogeneous landscape of high-canopied groves of towering trees and hanging vines shading the cool, soft, open forest floor; of dense, hot, snake-infested thickets blanketing the hard, wildly undulating, and fractured limestone surface of the peninsula; of occasional cornfields and a rare savanna; of pondlike sinkholes (*cenotes*) and lagoons; with mangrove swamps and floodlands buffering the forest from the coast.

Most trails through the forest were exceedingly narrow, and travelers upon them were repeatedly jostled, stung, and lacerated by the exuberant plant life inevitably springing up wherever sunlight could reach the ground. These were trails more suitable for men on foot than for horses or mules, too clumsy or tired to manage the incessant turns and shifts of weight required by fallen trees, tiny openings into subterranean caverns, precipitous hillocks and ridges, and the exasperating plasticity of rain-soaked soil. With its plague of mosquitoes in that malaria-afflicted territory, nighttime brought little respite to the weary traveler scorched by the pounding sun of a desert-dry March or April, soaked through by the sauna-like conditions of rainy-season summers, or chilled to the bone by winter storms that swept in from the north.

One could actually make a good life in the forest, choosing well just where to live—near a constant source of clean subterranean water, away from lands that did not drain well after rainy-season thundershowers, close to the flatter, deeper-soiled terrain in which cornfields will yield their best. But travelers, refugees, exiles, indeed all newcomers to the land, whether white men or Mayas, tended to experience the worst the forest had to offer. Many who lingered there perished with astonishing speed. If such outsiders found in the forest "a place of desolation and death," that had as much to do with the disruptions of war as with the perils of the tropical forest.

One of the last of the prewar explorers of the region, the American travel writer John L. Stephens, had an inkling of things to come when, while traveling in eastern Yucatan, he

> met a large straggling party of Indians, returning from a hunting expedition in the forests along the seacoast. Naked, armed with long guns, and with deer and wild boars slung on their backs, their aspect was the most truculent of any people we had seen. They were some of the Indians who had risen at the call of General Iman, and they seemed ready at any moment for battle.

General Iman was but one of many Yucatecan commanders battling other members of the state's ruling élite over issues of Yucatan's relation to the rest of Mexico, of who should govern the state, and such sundry political matters seemingly so pressing at the time. They armed Maya recruits to do their fighting for them and promised in return relief from the taxes and church levies so onerous to the Indian *casta* or caste. By doing so these commanders made a fatal mistake. Yet perhaps only an outsider like Stephens could clearly see "what the consequences may be of [Mayas] finding themselves, after ages of servitude, once more in the possession of arms, and in increasing knowledge of their physical strength." It was "a question of momentous import to the people of that country, the solution of which no man can foretell."[6] The answer was not long in coming, and the war that followed would greatly restrict the movements and labors of subsequent explorers in Yucatan and Quintana Roo. Precisely what the restrictions were varied, diminishing as the nineteenth century waned and depending upon whether one approached rebel Maya territory from the north, from the south and west, or from the east.

In the northern reaches of the Yucatan Peninsula lay the ruins of Chichen Itza. A colonial-era Maya chronicle available to nineteenth-century explorers seemed to place the city's founding at A.D. 360 or 432,[7] and it was also known that, by the time the first conquering Spaniards arrived upon the scene, Chichen Itza had long since been abandoned. The Spaniards had recorded precious little about the place (though at one point in their wars of conquest against the Maya Spanish forces took refuge there from annihilation), and much of what they had recorded was contained within a manuscript, Franciscan Diego de Landa's *Relación de Cosas de Yucatán,* still lost in a European archive as the first mid-nineteenth-century explorers ventured out from Merida to visit Chichen Itza.

When Stephens visited the place, it was easy to get to Chichen Itza and walk about the two or three square miles of densely gathered monuments. An old Spanish colonial road between Merida and Valladolid, two of the three largest cities on the Yucatan Peninsula, ran right through the middle of the ruins and the cattle hacienda within which they stood. Herds of cattle had apparently grazed and trampled the plain clear of underbrush, though the ancient mounds and ruined buildings were themselves topped by brush and trees and surrounded by fallen fragments of great stone serpents, carved fronting, and column segments dislodged or tumbled over the centuries.

Some buildings still stood intact, either at ground level or on low platforms, or at the summits of truncated pyramids, one of which, the hundred-foot-high Castillo, was the first structure glimpsed by explorers

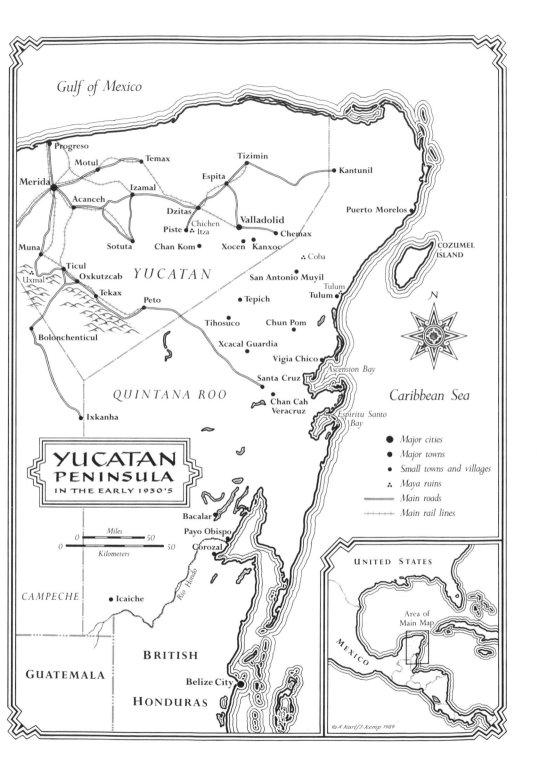

Gulf of Mexico

COZUMEL
ISLAND

Progreso
Motul
Temax
Tizimin
Kantunil
Merida
Acanceh
Izamal
Espita
Dzitas
Puerto Morelos
Piste ∴ Chichen
Itza
Valladolid
Muna
Sotuta
Chan Kom
Chemax
Xocen
Kanxoc
Ticul
Oxkutzcab
∴ Coba
Uxmal
YUCATAN
Tekax
San Antonio Muyil
Tulum
∴
Peto
Tepich
Tulum
Bolonchenticul
Tihosuco
Chun Pom
N
Xcacal Guardia
Vigia Chico
Caribbean Sea
QUINTANA ROO
Santa Cruz
Ascension Bay
Ixkanha
*Chan Cah
Veracruz*
Espiritu Santo
Bay

YUCATAN PENINSULA
IN THE EARLY 1930'S

● Major cities
● Major towns
• Small towns and villages
∴ Maya ruins
── Main roads
+++++ Main rail lines

Miles
0 ──── 50
0 ──── 50
Kilometers

Bacalar
Payo Obispo
Corozal

UNITED STATES

CAMPECHE
• *Icaiche*
Río Hondo

Area of
Main Map

MEXICO

BRITISH

GUATEMALA

HONDURAS

Belize City

© A.Karl/J.Kemp 1989

9

approaching the site. Forest clearing, excavation, and laborious reconstruction were not necessary for one to discern clearly the original form
of many of the major structures there—the Castillo; the Iglesia, from
which, Indians told Stephens, music mysteriously emanated each Good
Friday; a strange round structure known as the Caracol; the Gymnasium
(later named the Great Ball Court), an immense structure consisting of
two parallel walls 119 feet apart, 272 feet long, 28 feet high, and 39 feet
thick that by reference to smaller but analogous structures in central
Mexico was identifiably an arena of ritual sport.[8] The Temple of the
Jaguars rose above one corner of the Great Ball Court and housed vividly
colored murals depicting scenes of ancient battle. There were also the
Red House (local Indians called it The Jail), whose rear interior wall
still bore hieroglyphic inscriptions along its entire length; the Nunnery,
the most elaborately ornamented structure then visible at the site; and a
building known to Indians of Stephens's day as Akabdzib, Writing in the
Dark, or, better, Night Writing.

Though this latter is among the least-imposing and most spartan of
the principal structures at Chichen Itza, more than one nineteenth-
century explorer found it especially intriguing. Over the doorway of
one of its many interior chambers is a lintel with hieroglyphic inscriptions,
and overhead within the doorway, parallel with the floor, is a stone
carving of a seated person who is bracketed by further hieroglyphic
inscriptions and gesturing as though, it seemed to Stephens, engaged in
"some act of incantation, or some religious or idolatrous rite, which the
[building's name] 'writing in the dark' undoubtedly explains, if one
could but read it." "Physical force may raze these buildings to the
ground, and lay bare all the secrets they contain," Stephens lamented in
pondering the meaning of the gesturing and the glyphs, "but physical
force can never unravel the mystery that involves this sculptured tablet."[9]
Unable to read most of what had been carved in stone, nineteenth-
century explorers could largely only guess at the meanings and functions
of what they found (guesses informed, in the best instances, by analogies
drawn from the better-known Aztecs and by reference to a few relevant
colonial-era Spanish and Maya writings that did subsequently come to
light). Meanwhile, they continued their practical labors of describing
and depicting the ruins, inscriptions, and murals in increasingly sophisti-
cated and accurate detail, uncovering earlier structures hidden within
those most lately constructed, opening burial caches, and retrieving
sunken sculptures.

When Stephens ventured out to Chichen Itza in the early 1840s, it
was a friendly and comfortable place. He was welcomed there by the

hospitable hacienda owner, who lodged him in the new, clean sacristy of the hacienda church. Stephens studied the ruins amidst the shouts of men tending the hacienda's cattle, the frolicking of children from the nearby village of Piste who came to swim in the large *cenote* just north of the ruins, and the Sunday promenades of well-dressed men and women from that same village. Nor did he have any trouble recruiting laborers to clear the ruins before his companion, Frederick Catherwood, set to sketching them, for it was a time of hunger and fear of famine, and to Stephens's door came sufficient numbers of Indians seeking such employment.[10] The next wave of explorers to Chichen Itza, drawn there by the well-written and -illustrated book Stephens soon published about his most recent travels in Yucatan, found a natural and human landscape radically different from that which Stephens had described.

Battles and massacres during the early years of the War of the Castes had left a broad swath of destruction from southwest to northeast through the middle of Yucatan. Chichen Itza lay in a no-man's-land still subject to rebel attacks, and from it the government occasionally launched expeditions against rebel strongholds in the southern forests. En route to Chichen Itza explorers now passed through ghost towns and villages all but invisible under dense coverings of vines, bushes, and trees. One passed the night within blackened ruins of lost settlements still sheltering a few stubborn inhabitants who seemingly "prefer this imminent danger of death to the pain of abandoning their devastated home." At Chichen Itza itself, the once-thriving hacienda was "a sad ruin among ruins." Where the sounds of cattle and cowboys, children and Sunday strollers once echoed on a clear plain, birds and lizards were the only inhabitants of the now-forested site.[11]

Travelers to Chichen Itza in the 1860s, '70s, and '80s hoped to avoid any contact with the "barbarous" and "ferocious" Maya rebels, whose name inspired such terror among the inhabitants of Yucatan, both Indian and non-Indian. So they traveled there under military escort (expeditions "half artistic and half military," as one of them put it), posted sentries about the ruins to guard against surprise assaults, armed Indian laborers, and spent nights in fortified residences there (such as the old hacienda house, though the tall pyramid known as the Castillo was also a good redoubt) or at the nearest military outpost a few miles away in the destroyed village of Piste.[12]

The measures were effective, and the only northern explorer to see any rebel Mayas was the French photographer Désiré Charnay. In 1860, having just arrived in Yucatan, he was still in the port of Sisal when some captive Indians in detention attracted his attention. "Most of them were practically naked; the women wore a simple petticoat, the little ones wore nothing: all were thin: but well-built: they had an air of savage pride which I have never noticed among those individuals of the kind that I had found in the villages [of Mexico]." He was told that these were rebels taken in a recent campaign and awaiting shipment to join thousands of their peers in slavery in Cuba.[13] Edward H. Thompson, American Consul in Merida and archeologist resident at Chichen Itza, came close to meeting rebel Mayas as he returned from an expedition to the ruins at Coba. Upon entering the town of Dzonotchel, Yucatan, he "found it to be a shambles. The bodies of men, women, and children lay about the streets, some of them mutilated." Rebels had just struck the town in retaliation for the molestation of some of their women by chicle gatherers who had chanced upon a rebel settlement in the forest.[14]

Other than those brief crossings of paths, there would be no encounters between nineteenth-century explorers of northern archeological sites and rebel Mayas of the southern forests. So rebel Mayas remained for the foreigners shadowy figures lurking ominously beyond the cleared areas of ruins and roads, whose sporadic offensives could upset travel itineraries and research plans, but who were otherwise only grist for the dramatic fictions of memoirs and travel literature.[15]

Explorers entering rebel territory from the south inevitably had more intimate contact with the Mayas. Far from the battlefields of the northern frontier, these southern forests—wetter, taller, more vast than those to the north—had for many decades been undisputed rebel domain, traversed by a well-worn route of wartime commerce between settlements of British Honduras and such rebel towns as Bacalar and Santa Cruz. The German geographer Karl Sapper, for example, conducted explorations in the southern reaches of rebel territory in 1894 and 1895. He found his Maya hosts and guides most helpful and trustworthy, but then he was dealing only with those once belligerent Mayas who had since made separate peace agreements with the Mexican government. He did not travel further north into the territory of the so-called Santa Cruz Indians, whose "bloodthirsty cruelty and warlike readiness . . . have made their name exceedingly feared."[16]

Though in 1888 William Miller, Assistant Surveyor-General of British Honduras, managed under rebel Maya escort to arrive safely in the capital, Santa Cruz, he warned others who might follow him: "I do not think it would be possible for a white man of any other nationality to go there. The Santa Cruz Indians have a very bad name and there are a good many murders recorded against them, which cause people to be very careful about going into their country." And even after he had arrived there unmolested, his work was still severely restricted.

> It is impossible to get any information from them, as they strongly object to being questioned. Some very simple questions which I asked were answered, but were always supplemented by the counter-question "Why do you wish to know?" On one occasion wishing to hear of ancient Indian ruins, I was questioning several Indians in the chief's house, and getting unsatisfactory answers, pressed the question, when they turned down their hat brims and peeped at me from under them, and simply answered in monosyllables. This so frightened my interpreter that he refused to go on with the questions.[17]

Miller wanted to continue his journey further north and east toward the coastal village of Tulum, where, he had heard, Indians consulted a cross from which "the voice of God issues." Miller claimed to have also heard about a non-Indian Catholic priest who upon his arrival at Tulum had been taken before the cross to undergo divine interrogations. The cross was said to have ordered the priest's execution, and the deed was carried out. The men who accompanied Miller must have heard that report too, for they "refused to go beyond Santa Cruz, as they stated that every stranger had to interview the cross and they feared the ordeal."[18]

There are ancient Maya ruins at Tulum that stand on the edge of thirty-foot-high limestone cliffs rising out of the western Caribbean (about thirty miles from the sacred village of Chun Pom, which was the home of the prophet Florentino Cituk). Thick masonry walls once separated the small settlement, most likely of coastal-trading Mayas, from the forest on three sides, while on the fourth side ready access from the sea is to be had only through a narrow gap where steep, ragged cliffs descend to a small, sandy cove continually beaten by waves that have just traversed the second-longest barrier reef in the world. From the top of its most massive structure—a twenty-five-foot-high platform on top of which stands a two-room temple, the Castillo of Tulum—one gazes west over the endless, level expanse of green forest or east over the equally vast sea. The structures of Tulum are diminutive and crude compared to those of other ancient Maya sites like Chichen Itza, Uxmal, Coba, or almost any other place of some importance. But its spectacular natural setting and its long-preserved isolation have, for American and European spectators at least, endowed Tulum with a durable "allure" and "mystery" all its own.[19]

The Castillo at Tulum, 1842

John Stephens, whose books then enjoyed great popularity in the United States, ventured by sea to the ruins in 1842. More than three centuries after Europeans first set eyes upon them, some six centuries after their first construction, and despite the striking solitude of that "forest-buried city," the ruins seemed to Stephens so well preserved as to suggest only relatively recent abandonment. Stephens later told eager American readers: "I conceive it to be not impossible that within this secluded region may exist at this day, unknown to white men, a living aboriginal city, occupied by relics of the ancient race, who still worship in the temples of their fathers."[20]

The description Stephens published of the ruins of Tulum (illustrated by his English companion, Frederick Catherwood) sparked intense interest among later explorers and archeologists, but many decades passed before any could follow up on his explorations there. The east coast of the Yucatan Peninsula was, as a subsequent explorer put it, "one of the wildest and least-known parts of the New World," and the Tulum ruins were perilously close to the heartland of rebel territory; it was "as much as one's life is worth to land at Tulum."[21] If the reputation of the rebel Mayas around the town of Santa Cruz was bad, that of those around Tulum was worse. Would-be explorers avoided Tulum for most of the remainder of the nineteenth century, though loggers from British Honduras apparently operated near there, and at times Tulum was an important site for rebel commerce with British Hondurans as well as the target of Mexican efforts to cut off that trade and pacify the rebels.[22]

Tulum, however, was too enticing a site for explorers to keep passing by. In 1895 a yacht full of American scientists, including the Curator of Anthropology of the Field Columbian Museum in Chicago, William Holmes, approached close in "to secure a glimpse of the great ruin of Tuloom, now occupied by hostile Indians as an outpost." Holmes and his companions contented themselves with only the "distant survey" one could make from their yacht, since, having heard of "special symptoms of hostility," they thought "we would certainly be fired upon by the hostiles if we attempted to land."[23] At least ten expeditions to Tulum followed in the next thirty years, each restrained by fear and practicing avoidance, foreigners having to guess at the meaning of ambiguous signs of the presence and intentions of the unseen Mayas until finally they met and began to talk.

George Howe and William Parmelee, sponsored by Harvard University, landed at Tulum in 1911. They spent two days exploring the ruins, sleeping nights on their vessel anchored offshore, always keeping a watch out for hostile Indians, who, it had long been rumored, still used the ruins as a shrine of their pagan worship.[24] "To carry on work in this region," Howe thought it

> necessary to have the assistance of the Mexican authorities to the extent of allowing an escort of about thirty soldiers for work at Tuloom. . . . This would be absolutely necessary, as the Indians are extremely hostile and live in the immediate vicinity. I am convinced that any party not fully prepared to defend itself would certainly be attacked before working long at any of these places.[25]

Howe and Parmelee had no such armed escort, and they anxiously registered many signs of the rebel Mayas' presence. On the beach they found footprints and cut sticks suggesting someone had recently been searching for turtle eggs in the sand. From their vessel at night they spied up the coast a fire lighted and then extinguished a few minutes later. The next day they spotted a white flag waved from a hill two miles northwest of the ruins, in the direction, they believed, of the nearest rebel village. Howe recalled that the earliest Spanish explorers had reported the use of white and black flags by Mayas signaling to vessels along this coast. No matter, apparently, that that was almost four centuries earlier, for it was the same coast, and of all living Mayas, the rebel Mayas were taken by foreigners to be those most akin to conquestera Indians.

When during their second day at the ruins Parmelee told Howe of also having seen a white flag briefly waved from the principal structure of the ruins (the Castillo)—earlier that same morning and without considering it much worth mentioning at the time, apparently—they discussed the likely import of these signs. Given what little was known of rebel Mayas, their meaning could only be ominous.

> I have no doubt that the party camped on the point [where fire had been spotted] discovered our presence and sent a man up to the Castillo to find out our numbers when we came ashore, and then signalled back a report to the village. An attack, I believe, would inevitably have followed had we waited a few hours longer.[26]

Howe and Parmelee were then in the midst of removing Tulum's most interesting artifact, the so-called stele #1. The stele had been discovered by John Stephens during his visit to Tulum seventy years before, and it was one of only several such stelae as yet found that far north bearing Classic Maya long-count date inscriptions, in this case 9.6.10.0.0, corresponding to A.D. 564. Howe and Parmelee apparently intended to load it aboard their vessel and take it as scientific booty to New York City. But fear of attack overcame them when they had dragged only a few of the stele's several-hundred-pound fragments to the beach. They buried them there at what they took to be the high-water mark, and left the remainder back among the ruins where they had been found.[27]

The School of American Research in Santa Fe, New Mexico, sponsored an expedition that landed at the ruins of Tulum in April 1913. The American archeologists Sylvanus Morley and Jesse Nusbaum had made their way to the island of Cozumel in a Mexican gunboat, and from there they crossed over to Tulum in a rented sloop, accompanied by five armed Mexicans to guard against a Maya attack. Morley expected the worst from any encounter with rebel Mayas, aware of the decades of warfare with Mexicans and noting that "in this general hatred for outsiders, Americans have not been excluded."[28]

The expedition's small landing craft foundered in the surf of Tulum's beaches, soaking the passengers and rendering useless the muzzle-loading weapons they carried. They remained at the ruins only a few hours, noting a sign of the rebel Mayas' presence, as had Howe and Parmelee two years earlier. This time it was a small clearing in the bush just in front of the Castillo. Nusbaum reported that, within the walls enclosing the ruins of Tulum, "the jungle is so thick that one must cut his way wherever he goes except near the main castillo, where the natives, who make constant excursions to the temple on top of the pyramid, have cut away all vegetation."[29]

Neither of these expeditions to Tulum accomplished much of scientific value, as so little time could be spent exploring the site owing principally to anxiety over Indian intentions.[30] "Moving about through this jungle is hard work at best," Nusbaum reported to readers of the *Santa Fe New Mexican*.

> It is doubly hard when you are expecting to be attacked by savage Indians at any minute. Taking pictures is out of the question. Serious work can only be done when there is no danger of attack. The native Indians here, as well as in other parts of Quintana Roo, fight from ambushes only, rarely making their presence known. Hence the difficulty in subduing them. They could have wiped out our small party in this dense jungle growth with the greatest ease, and our excursion about the ruins was possible only as long as we could keep them from becoming aware of our presence there.[31]

Sylvanus Morley headed another expedition to Tulum, sailing from Belize in March 1916 under the sponsorship of the Carnegie Institution of Washington. The explorers' fears of attack had diminished somewhat with word of a peace agreement between the rebels and the Mexican government. So, during the four days of their stay at Tulum, two members of the expedition, Morley and a British archeologist, Thomas Gann, even dared to spend nights sleeping on the beach. But Morley could not get the crew of his rented vessel to come ashore and assist in labors there. "These cowardly fellows, with but one exception, flatly refused to leave the boat, and spent the days and nights discussing the 'Indian peril,' which was never acute. . . . Evidence of recent Indian visits to the ruins, however, was not wanting." This time that evidence included discarded palm-leaf slings of the kind Mayas used to wrap and carry the butchered flesh of game they had shot or trapped; broken turtle eggs; and candle drippings in some of the buildings. Members of the expedition mapped and photographed the ruins, made tracings of murals, and recovered stele #1, which they assembled, photographed, and buried in the sand to be retrieved another day. They did not stay long though, still not trusting entirely to the peace then supposedly reigning in the territory.[32]

None of these early visitors to Tulum met any Mayas, though they sensed their proximity and feared what at times seemed imminent encounters. Visitors stole in and out of the ruins quickly and quietly, attempting to get a little work done in the process. In the absence of any communication with rebel Mayas, and informed as these visitors were by tales of Indian cruelty, hostility, and ferocity, the most minimal signs of human presence were material for grim speculation about the activities and intentions of the unseen Other.

Such anticlimactic non-encounters, however, provided paltry material for the travel narratives those expeditions spawned. So over time and from the safe vantage points of Santa Fe, New York, Washington, and London, writers elaborated upon the minimalia, constructing a fiction of encounters where none had quite transpired. Though he had speculated on the recent abandonment of Tulum and the possibility of still-living aboriginal cities, Stephens had reported no signs of human presence at the coastal ruins of Tulum. On the contrary, the solitude and desolation weighed heavily upon his senses. Yet his traveling companion, Frederick Catherwood, later reported that they *had* found, in the innermost chamber of the Castillo, "traces of fire and copal, making it probable that some Indians had recently been engaged in celebrating their ancient rites, which they still adhere to when not within observation of the Spaniards." The Allison Armour expedition to Tulum in 1895 made no landing there and reported no sightings of any kind. But fifteen years later it was asserted that members of the expedition *had* spotted flags waved from shore, and in another fifteen years word had it that the expedition had actually been "turned back" by hostile Indians.

While George Howe reported that members of his expedition to Tulum in 1911 had spotted flags, fifteen years later the story grew to include actual sightings of hostile Indians creeping about in the bush. Sylvanus Morley reported finding discarded palm-leaf meat slings lying about upon their arrival at the ruins of Tulum in 1916. Another member of that expedition, writing years later, reported that the leaves were found deposited on the floor of a building they had swept clean only the day before, suggesting not only that Mayas visited the ruins from time to time, but that they had the visitors under surveillance.[33]

These many stories were told and written by foreigners about

Two anonymous Mayas at Tulum, 1922

themselves, not about the Mayas of whom they still knew precious little. They were fashioned to accent personal daring and the courage of pioneers in scientific research, and to explain the scant accomplishments of early expeditions. And they were fashioned above all else, of course, to sell books. Subsequent visitors to rebel territory concocted still other fictions of encounters with the Other. But at least they would have more substance to work with, once minimal signs of human presence and grim interpretations of Maya intentions developed into actual meetings and dialogues.

The honors of the first modern encounter with the elusive Tulum Indians fell to Prince William of Sweden in 1920. While touring the Caribbean on his yacht *Iberica*, Prince William and his entourage put in (with some typical difficulty—"our little dinghy came very near upsetting, with its irreplaceable load of cameras and sketching materials") at the Tulum ruins. They were met on the beach by a small contingent of Mexican soldiers, who escorted them up to the ruins.

> Hardly had we passed the huge wall which encircles the city on three sides, when a handful of Indians appeared. Thrusting the leader [of the Mexican escort] aside without ceremony, they proceeded to scrutinize the intruders at close quarters. We did the like. With hands on our revolvers we exchanged long and eloquent glances.

Uttering the word *ingleses*, "Englishmen," and gesturing at themselves, the foreigners assumed an auspicious nationality, and

> by means of signs and gestures we managed to make them understand that our visit was made with no hostile intent, but merely for the purpose of viewing the sacred ruins. Soon we were shaking hands, and cigarettes were brought out. When, further, the chief had been presented with a Swedish matchbox adorned with a figure in glaring colours, the completest understanding was established.

Prince William's Maya hosts let him tour the ruins, though they forbade any digging and the removing of any artifacts, "for fear lest the spirits should be angered, and great calamities be visited upon the tribe." "Indeed," the Prince later wrote, "they seemed quite eager after a while to show us round, and when we were not quick enough in apprehending the meaning of their signs, they would emphasize them by a friendly dig in the ribs with their guns."[34] The foreigners did not stay long nor did they ever manage much of a conversation with the Mayas.

Other expeditions to Tulum followed in 1922, 1926, and 1927, and when on several occasions rebel Maya did make appearances, both to investigate the intrusions and to worship in the Castillo, they conversed with visitors accompanied by interpreters of Yucatec Maya. As for the hostility that the foreigners expected in such encounters, if it was ever a legitimate fear, it had become outdated. According to Samuel K. Lothrop, who accompanied a 1922 expedition to the site, "the difficulties presented by the Indian population are fast disappearing and no trouble need be anticipated if they are tactfully handled," for "when the Indians understood our purpose they placed no obstacles in our way and even consented to work for us. We found them persistent and cheerful, if not intelligent, workers."[35]

While the threat of attack had seemingly passed, Mayas were still openly ambivalent concerning the arrival of foreigners there. At Tulum Gregory Mason, a member of a 1926 expedition financed by the *New York Times,* spoke through an interpreter with a man named Caamal, "ear-ringed chief of the Tulum Indians": "He says that thirty or even fifteen years ago you could not have landed here. You would have been surrounded by his people, all strong young warriors. He says those good days have gone, but he is glad to meet you, even under these conditions."[36]

Mason learned from other Mayas that some were unhappy with the foreign incursions, and Maya leaders had to consider dissension in their ranks as they measured what aid and tolerance to lend the explorers. Maya ambivalence was understandable not only in view of the decades of hostilities past, but also for the things then said about Tulum. Maya oral tradition had it that the first foreigners had landed there centuries before; that the King of the Mayas had paid the intruders little heed, since there were so few of them; that when he did expel them the foreigners came back in great force and conquered the land, while the king and his people fled eastward on a road that passes under the sea. Now here came the foreigners once again; though few in number, who could know where it would end?[37]

That aid or tolerance was extended at all stemmed from both the curiosity and the needs of the rebel Mayas. There were things they wanted to know about the foreigners and the nations they had come from, and there were favors they had to ask. Concerning Juan Bautista Vega, who had served as scribe under the prophet Cituk, Gregory Mason observed during his visit to Tulum that "he is an interesting character, a mixture of business man, mountebank, diplomat and seer. He is telling me about the social usages and customs among the people he rules, trying to get my opinion of them without giving me his." Vega himself was not Maya, but rather the sole survivor of a small party of fishermen from Cozumel who many years before (when Vega was ten years old) had landed on the coast at Tulum to cook their catch; Mayas suddenly appeared and massacred the intruders, sparing only the child Vega to raise among themselves.[38]

The British archeologist Thomas Gann, during one of his visits to the ruins of Tulum at about the same time, conversed at length through an interpreter with a Maya officer named Canul from the village of Tulum. (Canul had been among those Mayas who had "supervised" Prince William's tour of the ruins in 1920.[39]) Long past were the days of fearing such meetings with rebel Mayas; Gann claims to have summoned Canul from his nearby village.

> As we sat talking and smoking our cigarettes, the General drinking some of the single bottle of whisky we had saved from the wreck [of Gann's launch—yet another casualty of the rough surf off Tulum], in a pause in the conversation, like a bolt from the blue, and à propos of nothing in particular, he suddenly asked me the extraordinary question: "Does your English King talk with God?"

Canul went on to explain: they had been told that in her time Queen Victoria did speak with God, and he wondered whether her son had inherited the power. Informed that the king was Victoria's grandson rather than son, Canul said that in that case such inheritance "would be too much to expect." Still, his curiosity was not idle; at issue were protection and alliance, both royal and divine.[40]

During an earlier expedition to Tulum that issue had been raised explicitly. Sylvanus Morley had already visited Tulum in 1913, 1916, and 1918 when he returned with co-workers in February 1922 to continue research. As they walked up from the beach and

> pushed through the palmetto bush to the inner enclosure [of the site] . . . a most pleasant surprise awaited us. It had been largely and recently cleared and the Castillo stood up wonderfully clear. Climbing thereunto first another surprise awaited us. It had been nicely swept and in the inner chamber on the bench at the back stood a small wooden cross, perhaps 16 or 18 inches high, painted blue with some figures on it.

The cross was garbed in a miniature embroidered frock similar in cut to those worn by Maya women (i.e., 'ipil), and in front of the stone on which it stood Morley found white, yellow, and pink candle drippings. They left the altar undisturbed.

A day after Morley arrived, he was visited by Paulino Caamal—the same who would speak with George Mason four years later. Accompanied by other officials and their children, and after hearing the purpose of Morley's labors there, Caamal explained to Morley that

> he was glad to have us come so long as we were Ingleses [Englishmen], which for the moment we were. He explained at some length and in Maya . . . that they have wanted for some time to be under the protection of Great Britain and that long ago Queen Victoria had promised to receive them as such! Further that they were somewhat disgusted that so many years had passed since this promise was given without its having been put into effect.

Morley's British Honduran interpreter, Muddy, assured Caamal with a fanciful update on royal affairs: though the Queen had died, the "boy king" who had succeeded her was now grown (King George V—no need to mention Edward VII), so finally "something might be expected."

Caamal returned two days later as Morley had promised to give him some gifts then—"cloth, tobacco, etc. etc." Caamal and his companions themselves came as "Greeks bearing gifts, oranges, limes, camotes, fowls and sour oranges, the latter are good in tea."[41] Though one is, of course, to beware of Greeks bearing gifts, at this time Morley was "too busy to be very simpático." He arranged for another visit to take place the following week, asking the Mayas to bring some ancient artifacts that he would buy. They might also perform a rain ceremony for the foreigners to photograph.

> Muddy said the Cura [a Maya priest who came with Caamal] had no objection to "putting it on" (to speak somewhat vulgarly). His observation was that "these Indians would do anything for money." They are returning Tuesday or Wednesday next week, and we will see what they will do then.

A week later, Caamal returned with a large group of Mayas from Chun Pom. "A strange enough sight it was too. Some fifty odd Indians seated around on their haunches on the ground each and every one with a gun in his hands. It looked like a young garrison."

Morley and the Chun Pom Guard at Tulum, 1922.
Morley is standing toward the front, wearing a pith helmet and tie.

A garrison it was, the garrison of the shrine center of Chun Pom, which protected the sanctuary from intruders. They were armed with muzzle-loading guns and some Mauser repeating rifles, "all well kept," one observer noted. And they could draw upon a great hidden cache of gunpowder purchased from revenues generated by granting concessions to foreign chicle contractors working a narrow strip of the coast.[42]

They had not come to Tulum to perform for the foreigners. Instead, there was some serious talking to be done. Two of the three Maya officers in attendance sat under the cover of Morley's tent, a third sat apart and looked "dour and disapproving" ("and even refused a copita [shot] of cognac which I presently had passed around to everybody"). "The conference began by the [Mayas'] interpreter [Juan Bautista Vega] telling me that the Chun Pom people suspected us of felling the bush to build a pueblo [town] there for the Mexicans! That this would displease them, and they wanted to know what our intentions were and why we had come. . . . The situation for a little while was pretty tense."

The rebels' British allies had once felled trees thereabouts under commercial agreements the rebels had found much to their strategic benefit. But then Mexican and Yucatecan invaders would also have felled trees and cleared areas around the ruins during their military occupations of the site as well. Morley explained that they had come only to study the ruins and that he had done similar work in many other countries. He showed photos he had already taken of the ruins at Tulum as labors there had proceeded. He assured the Maya visitors (when they asked) that he had the permission of the Governor-General of British Honduras to do that work and that if their presence was "not to the liking of the Indians" he and his companions would go away. Cognac, cigarettes, and phonograph music were deployed also, until finally the group's ranking officer, Cristino Yeh, "deigned to smile which he had not done before, and one felt the tension lessen."

Vega told Morley that "everything was all right. They were glad to have us working here and they understood what we were doing, and hoped we would come again." (The Tulum officer Caamal later claimed that they had *ordered* Morley to return each year to clear the bush around the ruins.) The Maya officers were given some quinine to take back to the ill wife of the general of Chun Pom, and then they were off to take care of other pressing business—to collect money owed them by their chicle concessioners at a camp only a few miles further down the coast. Twenty of them returned the next day to pray before the small cross in the Castillo. "We had been careful not to move this, and I was glad enough that we had taken this precaution because they were very much in earnest," Morley noted in his diary. The returned visitors also "all had ailments to attend to."43

Topics previewed in such sporadic and fragmentary dialogues between Mayas and foreigners at Tulum were explored more fully in subsequent encounters between Maya officers and Sylvanus Morley, a pioneer and still-towering figure in the scientific study of ancient Maya civilization. Morley had become interested in the ancient Maya during his years as a student at Harvard University, and he undertook many expeditions to Maya ruins in Mexico, Guatemala, and Honduras from 1907 on. In pursuit of as-yet-undiscovered sites and unrecorded hieroglyphic inscriptions, Morley was unflagging and meticulous, despite the toll that life in the tropical forest inevitably took upon one's health. As early as 1914 Morley began encouraging the wealthy Carnegie Institution of Washington to sponsor a comprehensive, twenty-year-long research project at Chichen Itza, the "greatest city," he believed, of the "highest," most "brilliant" civilization of the ancient Americas.44

In the sixteenth century, the Aztecs who battled invading Spaniards in the central highlands of Mexico were at the height of their power, and their capital city of Tenochtitlan was the largest in the Western Hemisphere, one of the largest in the world, in fact. When Spaniards arrived there in 1519 its palaces were still occupied by an élite who commanded tribute from vast numbers of peoples in a far-flung realm. At its pyramids and in its temples a still-vital religion was practiced, macabre though it was in its voracious appetite for human sacrificial victims. Its markets were crowded and its armies were the terror of ancient Mexico. We have long known a great deal about the Aztecs of those years, for even as Spaniards struck their extraordinarily devastating blows at the head and heart of that Indian empire they observed and recorded much about its society, religion, economy, military sciences, languages, and more. In comparison, until quite recently we could know precious little of the ancient Maya civilization that had flourished centuries before the Aztecs had become masters of their own lives, let alone lords of a great empire. Colonial-era Spanish chroniclers and Maya authors writing in a newly acquired European script could shed some little light upon Maya customs, ways of making a living, governance, costume, warfare, and religion as they were in the few centuries ending with the Spanish conquest of the Mayas. But knowledge concerning any more ancient periods of Maya history awaited the modern advances of archeology and epigraphy.

By the time Morley began his archeological investigations at Chichen Itza, though the grandeur of that ancient civilization had been redis-covered a scant sixty years before, scholars could already discern that the ancient Mayas had excelled in the beauty of their art and archi-tecture, the complexity of their calendrical and numerological reckonings, and the accuracy of their measurements of the periodicities of the sun, moon, and Venus (perhaps of other planets, too). That the ancient Mayas had been tireless and accurate chroniclers of their own history had become evident to scholars, as before them now lay a seeming millennium of dated texts, inscribed in stone, stucco, wood, and bone, or painted on walls, pottery, and the pages of the several hieroglyphic codices that had survived book burning by early Spanish friars.

The glyphs for numbers and time periods and the complex workings of multiple, interrelated Maya calendars had already been deciphered, though the events to which the decoded dates referred remained a mystery still waiting to be solved. Another, still greater mystery awaited solving, too, as scholars had by then discerned that, for causes unknown,

Sylvanus Morley and his wife, Frances, 1931

the heartland ancient Maya civilization in the midst of its "Golden Age" had met with sudden "universal calamity" (around 600 A.D., Morley then thought). Construction of palaces and temples stopped, date-bearing monuments ceased to be erected, and all the great civic centers—Tikal, Copan, Palenque, to mention the greatest among them—were abandoned.

Chichen Itza, it seemed, was the product of a post-collapse renaissance in the northern reaches of the Yucatan Peninsula to which the "banner of Maya civilization" had been carried out from the darkness that had descended upon the desolated heartland. It was also evident, however, that Chichen Itza itself later suffered abandonment in civil war, later still to be resettled by the bearers of a foreign culture (that of the Toltecs, predecessors of the Aztecs in central Mexico, in whose favored forms and images the Castillo, Ball Court, Temple of the Jaguars, and other structures at Chichen Itza were built). Chichen Itza once again flourished until its primacy was wrested away by other ascendant centers of the north, before all declined into the chronic warfare and political fragmentation that lasted until the Spaniards came in the mid-sixteenth century.[45]

The project Morley proposed that the Carnegie Institution undertake at Chichen Itza was novel in the then brief annals of Maya archeology, emphasizing not wide-ranging and necessarily superficial explorations of the entire ancient Maya realm, but rather intensive study of all periods and aspects of a single great Maya "city." Morley's project would attack all outstanding problems of ancient Maya history, including Morley's own primary interests, such as the proper correlation of ancient Maya chronology and contemporary European calendars, or the meanings of the still largely unintelligible Maya hieroglyphic script.

In 1924 that project did finally begin. Through protracted negotiations the Carnegie Institution secured the approval of the Mexican government and arranged to rent the hacienda of Chichen Itza from its current owner, Edward H. Thompson, an archeologist and former U.S. Consul in Merida. Morley set up residence in the structure known as the Nunnery, not in the former hacienda house, much in decline since the days of Stephens and burned as recently as 1921 by irate Maya socialists. He began assembling at the site a staff of able colleagues and a labor force of scores of Maya workers, and several years later he was joined by his second wife, Frances Rhoads. Thereafter, from his vantage point at Chichen Itza, Morley continued his lifelong endeavor to chart the course of ancient Maya history as revealed through a complete-as-possible corpus of hieroglyphic inscriptions from all parts of the ancient Maya world. Research on Chichen Itza itself—along with affiliated sociological, anthropological, and medical studies of contemporary Maya that the Carnegie Institution also soon sponsored—made of that place and its environs for many years to come the most thoroughly studied part of the Maya world.

Sylvanus Morley was, his biographer tells us, a profoundly good-natured man, open and honest with all whom he encountered, and "uneasy over any case of hard feelings regardless of who was at fault." He was one to seek reconciliation and the repair of damaged relations and was extraordinarily effective and tactful in social interaction. "Although he was short in build, unprepossessing in appearance, and nearsighted," that biographer also notes, "he was richly endowed with a warm personality that made him remarkably attractive."

Morley left an indelible trail of good will among those who knew him in the course of his hectic life—his colleagues in archeology and anthropology, his acquaintances in government and business, as well as the Mayas who worked for him or spoke with him. Toward the latter Morley displayed a special fondness born of his appreciation for the intellectual and monumental achievements of their ancient civilization such that " 'My Mayas,' as he referred to them, was a term of affection rather than possession," and though centuries distant from their former greatness, in Morley's eyes they "still remain the finest aboriginal people of North America."[46]

When at forty-one Morley assumed the directorship of the Carnegie Institution's investigations centered at Chichen Itza, he had already several times made visits to former rebel Maya territory—his travels to Tulum, of course, as well as a 1918 excursion to the former rebel capital of Santa Cruz (then known to Mayas as Noh Cah Santa Cruz Balam Nah and to Mexicans as Santa Cruz de Bravo, after Mexican General Ignacio Bravo). From the mid-1920s on, the focus of most sustained contact between archeologists and the once-rebel Maya shifted from coastal Tulum to the much larger inland site of Chichen Itza. Morley's contacts with rebel Mayas had until then been brief, sometimes tense, affairs. Now he would talk at greater length with a different segment of the rebel Maya population—those in villages north and west of their former capital of Santa Cruz. In this new round of dialogues with once-rebel Maya, Morley's good-naturedness, frankness, and sentimentalism would be truly tested in novel ways.

II

RECONNAISSANCE UNDER COVER

SANTA CRUZ had been occupied by the Mexican army in 1901 and abandoned fifteen years later as revolution raged elsewhere in Mexico. When Sylvanus Morley visited the town in 1918 it was a "veritable city of the dead," home to but a single Maya household.[1] In 1929 a journalist found Santa Cruz only somewhat more alive under the command of Maya General Francisco May. Apart from the few Mexican officials residing there to regulate the only significant commerce of the region — the extraction and exportation of chicle, from which chewing gum was manufactured — the town seemed little more than a "camp of outsiders, of restless and discontent people, of people tired to exhaustion by the implacable and cowardly war of the tropics, of people who in the end get drunk in order to forget life and its poverty and its infinite boredom."[2]

But to Mayas of the surrounding region, Santa Cruz was a sacred place. Their miraculous cross of divine wartime revelations was still harbored there, and though it no longer spoke to would-be rebels, exhorting them to battle and pious living as it had done in headier times, it nonetheless remained the most awesome and revered presence of the divinity from whom human life and power flowed. Its presence marked the sacred center of the rebel Maya realm, and though they would not live in a town so desecrated by conquest at the hands of Mexicans, Mayas of the region still reported there every so often to serve at the command of their officers (and, ultimately, General May) in a rotating guard that protected and maintained the premises of the sacred shrine. Twice daily masses were said in Maya before the cross, and twice annually well-attended festivals were staged in its honor.

In 1928, in an effort to reassert Mexican authority, a small detachment of federal troops was sent to Santa Cruz from the island of Cozumel. Mayas of the region responded by denouncing General May, suspecting him of having sold them and their land to the enemy. They plotted his assassination and laid siege to the shrine center, where twenty-five terrified Mexican soldiers holed up in their barracks awaiting certain death.[3] Meanwhile, alarm spread through Maya villages of central Quintana Roo with reports that in the shrine center of Chan Cah Veracruz, not far to the southeast of Santa Cruz, a letter from God had appeared on the altar of the church announcing an imminent invasion of Maya sanctuaries by a Mexican army that would bring "suffering and crying." It commanded the faithful to unite and to assemble more frequently at the shrine center. A request for reinforcements went out to the distant, but notoriously bellicose, Maya town of Kanxoc in eastern Yucatan.[4] Though no outbreak of hostilities ensued, rumors and fears of imminent war remained current among Mayas in the years that followed.

Amidst that crisis of 1928–29 disaffected Maya officers from north and west of Santa Cruz—one Lieutenant Concepción Cituk and another Sergeant Evaristo Zuluub—stole into the town and removed the miraculous cross to a location more secure from Mexicans and turncoat Mayas. The cross and its adherents wandered north and east through the coastal region already visited by Morley, Gann, Mason, and others, finally turning southwest to settle at a small hamlet then known as Xcacal.[5] A church and sacred precinct were constructed to house the cross and those who would thereafter guard and serve it. This was not to be a *new* sacred place, one to add to the roster of rebel Maya shrine centers after Santa Cruz, Tulum, Chun Pom, Chan Cah Veracruz, Xocen, and San Antonio, central places in Maya sacred geography of the time. Rather, it would be Santa Cruz-in-*temporary*-exile, named as such in prayer but thereafter referred to for mundane purposes and in ordinary speech as Xcacal Guardia.[6]

With the region thus in turmoil, foreign explorers began arriving. In 1929 the Yucatan Medical Expedition of the Carnegie Institution set out from Chichen Itza and skirted the western frontier of Xcacal Guardia's domain for brief visits to several villages. The Indians they encountered were "not quarrelsome and . . . not likely to molest anyone against whom they have no grievance. They can be fiercely vindictive, however, when their sense of justice is outraged."[7] When the Grey Memorial Expedition of Tulane University, led by the explorer Frans Blom, crossed through Xcacal Guardia's territory in July 1928 it inadvertently offended someone's sense of justice. Upon arrival in the shrine center they found

the Indians were praying, and shortly after we found them all around a big meal, on the floor of the church. They understand Spanish, but pretend they don't and in every way show us that they don't want us around. By their houses are many chickens, but they will not sell any, and we are told that we will have to watch our animals carefully, as they otherwise will hide them for us.

Several of them came to look us over. An old man, and a boy of about eighteen wore no earrings, but a boy of twelve had one gold one in his right ear. A small boy of about four also had one ring in his right ear.

I got a photo but when the old man saw the camera directed towards him he fled.

There was no grazing or fodder for our mules in the forest around and the Indians would not sell us any corn. Only on the clearing by the church was a little grass and close by this stood about ten shabby looking stems of bananas, most of them blown to pieces or broken. Some of our mules started to feed on the banana leaves, and promptly an Indian appeared "muy bravo" [very ornery] and balled me out in Maya. When he carried on for a while and worked himself up to a fine frenzy, I opened up at him in English, which he understood just as much of as I of his language.

Then our interpreter stepped in and informed me that our mules were destroying his valuable banana crop, and he would claim 25 pesos for the damage. The Indian assured that he would shoot our mules and ourselves, which was no hollow threat from him. . . .

The excited Indian later returned and told us that Teniente [Lieutenant] Concepción [Cituk] would be in with his escort of soldiers that evening, and he would be sure to clear us out quickly. . . . Towards evening an Indian patrolled in front of our camp, armed to the teeth. . . . The night passed by without any adventure, and in the morning we found that the Indians with their rifles and shotguns had been sleeping in the church close to our camp. They had apparently meant what they said. . . . We loaded and left with all speed.

On the way out of Xcacal Guardia Blom and his party met Lieutenant (later Captain) Cituk and his guard returning to the shrine center. Cituk asked Blom's guides a few questions, "which they all answered without telling him where we came from nor where we were going," or that they were carrying a small fortune in silver pesos, presumably for expedition expenses. After that the foreigners hurried on north to the safety of the state of Yucatan.[8]

In that same year the American aviator Charles Lindbergh flew a Pan American Airways twin-motor Sikorsky amphibian on an experimental air reconnaissance of Maya ruins on the Yucatan Peninsula. During one leg of his flight near Xcacal Guardia, while accompanied by the archeologist Alfred Kidder, Lindbergh buzzed a mound near a clearing with an Indian hut, where he spied "an Indian woman in a pink dress and several naked children who ran into the house as we circled downward."[9] Lindbergh and Kidder flew on to a water landing off Tulum after circling the ruins to take photographs. They spent two hours inspecting the ruins on foot, during which time they too met and spoke with local Mayas before flying off to the east.

In 1932 Alfonso Villa Rojas explored much of once-rebel territory on ethnological reconnaissance under the auspices of the Carnegie Institution. Villa, born and raised in Merida, was teaching in a primary school in a Maya village in eastern Yucatan when the American anthropologist Robert Redfield recruited him as an assistant in field research. After collaborating with Redfield in his study of that village, Chan Kom, Villa was dispatched to explore possible sites of future research in central Quintana Roo. While on vacation from the college he was then attending in Merida, he spent three weeks visiting twenty-three villages west, south, and north of Santa Cruz. He intended to give special attention to the villages of Tuzik and Señor, which reports from schoolteachers working in the region suggested were organized differently from other southern Maya communities. Villa went accompanied by a guide who one of those teachers swore knew the territory inside out.[10]

In some villages Villa and his companion were moderately well received, as in Xpichil, previously visited by the Yucatan Medical Expedition in 1929 and by Redfield and Villa for a few hours only the year before. There Villa found "clean and polite" men who remembered him as the fellow who had accompanied "the American" (i.e., Redfield). They questioned him about his intentions and, apparently reassured, they laughed and conversed with Villa, except for the one Maya officer present, who remained "closed-mouth and observing."[11]

In other villages Villa met with what he took to be "feigned indifference." In Tuzik, with the menfolk out working in their fields when Villa passed through (as was so often the case during his travels), women showed themselves "little friendly but not shy," offering only typically monosyllabic responses to uninvited questioning.[12]

Where the menfolk were present, Villa was commonly received with overt hostility. Even as Villa and his guide dismounted from their mules in the village of Dzula, home of Sergeant Evaristo Zuluub, where they hoped to rest and eat after hours spent wandering lost on forest trails, "two half-naked Indian males approach us, only wearing shorts, and with a rude gesture and vulgar tone [one] asks us, 'What are you looking for around here?' To which my guide responds, 'We are taking the road to Payo Obispo.'" Though they were not, in fact, headed to that distant town in southern Quintana Roo, they were traveling in a generally southerly direction. "The grimmest of our interlocutors, looking at us in an impertinent manner, adds 'You lie! You must be Teachers, and you come here to observe us, but as soon as the Corporal comes we'll fix this; for now, we'll take the horses.'" (The federal government was then attempting to install its primary school teachers in Maya communities in Quintana Roo, though only in a few did Maya leaders accept the Mexican instructors who, they feared, would subvert Maya youths.)

They reluctantly surrendered their mounts. But Villa gave his stern hosts some cigarettes, and found they "alleviate a little the natives' tension and the conversation follows less hostile directions." A further gift of sweets put the "natives" even more at ease, and when after some time neither the corporal nor the village's ranking officer, Sergeant Zuluub, had appeared, Villa and his guide were released to continue hurriedly on their way.[13]

In the course of his reconnaissance Villa decided to conceal his true identity and purpose, and

> cloak with very subtle pretexts my presence in each settlement, as the first thing they suspect upon seeing me with a camera is that I am a spy of the Government who goes about investigating their way of life in order to later dominate them more easily. However, I have managed to overcome this suspiciousness with cigarettes and sweets.[14]

His pretexts sometimes worked, though never to more than temporarily allay Mayas' suspicions and reticence, as when Villa visited the shrine center of Chan Cah Veracruz, accompanied on this leg of his journey by a federal school inspector stationed in Santa Cruz, who hoped to make observations without Mayas' learning who he was. Upon

To Valladolid

Tepich •

Tihosuco •

To Peto →

N

Sacalaca •
• Saban

*Chichankanab
Lagoon*

Yaxche •

Chun Ya •

Cocoyol •
Chunyaxche •

Tulum
TULUM ⊙ ∴

Boca
Paila

Chun On •

⊙ **CHUN POM**

San
Antonio •

Kampokolche

**XCACAL
GUARDIA**

• Tuzik

• Yokdzonot

Santa Maria •
Hobonpich •

Xmaben •

Chunkulche

⊙ Señor
• Chan Chen Laz

Vigia
Chico

• Chan Chen Comandante

San Jose

Yaxkax •

Tabi •

• Xpichil

*Ascension
Bay*

Xiatil •

• Xhazil

Chunhuhub •

Dzula •

Chunhuas •

Chanchen •
• Pom

Sahcabchen

Chunbalche •

SANTA CRUZ

Yo'actun •

Komchen •

⊙ **CHAN CAH
VERACRUZ**

Kilometers

0 ▬▬▬ 15

0 ▬▬▬ 15

Miles

Yaxche •

San
Pedro •
• Xhazil

• Yokdzonot

*Espiritu
Santo
Bay*

San Ignacio •

• Kopchen

• Petcacab

⊙   Shrine centers

•   Villages

∴   Maya ruins

═══   Main roads

‒ ‒ ‒   Main trails

+++++   Small-gauge tracks

C E N T R A L
QUINTANA ROO
IN THE EARLY 1930'S

© 1989 A. Karl/J. Kemp

To Bacalar

arrival, Villa and the inspector were greeted with "vulgar gestures" from the shrine village guard and directed to leave immediately. Villa responded, saying that he represented an American company and that he had come to buy all of the chicle they gather in the next season. "The conversation," he noted, then "turned friendly and the faces, smiling."

From at least the turn of the century Mayas had been involved in the tapping of sapodilla trees (*chicozapote* in Spanish, *ya'* in Maya) from which chicle was derived. Tapping the trees was a technically simple though potentially hazardous chore. Having scaled the thirty- to sixty-foot-tall trees one then worked one's way back down the trunk, using a machete to incise its bark with two sets of descending, intersecting grooves (left to right, then right to left, then left to right again, and so forth). As the tree bled, the latex flowed slowly down the grooves into a bag at the base of the tree. The flow was greatest and most rapid during the rainy-season months of July through October, and even into January on occasion, so these were the prime months for chicle gathering. The latex so collected was taken to a small base camp, where it was boiled down and hardened into readily transportable blocks, which were accumulated by the chicle gatherer and sold to a chicle contractor for delivery or resale to representatives of major chicle-exporting companies.[15]

At the beginning of the century production was slight and the gum-chewing habit of North Americans still relatively new. After the First World War, however, the habit spread rapidly, and with it grew the demand for chicle from the forests of the Yucatan Peninsula, British Honduras, and the Peten of Guatemala. From 1918 to 1929, as North American demand burgeoned, so too did production in central Quintana Roo, though not at the rate that exporters would have liked. While chicle companies owned or held concessions to vast tracts of sapodilla-rich forests in British Honduras, Campeche, and northern Quintana Roo, in the once-rebel territory of central Quintana Roo one had to purchase from Maya producers and negotiate with Maya leaders.[16] As demand and prices fluctuated from one year to the next, so too did those Mayas' disposition toward outsiders, as Villa himself was quite aware.

> If they [prices] are high, the native shows himself more friendly and communicative with outsiders, believing that they are treating him with honesty and justice; if, on the contrary, prices drop, then he appears displeased towards strangers, and especially towards Government men to whom he attributes the manoeuvre [of reducing prices] as an act of ill-will.[17]

The members of the Chan Cah shrine guard told Villa they would want 60 pesos per hundredweight for chicle they had gathered, and even though the current price was only 15 pesos, Villa agreed. In fact, he told them, he would pay them in dollars. "Dollars! shout all, and the magic word passes from mouth to mouth like something cabalistic, of venerable power." Villa obtained an audience with the commanding officer of the shrine, Sóstenes Mendoza, with whom he spoke of similar things and from whom he learned that in that settlement they considered themselves British subjects. But, despite the Mayas' obvious pleasure with Villa's offer to buy their chicle, they would not accede to Villa's request to enter the church (under the pretext of wishing to present lighted candles before the altar of the shrine). And when chicle gatherers from Santa Cruz arrived, Villa and his companion hurriedly left, fearing the school inspector would be identified and their cover blown.[18]

In the village of Señor, Villa's ploy was equally effective. When a local man of some influence, Paulino Yama, learned Villa was a chicle merchant, "suspicious looks" dissolved into a flood of questions about the outside world, the Sino-Japanese War (i.e. the Japanese conquest of Manchuria), and distant nations.[19]

In the course of the next year Villa twice returned to central Quintana Roo. His brief visit to the village of Tuzik had confirmed that it should be the object of his and Redfield's attention, for it seemed "the best and most picturesque" of a cluster of villages most "stubbornly against receiving foreign influences or even to having contact with people from the outside world."[20] The customs of Mayas in those villages, Villa expected, would bear greater resemblance to pre-Hispanic practices than one could then find among Mayas anywhere else on the Peninsula. The data from ethnological study of those villages would be compared with the findings of Redfield and his co-workers in other Yucatan communities, and the results of that comparison, they expected, would shed light on the rate and nature of social and cultural change as general processes in human history.[21]

The objective of Villa's second and third visits was to "gain the confidence and sympathy of the people" in Tuzik. The very traits that made Tuzik and its neighbors most desirable objects of study — "the habitual xenophobia of their inhabitants" — also implied special obstacles to research there. Preparing for a second excursion in the region, Villa and Redfield discussed the best way to proceed. It seemed to Villa that under no circumstances could he reveal that he was, or had ever been, a schoolteacher, the likes of which local people so detested that some referred to them as the "greatest demons." Rather, he had best

Alfonso Villa Rojas

present himself as a chicle buyer or a traveling merchant. Redfield agreed but suggested that after Villa had gained the Indians' friendship he might tell them he had *once been* a schoolteacher but had abandoned the profession in disgust and had become a merchant instead. That way he could avoid problems that would surely arise should Mayas learn from some other source of Villa's pedagogical past.[22]

So Villa provided himself with a trusted companion and guide in Edilberto Ceme (from Chan Kom, Yucatan, where Villa had earlier taught school and assisted in Redfield's anthropological research) and three mules laden with merchandise to sell in the villages they would pass through. Traveling south through the forest proved arduous, as trails adequate for travel by people on foot had to be widened by machete to accommodate the mules. Villa was well received in Tuzik, since along the way he had met a Maya with relatives there, who sang the praises of Villa-the-merchant and fed him in his sister's house. Villa and Ceme were lodged in the family chapel of the principal officer of Tuzik. The officer was not home at the time, but his wife gave reluctant permission once Villa contributed a dozen candles for the chapel's altar, the usual practice of itinerant merchants so lodged in communities thereabouts.[23]

As they would in each of the villages they visited, Villa and Ceme decorated their borrowed dwelling with colored paper and balloons, spread their wares out on tables and benches, and started up a phonograph they had brought with them. Attracted by the music, villagers trickled in to inspect the merchandise and chat with the strangers, registering surprise at the variety of things this new merchant had brought: cloth, thread, button. needles, mirrors, earrings, combs, shirts, shawls, pants, blankets, scented soaps, scissors, cups, plates, bowls, aluminum spoons, flashlights and batteries, napkins, two hundred rubber balls, and more. Women showed particular interest in the shawls, fabric, earrings, and embroidered strips for the borders of their traditional white frocks (*'ipil*), while the men seemed most interested not in the blankets, machetes, and axes, but, rather, the balloons. And, though Villa made no note of this in his diaries, the men were likely also interested in the ammunition that Villa brought—more than twenty pounds of cartridges for twelve- and sixteen-gauge shotguns and for 30/30 rifles.[24]

In most villages the inspection of Villa's wares proved a festive occasion, though Villa once despaired that "God only knows the patience and good temper needed to deal with these people." His customers were unfamiliar with modern Mexican currency, pesos and centavos, so Villa had to translate prices into the colonial-Spanish system of reales and medios, and most were very choosy about the merchandise, handling it and discussing it *ad nauseam* with bystanders and relatives. Even after all that, few purchases were made, since a recent sharp downturn in the chicle trade had left those Mayas very short of cash. "The women feel the worst," it seemed to Villa, "because they cannot buy everything that pleases them."[25]

Villa labored at concealing the true purpose of his coming. For fear of arousing suspicions, he dared not linger too long in Tuzik and so moved on to make brief visits to several other villages just as a real traveling merchant would do. Villa told people he was from the Yucatecan port of Progreso, confident they would never have heard of the place. To have truthfully declared himself come from Merida would certainly have suggested he was a government spy, since those Mayas knew that that city was the seat of government in Yucatan.[26] With other traveling merchants whose paths he crossed in his travels, Villa kept up appearances also. Finally, he took extraordinary measures to conceal his note taking: "To remove all suspiciousness I waited until the late hours of the night and once in my hammock, covered myself up completely with my blanket, lighted a small flash light and wrote up rapidly and briefly my impressions of the day."[27]

Local Mayas kept Villa under close surveillance during his visits. While common people enjoyed the fair he put on in each locale, officers apparently observed carefully. Of one such officer Villa noted: "The Comandante, like the good Indian he is, the less he talks, the more he notices, and the more he notices, the less he talks." In the village of Xmaben Villa met the most influential officer of the region, a captain, who while others gathered about Villa's wares and balloons "was the only one who was silent and wary. He watched me every minute. When he left he said to us *'hasta mañana'* [until tomorrow]."[28]

The captain wanted to know more about this stranger who called himself a merchant. The next day when Villa was in Señor, "six of the captain's men arrived from the shrine center. They were very well armed," and told people they had come to buy oranges, but Villa reckoned they were sent to check on him. They chatted amiably with Villa for a long spell, consulted with villagers with whom Villa had conversed earlier, and then returned to the shrine village. "I must employ great caution in order not to arouse suspicion among these people," Villa reminded himself that day.[29]

During his several weeks of reconnaissance, Villa accumulated snippets of information about current social and political conditions in the region, and about religious practices as well. Women seemed to have been very open with him. They were his most interested customers and were around during the day while the men absented themselves to work in their cornfields. With the menfolk gone, Villa found women positively "loquacious," "smiling, bold and coarse in speech." He was struck by how they would come to talk with him with only their skirts on and how "in their conversation they do not hesitate to speak quite often of the sexual act in its various aspects. Of course I do not encourage them in talking along those lines." All told, they struck Villa as "gossipy, shameless, and lascivious."[30]

In his guise as friendly merchant, when menfolk were around Villa was unusually free to observe a range of male-female interactions. In the village of Señor

> the hut next to the chicken house in which I am staying is inhabited by a young couple with a small child a few months old. Thanks to my vantage point I have been able to observe the attitude of this young couple toward each other. Rarely, or to be more exact, never before have I seen among the Indians such extreme affection. Both husband and wife caress each other tenderly and they spend most of the day in their passionate courting, which resembles that portrayed in moving pictures or in novels. The fascination of his wife is such that the man appears to have forgotten his working.[31]

It was a rare glimpse of Maya romance. In still another village, on another occasion, Villa witnessed a more familiar scene from married life in Maya villages.

> Here I was present at a family quarrel. It happened, for reasons of which I am ignorant, that the wife of Yum Andres was on that day in such bad humor that she wished to do nothing for her husband when he returned from the milpa [cornfield]. "If you want to eat in a hurry, you'll have to wait on yourself," she cried in a loud voice. "There are tortillas in the *jícara* [gourd] and onions in the caanche." Her husband discreetly did as his wife told him, but as he was going for the onions, she became even more angry, and yelled out, "Mehen kizin [little devil], it seems that you haven't feet, you move so slowly." The patience of Yum Andres was exhausted, and turning on his wife he struck her until she cried and began calling for her mother. The mother, hearing the cries of her daughter, came at once and was evidently quite ready to enter the fight. However, it did not come to that, thanks to the return to

discretion of Yum Andres, who moved over and ate in silence. A few moments later he said to me, "These daughters of the devil are crazy. They only want to fight."[32]

Discreetly monitoring domestic happenings within his ken was one thing. Learning about matters religious, military, and political was another thing altogether. Villa found local Mayas closed-mouthed in the face of any inquiries about their practices, especially those of the rotating guard service, in which all adult males took turns protecting the shrine center and executing religious observances.

> It is interesting to observe the profound secrecy which they try to preserve with regard to this practice. There isn't an Indian, no matter how friendly and confiding he appears, who will give direct information about the place where his "guardia" [guard service] takes place or about the rites practiced in their churches.[33]

A young man who cut Villa's hair one day talked more than he should have about such things, it seems.

> We conversed on various matters [and] in this way I learned that he performed his *guardia* in a village which he limited himself to saying was called Noh-Cah [great village]—where the *jefe* [chief] lives. After further conversation I was able indirectly to lead him to the point where he would tell me the whole name of his famous place, which turned out to be Noh-Cah Tixcacal [i.e., Xcacal Guardia]. "But no one can enter there," he said, "not even the merchants, because the people give them a beating and throw them out." When I asked where it was, he said "It is to the north, about two leagues from here." This was entirely false, since information from other better sources has located it between Señor and Xmaben. [Villa's "better sources" were not quite accurate either.]

Villa went on to note that "my informant told me these things in a frightened manner, oppressed, perhaps, by a fear of the dislike the *Santo* [divinity] would have for his revealing the secrets of the Sanctuary." But it was done. At last Villa knew the name and location of the shrine center of the group of villages he intended to study. When ten days later he chanced upon the trail to that village he thought better of entering it, "as the time seemed inopportune."[34] A visit to that sacred place was postponed indefinitely.

From still another villager reticence turned to a stream of revelations in a moment of rage against federal teachers. "The Teachers are emissaries of the *Federales* [federal soldiers]," Paulino Yama of Señor explained to Villa, "who now have occupied Noh Cah Santa Cruz, the largest of our *pueblos*. But this is only temporary. Already the hour is approaching when we will gain back our liberty as it was in those times when this country had no masters but ourselves." "Here he stopped," Villa noted in his diary:

> and the rest watched me to see what effect his words should have on me. Upon seeing that I acquiesced . . . [he] went on to say "we are not willing to have the Government mix into our affairs. Isn't it the Government that has stopped the buying of *chicle* so as to impoverish us and trample us into the ground? Isn't it the government that sends airplanes so often to observe us and to see the way in which we make war? Why are they making the landing-field in Santa Cruz? Only so that they may be able to dominate us with many airplanes when the war begins. But we are not sleeping. We have prepared for some time. And now everyone has at least his Mauser, 2000 cartridges, and three arrobas [hundredweights] of powder. As for the airplanes, there aren't enough of them to bother us. I am sure I can bring them down with a volley from twenty-five soldiers. I am practicing. I have been able to bring down *zopilotes* [buzzards] from high up."

As Yama railed on against his enemies, Villa was struck by the transformation wrought in this speaker whom he had previously thought "meek and peaceful." "Don't you know anything about the next war? No! Then it is well that you know that it will be hard for January to begin with us still at peace." "This appeared to mean a great deal to the others," Villa noticed, "and they gave him meaning[ful] glances which put a finish to his tirade. Nor would he speak again but regained his usual deceptive air of meekness." Again, it seems he had already said more than he intended. Meanwhile, Villa was left wondering, "Were his prophecies true ones? Would these men dare throw themselves into an armed struggle in which without any doubt they would lose?"[35]

Thanks to the observations he was able to make and the indiscretions of occasional interlocutors, Villa counted his reconnaissance a limited success. Though he only made "a profit of fifteen percent upon the net value of the merchandise sold," he did succeed in establishing friendly relations with some Mayas of the region. Villa was left hopeful regarding the prospects of future fieldwork there, but still unsure whether "the natives will allow me to stay with them in the village selected [Tuzik] or whether it will be necessary for me to resort to other measures."[36]

Something else would have to be done. Though posing as a traveling merchant worked well enough to get Villa into villages, people there were so short of cash that any demand for Villa's wares was rapidly exhausted, leaving him with no excuse for lingering. It was two years before Villa would return again to the region, and when he did, he came in a different role, made possible by those Mayas' subsequent dealings with the Americans at Chichen Itza.

III

ILLUSIONS OF
ALLIANCE

EARLY IN 1934 word arrived in Xcacal Guardia that there was an American at Chichen Itza. Some officers said that he was selling people into slavery, that Americans were bad like the Mexicans. What else could one expect of people who come from the interior (i.e., from central Mexico) and from behind the water? But other officers said the American's thoughts were good. He had come to see if the old ones were all dead, if the *masewal,* as Maya rebels called themselves, were extinct.[1] And for some reason they were taking mud out of the sinkhole there. Americans were then called *čačakmáak,* "very red men."[2] But one who recalls those first reports says "we had never seen one and didn't know what color they were—red, blue-green, black." Several men set out to investigate.

When rebel Mayas spoke with foreigners at Tulum, they did so as the ambivalent hosts of trespassers. Now *they* were going out from their homeland in search of the foreigner, an American, whatever kind of being that was. They would have to trek several days across the no-man's-forest that lay between rebel territory and the enemy-controlled north. The journey would take them past scattered cornfields and the camps of chicle gatherers, around the stone barricades of wartime forest skirmishes, and through the overgrowth of ruined towns surrounding the blasted hulks of colonial-era churches and the once great houses of the wealthy and powerful. Some of the ruined settlements were already stirring with new life.[3]

They would have heard of Chichen Itza, though they had never been there. The city was once premier on the Yucatan Peninsula, and even

45

after the Spanish conquest it still attracted Maya pilgrims. Rebel Mayas of Morley's day, however, could only dimly recall that glorious past as it was encoded in stories of ancient kings and the strangely powerful beings of a previous creation who had multiple connections to that place. Colonial-era prophetic and historical books in the Yucatec Maya language, the so-called Books of Chilam Balam, devote precious pages to the saga of Chichen Itza and the fate of its ruling élite, the Itzas. But the Mayas who sought out Morley most likely knew little of that either. Finally, they may have recalled stories of a stone archway of the colonial-era estate at Chichen Itza under which Maya rebels returning south from attacks in Yucatan would pause to divide up the spoils of their conquests, including white female captives to be taken as wives and white males to serve as porters and slaves.[4]

After several days on the trail, the men from Xcacal Guardia arrived at Chichen Itza. They were wearing pleated blouses with billowing sleeves gathered up at the wrists and each with two rows of small buttons down the front, long trousers, palm hats, single gold earrings dangling from their left ears. Leather straps circled their waists and crisscrossed their chests, and from them hung waterproof traveling bags, machetes, and other paraphernalia of forest farmers and hunters. The straps gave them a military look, and today they say it was by their clothing and ornamentation that Morley recognized them as men from the south, the area of Santa Cruz.[5]

Morley's visitors explained to him that while, yes, they were from the south, they were no longer under the command of General Francisco May; rather, they had separated to establish their own group. "Do you have a leader?" Morley is remembered to have asked them. "We do. How could we not have a leader?" "Well, I need to see him, to talk with him," Morley said. The visitors were wary.

> Ok. But only if it's on the level, then good.
>   But if . . .
> As they say: A broody hen with many chicks, the mother
>   is eaten and the young ones go around crying for her.
> Well, because of those little ones, that which ate the
>   revered mother is discovered,
> and it gets fucked too,
> that thing that ate her.

Morley was not disturbed by the menace in this rustic allegory. All the same, he is said to have told them, everything was on the level. He wrote a letter to be taken back to their leader. He also gave them gifts — cloth, medicines, tobacco, sections of used automobile tires from which to fashion soles for their sandals — and invited them to return again.[6]

Back home Morley's letter was presented to Xcacal Guardia's principal officer, a captain, who fetched his secretary to read it: "The man at Chichen Itza asks who our leader is. We have five or six weeks to respond. After that, he will assume that the letter never reached its destination." Or that, at least, is how they tell it today.

Some of those present counseled against responding and revealing the names of their shrine center and its leaders. It could be treachery, they said. Morley was, after all, a *ʔùul,* a foreigner, and so probably also a "natural enemy, a hypocrite, and a liar." And all the officers would have known of a divine injunction against any dealings with such people. In a latter-day postscript to a mid-nineteenth-century revelatory proclamation, the "Divine Commandments," the officers are warned by their Lord: "One by one [I will] punish you with fifty [lashes] because you are talking about mixing with the enemy, although you see how the enemy exhausts me, you say that no harm will come to you through them, because I am advising you my children, don't say that, it is what the created enemy says, it is what you say because he has money and not what my true Lord says."[7]

The seemingly ancient commandments were publicly read at high masses celebrated during shrine village festivals. Attendance at such masses was great, and during the reading of the commandments officers and common people knelt and bowed their heads.[8] But, despite the sacred warning, the captain declared to his fellow officers that they *would* respond to Morley's letter. The captain could apparently claim the sanction of a different set of revelatory texts for his decision. Was it not prophesied, they say he said, that such contacts with the enemy would come to pass? That at Chichen Itza

> there will be the coming of one poor man.
> Though *ʔùul* he calls himself,
> he will come out to give his thoughts to the poor ones,
>   the masewal,
> so that they can stand up,
> so to explain what must be when the day arrives,
> so to empower the king for us, so that the commandments
>   and the law may be obeyed.

Such prophecies, they believed, were inscribed in the ruins of Tulum, where ancient hieroglyphs foretold union between Americans and Mayas in war against the Mexicans. Also to be seen there are the images of two individuals, one upright and ascending, one upside-down and falling—signaling the future fates respectively of the Maya king and the king of the foreigners. The long-vanished king of the Maya would return someday with the *čak winkob,* the "red people"—people who were very tall, or who had eyes like those of bees, some said. In any event, Mayas would recognize those blessed people with whom they were to form a future alliance. They would be the ones who could decipher the ancient script, thus signaling divine approval and shared ancestry.[9]

So they would write to this fellow at Chichen Itza. In any event, the officers said among themselves, if they kill us there we will kill them here—a maxim of social intercourse forged through what for these men had already been a lifetime of hostilities.

Eleven months later, toward the end of that year's agricultural season, a subordinate of the Maya officers of Xcacal Guardia returned bearing a letter[10]:

> It is necessary that I make this list on the paper. It is drawn up in Chunkulche village on 18 of November of the year of 1930 years [actually, it was 1934]. Thus then the holy hour in which it was that I raised a commission to come to your place in Chichen town, in which it was that you received it with goodness and love, in which it was that you put your letter in their hand. So also I put it in the hand of my commission [this time]. So too, upon receiving it [your letter] I was very happy to receive it. So also I answer another to you also. I put a letter in your hand, you who are here in Chichen town.

The letter was signed by two officers of Xcacal Guardia, Captain Concepción Cituk (no relation to the prophet) and Sergeant Francisco Chaac. It was also signed by their secretary, Apolinario Itza, and by the young subordinate who brought it, Juan Bautista Poot. The officers were men in the middle years of life by our reckoning, elderly men, however, in their time and place. Chaac was forty-five; Cituk, fifty-four; Itza, forty-two.[11] (Sylvanus Morley was then fifty-three.) Epidemics of the early part of the century had decimated the elderly, so that by 1935 there were only fourteen men over fifty years of age in a population of more than seven hundred people in villages affiliated with Xcacal

Guardia. The officers, moreover, no longer resided in their natal villages. All had abandoned settlements further south at the turn of the century when the Mexican army under General Ignacio Bravo advanced in the final and successful offensive against the rebel capital of Noh Cah Santa Cruz Balam Nah.[12] It was from their new villages that the officers of Xcacal Guardia sent letters to Morley, in this instance from Sergeant Chaac's village of Chunkulche.

Officers at Xcacal Guardia commanded subordinates, men and their wives, in matters both civil and religious. All adults in the villages affiliated with Xcacal Guardia belonged, principally by descent through the male line, to one of five "companies." Each company had several officers, and the full complement of officers of all companies, when assembled, made up a council that looked after the scheduling and execution of shrine village ceremonies and everyday guard service around the sacred precinct of that center. The council of officers also adjudicated civil complaints and punished offenses—sometimes by whipping the guilty—that could not be dealt with at lower levels of company organization. And they discussed and set "foreign and military policy," which is to say dealings with non-Mayas who entered the region for trade or to otherwise use the forest, with federal authorities then ensconced in Santa Cruz, and, evidently, with Americans at the ruins of Chichen Itza.

Captain Cituk of Xmaben was the most influential of the Maya officers serving Xcacal Guardia. One other, Commander Herculino Can of Chan Chen Comandante, by rights outranked him, but age and collaboration with the federal government in the matter of establishing schools had undermined the commander's influence in Xcacal Guardia, leaving Cituk as the chief person to reckon with. By local standards Cituk was poor, even to the point of having sometimes to work as a common agricultural wage laborer for his own subordinates. Yet among Mayas of the region he enjoyed great prestige for his wartime "boldness and valor," and among outsiders his reputation was that of a "fierce and tenacious enemy of the white man," and the "wildest," "most hostile," and "most brutal" of all the Mayas in Quintana Roo.[13]

Captain Cituk and his fellow officers addressed Morley in the only language they knew, Yucatec Maya. It was Cituk's secretary, Apolinario Itza, who drafted most of their letters to Morley and who read most of the responses. There was, with one exception, no other scribe who could do it. In Apolinario Itza intersected channels of communications with both foreigners and the divine. Although True God had long since ceased to address Maya audiences audibly and in public, officers still received letters from Him "dictated" to Itza, presumably in extraordinary states of divine inspiration or possession. And it was Itza who read aloud the "Divine Commandments" to Maya audiences in the shrine center of Xcacal Guardia.[14]

That first letter was not the most competently crafted of the officers' letters—or "list," as they called it on this occasion—to Morley. Perhaps they had not yet found words to suit their motives in dealing with this foreigner. They were not even sure yet how to address Morley, calling him "Mr. Don Chief," since some had heard his Maya laborers at Chichen Itza call him *jefe*, "chief," or "boss." Morley's translators, though fluent speakers of Yucatec Maya, also had their troubles with the correspondence. They had to decipher the handwritten script; aggregate disarticulated syllables into words and the words into clauses and sentences; identify person, temporal and spatial references in the written text; translate Yucatec Maya words and constructions whose usage may have varied regionally; and so on.[15] Sometimes what Morley read in translation was a hopelessly garbled version of what the officers had written. More often the errors introduced noise, as it were, into the channels of this dialogue, which distorted but did not obliterate the intended messages. In the passage quoted above the message was clear enough—the officers were responding to Morley's past letter.

If Morley had any doubts about the officers' purpose, those doubts should have faded once he had read on:

> Mr. Don Chief, there is something I make clear to you. To the suffering of God, already the town where we are here [Santa Cruz] along with all the land are all taken from us by the Mexicans. Already they are all taken from us. All they want, they are doing to us. We who are here in the village want that there be well delivered to us the place to all the ends of the territory of Santa Cruz as it was long ago. Because we, we are used to governing ourselves here in this town. Because we, we do not want Mexicans to come in to govern us. We are used to governing ourselves in our town, since long ago, thus in the present. Therefore also there is my telling you, Mr. Don Chief: do not believe that we have all surrendered to the Mexicans.

The rebels were not extinct; others *had* surrendered, the officers wrote Morley, but not they. Only five years earlier the Xcacal Guardia group had split off from the unified command of General Francisco May based in Santa Cruz. The reoccupation of that town by federal troops in the

Captain Cituk

u tian ya 5in co tte 3un nia tihabil de
y9o 36 An mon cu Kanan tal u liic
in car ta Vay tu cah gixla cah u liic
bal in Sarler des u tial in Kaat yan diil
tic ti te ech 3r Bou ge pe ya ni le eck
tu ca gil chi chem 3r Dro 5ir ba no
doc tor Mo le tio la in Vuic bix cu
20 cot le al le Ora do cax ti que letun
ti cin uiyic tii tech bix cu bin 20cool tun
tumen tene le ale gro cu met ma uche
leti val caa pach tic tac belaa e yo
la tun in villic tun ua yucha cil asa
ic jum pel ayuda ti cuyum jajadios
uaye x ca cal ca jeeh tumen yo lal u nu
ma nia ciyum jajal dios patal uayee
tumen ton yan tal u yic yalaal binu
calaa chaa bil ton tumeen me ji canoab
le tun ti cin sa si cun sic tii tech senior
don sir bano doc tor mo le yo la ci uiyic
teche uayucha cil A metic jum peel ayu
da ti toon uaye tiyo lal le lumo culaa
chaabal tii toonoo uaye tiyo lal cu uiyic
tun te chee ua yucha cil u pa tal ton
elumaa tux manal je bix uchee
letun ti cu uiyic techee ua yucha cil
abe tic u cuen tai lee utial caa pataa
tii ciyum jajal dios yetel tii toon
tumen tonee jum pel un mi nion Kaat
cax te ta uetel jach la tu ja ji in
than jach tu ja ji in tucul tin puc sikal

Officers' letter to Sylvanus Morley, June 5, 1936

52

late 1920s along with the increasing accommodation of General May to a kind of power sharing with the Mexicans led to that split and to fears of Mexican usurpation. The appropriate response to the challenges of those times seemed evident enough to the officers who wrote Morley:

> The United States and England, where is Madame Queen Victoria ["the Virgin Mary," Morley's translator mistakenly transcribed this]—Mr. Don Chief I ask of you the favor of your giving me the flag [of those nations] for us here, because we want to become one nation with you too. Therefore I ask you for the flag.[16]

As they would on many subsequent occasions, in this letter the officers alluded to their predecessors' dealings with the British in Belize:

> Mr. Don Chief, that is what I make clear to you, too. Because the words made in the town of Corozal and [unclear], that is what we want to know—how will it end? Because we, that is what we pursue even today.

Even more to the point, they wrote:

> I want you to know that here it happens that I negotiate with you, like long ago [with the British]. Because I, I am very sincere in my talking with you. Mr. Don Chief, I want to speak with you about the weapons. A thousand weapons I ask of you, with [unclear], their accouterments. There is my asking this of you, Mr. Don Chief, so to protect ourselves a little here in this village, Mr. Don Chief.

In asking for a *thousand* weapons, even though the five companies of Xcacal Guardia included only 150 "soldiers," the officers surely had in mind one of the Divine Commandments uttered back during the War of the Castes by their Most Holy One, around whom besieged rebels had once rallied and whose pronouncements directed them on the battlefield as well as in the governance of their sacred capital and forest villages.[17] Many of those Divine Commandments had long ago been set to paper, and subsequent generations of Maya officers still heard them read aloud in such shrine villages as Xcacal Guardia. So even in the 1930s the divinity seemed to exhort them in wartime tones:

> And another thing
>   That I command
> For you,
>   Ye my beloved Christian villagers.

53

> One thousand weapons
>   And one thousand of their bearers
> In order to surround their ranch
>   That Kampokolche.[18]

No matter that the settlement of Kampokolche lay abandoned and in ruins from fierce fighting eighty years before, fighting spurred on by this commandment at the time of its first utterance. Such divine words have a timeless quality and seem continually to refer to an ever-shifting present moment. And if to the Maya officers of Morley's day it seemed foolhardy to challenge the Mexican army when they were so few, from the same source came divine assurances of a similarly timeless nature:

> Because even though they are going to hear
>   The roar
> Of the firing
>   Of the Enemy's guns
> Over them,
>   Nothing is going to cast harm
> Upon them.
>
>   . . . .
>
> Because know ye,
>   Ye Christian villagers,
> That it is I who accompany you;
>   That at all hours
> It is I who goes in the vanguard
>   Before you,
> In front of the enemies,
>   To the end that
> There not befall you
>   Not even a bit of harm,
> O ye my Indian children.[19]

Though from that past assault on Kampokolche rebels had withdrawn with grievous losses, the officers of Xcacal Guardia in the 1930s still "believed . . . in the invulnerability of their armed forces," although, it seemed, "less firmly" than before.[20]

In that same letter, the officers asked Morley for an airplane, too, for the commission to return home in.

Morley responded several days later. He did not address the matter of arms for now, since his translator, unable to read the Maya scribe's handwriting, had mangled that part of the letter. In place of the passage requesting a thousand guns, Morley read instead, for example: "It is necessary for us to ask you to write us also, so that we could ask you what goes on there, and we'll also tell you what goes on here with us."[21] Mention of the talks at Corozal, Belize, was also lost, as well as the request for an airplane. What was left of the officers' words to Morley could be summed up succinctly: "The letter asked us to enter into correspondence with them, and to carry on friendly relations." So, limiting himself to expressions of happiness for having received their letter and commission, Morley told the officers he was sending back twenty-five meters of cloth to be distributed among the letter's authors, as well as quinine and purges, tobacco, more tire sections, and twenty-five pesos to defray the costs of their next visit to Chichen Itza. The cloth was, Morley explained in Maya, "a sign of my love for you, and of my hope too."[22]

Hope? Describing these visits in a letter to the head of the Historical Division of the Carnegie Institution, Morley told of the "friendly and rather pitiful" letter he had received from the hand of a young Maya subordinate from the village of Xmaben—Juan Bautista Poot, "who wears a most gorgeous gold earring in his left ear." He went on to note that "in establishing this contact I have had in mind especially Alfonso Villa's future work. I think that [Captain Cituk's village of] Xmaben, which is within two or three leagues of Tuzik, may be his entering wedge."[23]

In the letter sent back with the commission and the cloth, Morley invited the Maya officers to come to Chichen Itza in January of the following year. That visit did not take place, but another commission bearing another letter was dispatched by the officers in February 1935. Cries of persecution were repeated, but the men provided no additional detail. The officers wrote, however:

> There is my making clear to you, also—I [one officer spoke for them all], that I deliver myself just like that to Mexicans, *never.* That is what I make clear to you also, Mr. Don Chief, nor may there be your saying I have not made clear to you what is being done to us by Mexicans, to us here in the village.[24]

The bluntness, even anger, of this passage was tempered by a prior assurance that "we all like you in that town of Chichen"—an assurance that was not in the Maya original, but that Morley's translator inserted, quite gratuitously.[25]

The commission may have been instructed to bring Morley back to Xcacal Guardia: the final line of the letter is ambiguous, and what Morley read in translation was that they were to "enlighten" him further on the matters at hand. Morley did not then go to Xcacal Guardia, though he told one of the visitors that a friend of his would visit Xmaben later in the year to gather information about the village and the corn farming there. Meanwhile, by querying his latest visitors at length, Morley was able to learn the names and approximate locations of the five places on the Yucatan Peninsula that those Mayas considered most sacred (Chun Pom, Tulum, Xcacal Guardia, Chan Cah Veracruz, and San Antonio), the names and villages of residence of the Xcacal Guardia officers, as well as the names of the villages associated with that shrine center, the water sources, number of houses and adult males in each one.[26]

Morley was pleased with his developing relationship with the Mayas around Xcacal Guardia, and the prognosis for future intensive study of them seemed good:

All these men have assured me that our people will be welcome there and no harm come to any of us. Indeed Frances [Morley's wife] and I are thinking of going down there ourselves sometime. None of these boys have gone away from here empty-handed; a little money, a lot of medicine, quinine, disinfectant for wounds, and "sal ingles," manta for shirts, and discarded automobile tires for sandals. I believe as they indeed assured me that our representatives will be able to go into that region and work among them.[27]

Letters were exchanged over the following months, Mayas writing to Morley more often than he wrote to them (Morley was away in the United States during most of that time), the officers expressing in varying detail their fear of, and anger toward, "the Mexicans."[28] In May they wrote:

How very happy I would be if you came quickly. The favor I ask—mercy from you, that there be your coming quickly. Because now the Mexicans are going around doing many bad things to us here where we are. Give a little thought to poor ones, Mr. Chief. For that reason I ask you to come quickly, Mr. Chief, because the garrison where we are here, they are displacing us, they are harming it also, really. Because there is one village from where the people have already been displaced by Mexican order. It ends up, they come to think, really, that the little community is like a community of wild animals.[29]

Once again the officers asked for arms, for "contraband" as they called it this time, and for a flag, "so to protect ourselves here." And once again the translator spared Morley from having to read this. Deciphering an "o" as an "a," an "r" as an "n," associating the syllables thus and so, and the officers' "the contraband we ask of you" could be read as "the fourth time we ask you so that the flag protect us."[30]

In September 1935 Alfonso Villa returned to central Quintana Roo. Since his earlier reconnaissance in those parts, the young schoolteacher and field assistant to Robert Redfield had been sent to the University of Chicago for more formal anthropological training. During that hiatus in his research, Mayas had begun their visits to Chichen Itza, a fact that he and Redfield considered as they pondered appropriate covers for his future activities in Quintana Roo. At first it seemed that Villa might do well to return there acting as a chicle contractor. As Redfield explained it to Morley:

> Alfonso tells me that in spite of the great advantage which ought to result from your cultivation of their good will, it will probably not be wise for him to return to those Indians in the role of collector of information. That is still too strange and suspicious a procedure for them to understand. Alfonso therefore suggests that he come in some role which will enable him to declare that he represents the chicle interests, because towards those interests they are, on the whole, friendly. Alfonso suggests that Dr. Kidder [of the Carnegie Institution] . . . or perhaps yourself, if you would be good enough to take the time, explain the matter to some representative of the Mexican Exploitation Company, and secure from that company their willingness to give Alfonso some nominal connection with their concern.[31]

Morley evidently preferred that Villa go as his personal friend, whom he was sending to gather information among the villages of Xcacal Guardia. He provided Villa with a letter of introduction that said as much.

The village of Tuzik was Villa's destination in central Quintana Roo, the place where he hoped to base himself while conducting research around Xcacal Guardia. It was an outlying settlement of the Xcacal Guardia group, an especially conservative and "picturesque" community, as far as Villa could tell from his earlier visits. The ranking officer there was a corporal, whose company superior, a commander, lived in a village some ten miles to the south. One hundred and sixteen people inhabited Tuzik, scattered among twenty-three large, sturdy, wattle-and-daub thatched-roof houses. Each cluster of houses had its chicken coops and pig pens, elevated wooden platforms on which herbs and small vegetables were grown, and very well kept walled patios, in which grew fruit trees of many kinds — oranges, bananas, papayas, custard apples, plums, tamarinds. Some clusters of houses also had chapels in which the important crosses of the extended family were sheltered and honored. The family's dead were buried around the chapels, and children seemed to like most to play over their unmarked graves.

These extended-family compounds surrounded a plaza at the heart of the settlement, grassy and clear except for flowers and some tobacco planted there, and several towering trees that had been spared when the site was first occupied three decades or so before. The centerpiece of the plaza was a long, narrow, wattle-and-daub, thatched-roof church in which the reputedly most miraculous cross, patron and protector of the entire village, was sheltered. The plaza ground was actually the limestone roof of an extensive water-filled subterranean cavern accessible through a small opening over which a circular concrete curbstone and cross-post had been erected and from which village women drew their household water several times a day. To that tiny oasis of dwellings, gardens, well, and church, ringed by guardian crosses at each of the entrances or exits of the settlement, and against which the wall of the tall forest pressed in from all sides, Alfonso Villa slowly made his way.[32]

When Villa arrived in Tuzik people recognized him as the merchant who had passed through "many years ago," and he was promptly surrounded by women who came out of their houses to investigate. Addressing himself to the only four men to be found in the village in the morning hours, Villa explained he had come "in name of the Americans to deal directly with the chiefs." He carried, he said, a letter from Dr. Morley at Chichen Itza for Captain Cituk and (now) Lieutenant Zuluub. With no one else would he discuss the nature of his mission while waiting for those two officers to return from a trip to Tulum, where they had gone "to burn candles," as they say. The villagers put Villa up in the church, brought him food, and by and large treated him very well, figuring he must be a "person of some importance."[33]

Two days later twenty-five armed officers and soldiers converged on Tuzik and escorted Villa to Xcacal Guardia. They thought it better that Villa await the return of Cituk and Zuluub there, in the shrine village itself, where his presence among them could be kept secret from the chicle gatherers and traveling merchants who occasionally passed through such peripheral villages as Tuzik. Villa spent the first night in one of the shrine village's five barracks, and the next day was moved to a lodging on

The Guard at Xcacal Guardia

the outskirts of Xcacal Guardia, away from "all curious observers" and, presumably, safely away from the church at the heart of the shrine center as well. "Because of this air of mystery with which they are surrounding my person, and also for the questions they direct at me," Villa informed Redfield, "I have come to understand that they are giving my visit a political significance." "As for me," Villa noted in his diary, "I endeavor to do whatever they tell me to and keep secret the true object of my trip to this place."[34]

Villa was treated well while waiting for the return of the captain and lieutenant. No longer posing as a traveling merchant or chicle buyer, but greeted, instead, as an emissary of the Americans, he found that doors once firmly closed were slightly opened, and people spoke more freely. Minor officers told Villa of their irritation with the annual invasion of chicle gatherers, and they made requests for weapons. They also chatted about the weather and the price of hogs, and cracked jokes.[35] And, when Villa asked to view the interior of the shrine village church, under his usual pretext of wishing to make a votive offering of candles, where once the answer was a polite no, this time his request was granted.

> Once in the Temple, the first thing I discerned in the shadows was a sentinel who, armed with a 30/30, protected the entrance to the sacred chamber called "Heaven" in which is kept the miraculous Cross, protector of the whole group. It was not possible for me to get that far, since another individual stopped me in the public room, telling me to turn over to him the candles for him to light. Doing that, I gave him the candles and he took them to the altar, not without first saying some words in a low voice to the sentinel who guarded the entrance shielded by an opaque curtain. Shortly after the same individual indicated that I could now leave the Temple.[36]

Nine days after his arrival the Tulum pilgrims had returned, and Villa had his first audience with Cituk and Zuluub. He explained to them that Dr. Morley was his boss, that desiring better friendship with them Morley had sent him there to act as his representative, and that he was to study them in order to determine if any help could be offered later on. For this, Villa said, it was necessary for him to live among them for at least two months.[37]

Villa then presented the officers with Morley's letter. Zuluub asked him to read it out loud. "Captain Concepción Cituk . . . my very beloved and good companion," Morley had written:

After wishing health to you as well as to all my good companions in Xmaben, Señor, La Guardia, and all the remaining villages in your land, with so very much love.

This letter is to introduce him, the foreigner [ʒ́ùul] who delivers it to you, Mr. Alfonso Villa R., who has joined himself to my work here in Chichen Itza, under the Carnegie Institution of Washington.

I want Mr. Alfonso Villa to go there to do some work for me there in your villages.

I want him to take your fame [record life histories?] for a printed-paper (Libro [book]) that I am writing, therefore it is necessary then that you explain everything to Mr. Villa so that he may serve me.

I want to know everything about you; my companions, how do you make your living there, how many are you in the village of La Guardia, and how many of you are there in each of the remaining villages; how do you make your cornfields, how much corn do you gather from each of your cornfields?[38]

Villa was unhappy with the letter of introduction Morley had drafted, and complained to Redfield from Xcacal Guardia: "To tell them, as Dr. Morley says in his letter that 'I come in search of ethnographic data for a book that the Carnegie Institution plans to publish' is something which does not convince them since it is not within their grasp to understand it. For them 'book' is synonymous with 'Teacher,' which is a 'spy' of the 'Government,' which is considered as the greatest enemy of the group."[39]

If the letter did raise such suspicions in the minds of officers and common people, their hopes for help from the Americans inclined them to suppress such thoughts. When Villa had first visited the villages around Xcacal Guardia he had found Mayas quite fascinated with the British.

In spite of the distance from here to Corozal [in British Honduras], some Indians have shown me in their huts fine cloth, beautiful shawls embroidered in silk, expensive jewelry, and other things which have come from there. . . . Almost everyone knows about the British colony, and they appear greatly interested in it. . . . From having been mentioned so much, the names of George the Fifth and of Queen Victoria have taken on curious connotations close to the fantastic among these people. Almost always they refer to them as omnipotent beings not far from the Gods.[40]

Since the Maya officers' first contacts with Morley and other Americans at Chichen Itza, there had grown up a similar fascination with Americans and America. Morley had come to be thought of, Villa observed, as a "superman, or better said, as an emperor who possesses numerous horses, automobiles, motorcycles, airplanes, machine guns, servants, luxurious living quarters, and, in sum, all that, in their infantile imaginations, should surround an all-powerful person." Americans as a whole were deemed "miracle workers for whom there exist no secrets nor impossibilities," whose "town" is like Heaven and "perfectly impregnable," surrounded as it was believed to be "by a magnetic ring so powerful that it repels the weapons and metallic objects of those who would cross it without permission." As Villa rightly noted, "This is the ideal defense for the Indians who live in constant fear of being attacked by the Mexican soldiers."[41] So of course Cituk responded to Villa by saying they, too, wanted to be friends with the Americans, and they would let Villa gather the information he required, expecting, however, that the Americans would help them by buying their chicle. As for letting Villa live among them, Cituk would have to consult with "all the people."[42]

An assembly was promptly called for the next day. After a mass at which the head priest personally officiated, all the adult males of the villages associated with Xcacal Guardia gathered in the long-house adjacent to the church. Toward the conclusion of their meeting they invited Villa in to present himself and read Morley's letter out loud (twice). Ad-libbing, Villa told his audience that "as representative of the Americans, all of them could be certain of always finding me a loyal and sincere friend, disposed to help them in all that is possible for me." And he told them that the "Americans only desire the moral and material betterment of all men, etc."[43] Aided by demonstrative gestures of approval from Cituk and Zuluub, Villa persuaded the assembly to let him set up residence in Tuzik. To conclude the meeting, Lieutenant Zuluub strongly recommended that his colleagues and subordinates not let leak to outsiders any word of the matters dealt with at that meeting, or even mention Villa's presence among them.[44]

Back in Tuzik, Villa was put up next to the house of the ranking officer of that settlement—in an old hut that had been used as a pigsty—a choice presumably dictated, again, by a desire to keep close watch on the visitor and to keep him away from itinerant merchants and chicle gatherers.[45]

A month later the officers sent a delegation of their sons to Chichen Itza to check on the authenticity of Villa's story and letter of reference. Villa followed them the next day. Villa, Redfield, and Morley had in correspondence discussed how important it was to make the officers think that Villa and Morley were the best of friends and that by dealing with them Mayas could improve their lot. So, when the most recent visitors arrived, Morley "impressed them right." His wife took pictures of Morley, Villa, and the officers, "in groups, singly, Alfonso and I with them, Alfonso and I by ourselves, arm in arm," and the photos were sent back to Xcacal Guardia to convince still skeptical officers. Meanwhile, Redfield wrote the head of the Carnegie Institution's Historical Division, Alfred Kidder, to see if the institution could do something quickly to improve the market for chicle gathered by Mayas around Xcacal Guardia, "so that they might feel that the coming of the delegate of the Americans has resulted in immediate benefit to them."[46]

To Morley, Redfield, and Villa things looked to be going very well indeed. Metaphors of warfare seemed appropriate to describe Villa's early accomplishments: "As will be seen," Villa wrote his mentor Redfield from Xcacal Guardia, "at last we have achieved our objective. However, much of the success of this conquest belongs to Dr. Morley." Redfield responded: "It is a great satisfaction to me to hear that the first battle has been won and that you have secured a foothold not only in the group of villages which you plan to study but also in the village of the sacred shrine itself." As for Morley, he anticipated that a "fine publication" would result from Villa's research, adding that

> it's time all that quinine, Epsom salt, chlorocane tablets, rubber automobile tires, bolts of unbleached cotton, cigarettes, cans of California peaches and old Saturday Evening Posts etc. should bear harvest and indeed they seem to have. I do not understand it all, but A. [Alfonso] says there is an old legend mixed up in it to the effect that some day there will be a white man who will treat them kindly and in a friendly way and that they will know who he is by the fact that he can read the ancient letters in the temples. I have always received these different delegations from down there on the back corridor of our house here which is always cluttered from one end to the other with parts of my Peten [hieroglyphic] inscription book. He [Villa] says the word has gone forth among them that I can read "these ancient letters" and voilà he said "Ud. está como un Messiah entre ellos!" [You are like a Messiah to them!]. Pues quién sabe [Well, who knows], but if it helps his work along it is O.K. by me.[47]

IV

ZULUUB'S
PLEA

OF THE MAYA officers' many letters to Sylvanus Morley, none were more eloquent than those authored by Lieutenant Evaristo Zuluub. Among outsiders Zuluub had a black reputation, and before Alfonso Villa had ever met him he had heard Zuluub was an "irascible and gross man," "despotic and cruel" toward the "people of his tribe," "a tenacious enemy of education and leader of the malcontents," disliked even by the Maya officers of neighboring villages whom he seemed to want to dominate.[1] In 1929 Zuluub, then a sergeant, had joined with Concepción Cituk to steal the rebel Mayas' most sacred icon—the Most Holy One Our Lord Three Persons—from General May's sanctuary in Santa Cruz, eventually to shelter and serve it in the new shrine center of Xcacal Guardia. By 1935 Lieutenant Zuluub was a man with a price on his head, his village of Dzula having been attacked, looted, and burned two years earlier by federal troops, who continued trying to apprehend him for the alleged assassination of a subordinate.

About the burning of Dzula stories are told today that differ radically in key details, the disputed versions recording subsequent and present antagonisms among Mayas as much as the facts of the case at the time. All agree that a man was murdered in Dzula and that Zuluub was accused of having ordered the killing. Federal troops were dispatched from the state of Campeche to apprehend him and prevent any greater outbreak of hostilities. En route the Mexican soldiers gathered up Maya men from the nearby villages of Xpichil, Xiatil, and Yo'actun and brought them along to assist in the attack. Upon entering Dzula the invaders were fired upon. They returned fire, and during the next hour

Lieutenant Zuluub

several residents were killed and the village was burned to the ground. Lieutenant Zuluub and most of his people fled into the forest, eventually to make their way to refuge in the shrine center of Xcacal Guardia.

Zuluub's enemies say the accusation was true — that he ordered the murder of a resident of Dzula, where he was the principal officer, simply because the man wanted to move his family and belongings to another town and was caught attempting to do so without Zuluub's permission. Zuluub's kin and friends say the accusation was false — a man *was* murdered, but by another man whom he had cuckolded. Zuluub's enemies say that villagers from Xiatil, Xpichil and Yo'actun had been rounded up against their will by the federal soldiers in order to prevent anyone from spreading the alarm; upon arriving in Dzula the hapless Maya contingent fired their weapons high over the heads of the Dzula villagers so as not to shoot any "of their own kind." Zuluub's kin and friends say the Maya collaborators were willing participants in the assault, who had long envied and hated the hardworking and prosperous people of Dzula, and who, while the village burned, stole everything they could lay their hands on. Zuluub's enemies say he managed to escape by donning his wife's clothing and calmly walking out through the attackers, who took him to be an infirm woman. Zuluub's kin and friends say that is not true. It was a *man's* shirt he put over his head as he ducked out the back door of his house and into the forest.

On this latter point Zuluub himself, it seems, had a still different story to tell. While fleeing from attacking soldiers, dressed as he normally was, no women's clothing or shirt over his head, he stumbled and fell. The soldiers caught up with him and no doubt would have killed him, but before they surrounded him he removed the gold earring that an officer wore in his left ear as insignia of his rank. Without the earring, Zuluub looked like any commoner. The soldiers asked him where Lieutenant Zuluub had gone, and Zuluub sent them off to the east while making his escape into the forest in the other direction. Whatever the merits of such disputed tales of treachery and sympathy, cowardice and valor, all who knew Zuluub do agree: he could be a fierce and implacable foe of any who antagonized him.[2]

In September 1935 Zuluub sent a long letter to Sylvanus Morley and Alfonso Villa:

Xcacal village of Guardia, 20 of September of the year of 1935 years. My exceedingly beloved ones you are, Mr. Don Chief in the town of Chichen. Thus then this holy hour, thus then this holy day, there is the great necessity of my making this letter for me to give to you, for you to know I have already received Mr. Don Alfonso Villa here in the village of Xcacal, here in the village of Guardia. I have already spoken with him, I have already conversed with him. How exceedingly happy was my heart as I received him. So, too, are all the troops [under Zuluub's command], also, with goodness, with love, with propriety. Mr. Don Chief, how very happy I am also to have already received your letter, so that I know what it is you say as well. Here in the village of Guardia I am very happy. Thus is the hour exceedingly good, exceedingly beloved. But also *I* have here goodness and love and propriety, also, here where I perform guard service, here in the village of Xcacal, where I take care of the Beautiful Most Holy One, where it is that I worship it, where it is that I adore the Beautiful One Our Lord Most Holy Beautiful Cross ✝ ✳ ✗   Jesus Mary in the beautiful name of Our Lord True God the Father with God the Child with God the Holy Spirit Amen Jesus. Thus then the truth of my words to you, Mr. Don Chief. I, Don Evaristo Zuluub, I speak with you also from here to the town of Chichen.[3]

Speak, of course, is just what Zuluub and the other Maya officers did, as their letters to Morley were dictated with an attending secretary transcribing their spoken words, syllable by syllable, line after line, continuously, without punctuation or paragraph (which I have some-times added in my translations). In his oral delivery Zuluub made elaborate use of parallelism and the repetition of phrases, a rhetorical style common to formal and sacred discourses in Yucatec Maya. And his opening salutations and protestations culminated in a powerful incanta-tion of deity names (breaking, for a moment, to represent the trinity graphically as well) by which means he pledged sincerity under penalty of divine sanction (an oath-taking known by the Spanish word *juramento*).

Zuluub continued, describing the hardships of his people, including his wife, six children and stepchildren, their five spouses and six children, as well as the one hundred and forty other individuals who had departed with him from the burning Dzula[4]:

Thus then this holy hour I am going to explain to you then what it is that is being done to me here in the village of Xcacal. How they [the Mexicans] hate that I make a little living here! They are preventing me from farming a little with my people and from going about looking to make a few pennies from the chicle around the holy village. They are working it all on us, all the holy forests. There is my telling them not to work all of it, to leave me some to

67

work a little with my people. They are not agreeing. The first thing they say: "You, you know nothing. That this land and forest, they belong to the Governor and the President. Thus even Santa Cruz. Where you go to work the forest, the federal soldiers [will] rise up to confiscate your chicle. It is just taken like that. You, nothing do you know. You cannot talk. You, you are nothing." They rule here in this land, here in this forest, here in Noh Cah Santa Cruz. Even here in Guardia, they are not letting me find a few pennies so I can pay my debts and those of my people. For many things I have borrowed with my people [in exile]. Where then do I go to make my living with my people? Nowhere, because the Mexicans, they rule here now.

Zuluub's troubles were not his alone or peculiar to his exile. The chicle business had engendered a host of problems for all Mayas around Xcacal Guardia. Though Mayas were principally slash-and-burn corn farmers and occasional hunters, many of them had for decades earned money from the chicle trade. Some of their leaders made fortunes through control of the gathering and export of chicle from the territory, and Maya attacks limited the operations of outsiders who sought to do the same.[5] But with the boom in the trade in the mid-1920s, the federal government—which had quit the reconquered territory during the Mexican Revolution—had taken a renewed interest in the forest and its population. As it had before the revolution, it began once again to grant its own concessions and collect royalties. To enforce its prerogatives in that trade, in 1929 the government sent detachments of troops back into Santa Cruz and other bases in the territory to stay, this time permanently. Meanwhile, thousands of chicle gatherers from Yucatan, Campeche, and other states annually trekked into central Quintana Roo during the chicle-gathering months between July and January. At a time when the permanent forest population numbered only ten thousand, up to six thousand gatherers arrived each season to work the forest, which the federal government now claimed as the nation's under Article 27 of the revolutionary constitution of 1917.[6]

The combination of those developments—most notably the reoccupation of Santa Cruz by federal troops and a subsequent decline in the price of chicle—led to sharp dissension in the ranks of Maya officers and their repudiation of the authority of Francisco May. During a 1918 visit to Mexico City, May had received the uniform and title of general in the Constitutionalist Army of Mexico (then enjoying success in the continuing revolution there) in de facto recognition of his local authority and to encourage his cooperation in pacifying his fellow Mayas. He was also granted exclusive control over seventy-nine square miles of forest, and the exclusive right to ship chicle along a then-abandoned rail line from Santa Cruz to Caribbean docks at Vigia Chico. May became a rich man in the process. Not only did he control chicle exports through Santa Cruz, but he owned the only general store in all of central Quintana Roo, from which he sold goods at very inflated prices. Outsiders viewed him as a "capitalist exploiter of his own people."[7] Mayas called him a traitor, suspecting him of having sold them out for the sake of self-enrichment. To the west and north of Santa Cruz, General May's subordinates eventually plotted his assassination (a deed never consummated). Zuluub was among those conspirators in 1929 whose dissension General May's secretary described in these terms:

> The anger of the Maya leaders had its origin in the permits which the federal government was giving to people from other places for the exploitation of the resin of the sapodilla tree. . . . The concessions . . . must have seemed to them threats against their ancient property rights, all the more so as, in effect, the concessioners were very abusive, including robbing them [local Mayas] of their corn harvests, and on some occasions the Indians, agitated, had arrived at the extreme of attacking chiclero camps in revenge, killing the workers whom they found.[8]

When in 1928 Frans Blom of the Grey Memorial Expedition engaged in a shouting match with a Maya near Xcacal Guardia because of the destruction of banana plants, he and his men came close to losing their lives for the crimes of others. Mayas around Xcacal Guardia in the mid-1930s still launched occasional attacks on the chicle camps of outsiders thereabouts, always first celebrating a mass at their most holy shrine.[9]

Once he had uttered a full page of written text in his letter to Morley, Zuluub counted the continuation a subsequent letter, repeating the formula of place and time with which he had begun.

> And my second letter. In Xcacal village of Guardia, 20 of September of the year of 1935 years.

He then went on describing the plight of his people:

> Because Mr. Don Chief, two years ago they drove me from my village of Dzula. Then was when they came to do me evil in my village of Dzula. Then was when I came out to Guardia. The holy

days [since then] are piling up, the holy hours are piling up. I am poor, then, beneath the right hand of True God. Not even holy corn [have I] for my sustenance with my people and with all my womenfolk. They are poor. And all the little angels [children]. We are as poor as can be. Not even a little clothing, not even guns do I have. Not even a machete. Nothing do I have. Poor are we beneath the right hand of Our Lord True God. Because we, nobody do I go about to bother in the towns of Yucatan.

After thus having appealed to Morley's sympathies, Zuluub got to the point of his letter:

The favor I am asking of you, Mr. Don Chief—that there be your settling accounts for me, that there be your making justice for me well, Mr. Don Chief, for everything the Mexicans do. Help me with the favor I ask of you, that there be your giving me aid, that you give me weapons, all the accouterments, the wherewithal for war. That there be your removing from me the evil men who are there in Noh Cah Santa Cruz, the Mexicans, because they are evil people. I, that is what I ask. That I be left well in peace. May there be your giving me one of your flags here in Guardia, so that I can protect myself with the Beautiful Very Holy One, so that you help us.

Zuluub also asked that Morley help by removing Mexicans from their posts at the ruins of Tulum, where he and other Mayas occasionally went on dutiful pilgrimage. Zuluub could not have known of Morley's role in opening those ruins for such foreign visitation and occupation over the previous three decades.

And all the men who are at Tulum, may there be your removing of all the people who are at the coast, because they are at the Castillo, supposedly, on the Castillo, there they have shut themselves up, supposedly.

Then, in words faintly echoing those today attributed to the turn-of-the-century prophet Florentino Cituk, Zuluub implored Morley to

open a road for you to get out to us some things needed for me to buy with my people, Mr. Don Chief. Because I, that is what I ask of you, that there be your speaking for me with the United States, and even with Mr. King and with the place of the Queen, with the

70

place of England, even with the place of Mr. Lord Englishmen, so that I may know if what I say to you can be, if my words are correct with you, also. Speak also on behalf of Our Lord True God and on my behalf also, that there be your removing the men at Tulum village, because they have put a watchman there. Thus then, mercy I ask of you, that you speak in my favor. I, Mr. Don Evaristo Zuluub.

The rhetorical device of parallelism and repetition operated on multiple levels of Zuluub's long letter. Even as couplets and triplets echoed and intensified words and phrases within short passages ("thus then this holy hour, thus then this holy day"), Zuluub would oscillate between successive, ever more detailed descriptions of his persecution and repeated urgent requests for Morley's aid:

In Xcacal village, 20 of September of the year of 1935 years. And my third letter. Thus then how very happy I would be should you get out to me all the things I ask of you—the guns and the accouterments—so that I can protect the Beautiful Very Holy One here in Guardia. And a flag I ask of you, so that I can protect myself from the Mexicans. For the holy days are piling up, the holy hours are piling up since I came out here to Guardia, here to the village of Xcacal. Daily they rise up to come and do another bad thing here to me and to my people. To catch me they think. The hour has not arrived that True God lets them catch me. For never will there be my delivering myself to them for nothing. Already twenty times they have come here to the village of Xcacal. To Chunkulche they approach in order to close off the roads to me, to wait for me. They approach two leagues about here. Then all the pigs and fowl there they take to eat, supposedly. Just like that, then, they take them. They are told not to take them, to pay for them. They pull out their pistols, they press the barrels against a person's heart. They aren't going to pay at all. Whatever they will, it is done immediately. Because of them [undecipherable word], because they are very evil men. They are doing everything to us here, Mr. Don Chief. That I make known to you, that which the federal soldiers do to us here in Santa Cruz, Mr. Don Chief. I, Evaristo Zuluub.

Lest Morley or Villa fail to understand precisely what the federal soldiers were doing, Zuluub had a sergeant of his company write further on the matter that same day[10]:

In Xcacal village of Guardia, 20 of September
of the year of 1935 years.

Thus then this holy day, thus then this hour, there is my making
of this one blessed letter, in order then that I put it in your hands,
in order then that I let you know what they really do to me, these
people, these federal soldiers, these Mexicans. Because they stole
holy corn and five bushels of holy corn, they took it all from me,
five fields of corn, holy corn, they took it all. And half an acre of
sugar cane, they ate it all on me in my village of San Jose, there in
Tabi [a hamlet]. As soon as they stop there in front [of my fields] it
happens that they enter in order to cut sugar cane. Just like that it
happens they eat it all. So, too, the holy corn, because when
Lieutenant Mr. Don Evaristo Zuluub left his village of Dzula, that
was when they got on my back, also, because I am with his party.
Only because I had been sent away [that day] they did not kill me
when they confiscated from me everything of mine. Mr. Don
Chief, Mr. Don Alfonso Villa, I, Mr. Don Pedro Huuh, Sergeant,
that is what I want, that there be your making [settling] accounts
for me, that there be your making good justice for me, that there
be my being paid for the holy corn, all of it.

Such depredations by enemy soldiers on patrol had plagued and
enraged Maya rebels from far back in the nineteenth century. Since the
very beginning of the Caste War, destruction of cornfields and food
stocks was a strategic goal of the expeditions sent to subdue the rebel
Mayas. (It was a policy dictated, as it is the world over in warfare, by a
desire to starve the rebels as well as to provision the invaders.) During
the first decade of this century Maya cornfields continued to be targets
of federal army patrols. As late as 1909 two British travelers in Quintana
Roo observed that "the 'war' is now as far as possible restricted to the
occasional 'potting' of an Indian and the burning of his *milpas* or
maize-fields."[11]

In the next two pages of his letter to Morley, Zuluub elaborated a
historical precedent for his request for military aid, invoking rebel Maya
trade and diplomacy with the British during the War of the Castes and
intoning the names of revered and infamous leaders of that time:

In Xcacal village of Guardia, 20 of September of the year of 1935
years. And my 4th letter. Because he, the police commander
Sebastián Canul and [undecipherable], they are the leaders of this
thing [the persecution of Zuluub]. And another thing I tell you,
Messrs. Don Chiefs, those there at Vigia Chico and Payo Obispo,

and Bacalar, may there be their removal from there, because those places belong to Santa Cruz. So I say to you, may you do the favor of removing all the people there at Vigia and Payo Obispo and Bacalar because they were garrisons long ago of our late honorable fathers, the leaders, fathers of the old ones in the district of Bacalar long ago, in the time of the late Mr. Don Bernadino Cen and in the time of the late Mr. Don Román Pec, long ago here in Noh Cah Santa Cruz, Mr. Don Aniceto Dzul and Don José María Akiib and Don Ilario Cab and Mr. Don José María Canul and Mr. Don José María Heron Tuk, and Mr. Don Felipe Yama and Mr. Don Reymundo Méndez. They kept guard in the district of Bacalar. From long ago talks were happening with the English lords in the time of Mr. Don Englishman, Mr. Don Mister Andrés Sin in the town of Bacalar and in the village of Oxualakin and in the village of Tzucanela and Dziris and Chan Corosal and Chaac Likin and Caldera and Chan Santa Cruz and Noh Bec, the riverine camp of the Englishman Don Mister Andrés Sin. All that time were speaking our fathers-leaders long ago, Mr. Don Leonardo Pat, long ago. I, Evaristo Zuluub, thus then I tell you also. Because I, that is what I want also, that it be like long ago.

And my 5th letter.
In Xcacal village of Guardia, 20 of September
of the year of 1935 years.

Thus then, Mr. Don Chief, I, that is what I want, that there be your removing of the Mexicans from everywhere they are, so that things are left like long ago when our great fathers were speaking with the English gentlemen. So, too, I want that we speak with you also, all of us, so that things are left like long ago, so that everything is left good as in the time of our late, honorable fathers of long ago, in the time of Mr. Don Juan Bautista Chuc and Mr. Don José Crescencio Pat, and Mr. Don Venancio Puc and Mr. Don Atanacio Puc. They, all the great ones here in Noh Cah Santa Cruz, they spoke with Queen Victoria and the English leaders in the town of Corosal long ago, with Secretary Don José María Cach and Mr. Don Julián Us and Mr. Don Isidro Uh and Mr. Don Augustín Barrera and Mr. Don Atanasio Caamal. They were the secretaries [the scribes and advisers] of our fathers-leaders long ago.

Once again, now unmistakably invoking the words of the prophet Florentino Cituk, Zuluub addressed Morley:

There were many secretaries long ago, but today we are poor. There are no secretaries. There are only a few, but there is nowhere for my speech to occur now. All the road openings, they are all closed by the Mexicans. Therefore I say to you, may there be your opening of the roads for us, for us to speak with you, for you to bring us what we need here in Guardia, Mr. Don Chief. Thus is the truth of my word to you, I, Mr. Don Evaristo Zuluub.

Zuluub might well have ended his letter right there. But he went on to address specifically the irritating matter of chicle gathering by outsiders in the forests of central Quintana Roo.

And my 6th letter.
In Xcacal village of Guardia, 20 of September
of the year of 1935 years.
    And another thing I say to you, Mr. Don Chief, concerning the chicle gatherers. They have already really gone into my village of Dzula. A thousand chicle gatherers are jammed in there. They are working all the forest of my village of Dzula. May there be your making accounts for me. May there be your making justice, because for two seasons it has been theirs, and for two years now just like that they make money, just like that they take money out. For that they came to do me evil, so that the forest would remain theirs, so that they could make money just like that. Therefore I say to you, if they are taking that chicle to you there, take it from them just like that! Because that stuff is mine, from the forest of my village they extract it. Take it from them just like that! Don't pay them! I will settle it with you [in return] for the guns I ask of you. Because that stuff is my money and my people's. They're taking it just like that, Mr. Don Chief. Therefore I tell you about how everything is, about what the Mexicans do, Mr. Don Chief. I, Evaristo Zuluub, I speak then with you thus. Everything I am explaining to you, how everything is, about how everything is that the Mexicans do here in Noh Cah Santa Cruz, here in Guardia, Mr. Don Chief, Mr. Don Alfonso Villa, Our Very Lord True God may He keep your holy souls. He is eternal, He is infinite, there is none other than He. Mr. Don Chief, I am Evaristo Zuluub.

As Morley and Villa came to know Zuluub better, they developed an opinion at odds with the dark rumors they had previously heard. They found Zuluub a man of "humble and inoffensive appearance" and began to "doubt the authenticity of the multiple crimes attributed to him."[12]

The truth, they would come to find, was something else still. Zuluub's subordinates had good reason to fear his anger, and Zuluub's relations with his peers among Maya officers were sometimes tense. In his exile in Xcacal Guardia Zuluub was second in authority and prestige only to Captain Cituk, but he and his family and company members could never forget that they lived there, farmed and hunted in the forest thereabouts, and bled chicle from local stands of sapodilla at the hospitable sufferance of others who had settled those forests long before. Political tensions among Maya officers directly affected the livelihood of the exiles of Dzula, and minor incidents among farmers, hunters, chicle gatherers and neighbors might engender political conflict within the ranks of officers.

In any event, while living in Tuzik Alfonso Villa made special efforts to get close to Zuluub. By December 1935 he had obtained Zuluub's "complete confidence and sympathy," or so he thought, and had persuaded Zuluub to work with his scribe on an autobiography. "In this labor of getting closer, the most difficult thing has been to disabuse them of the aid that they expect from the Americans without weakening the force of their prestige [among Mayas]."[13] That effort would continue to prove very difficult.

V

ROYAL

TREATMENT

In December 1935 a high-level delegation of Maya officers finally responded to repeated invitations from Sylvanus Morley and went to meet him at Chichen Itza. Morley had hoped the officers would come to "see Alfonso's relation to the [*Carnegie*] Institution and pave the way for the important work that he has commenced down there."[1] The officers came, instead, to pursue face to face the matters raised in the past year's correspondence.

Their arrival was preceded by a letter from the aged, half-blind, reclusive head priest of Xcacal Guardia, Pedro Pascual Barrera. Barrera, whose titles were "Patron of the Cross" and "Great Father," was the supreme servant of the Most Holy One, the miraculous cross of Xcacal Guardia. He and all his followers considered themselves good Catholics, though the Roman Catholic Church would scarcely accept the claim. That mattered little, however, to those Mayas who had long been self-reliant in their dealings with the divine. Barrera's father had been patron, as had his father before him, when the cross was still sheltered in the town of Santa Cruz. In fact Barrera's grandfather, José María Barrera, was reputed to be the founder of Santa Cruz and of the cult of the cross that arose there in the early years of the War of the Castes. In those early years the patron was premier within a triumvirate that attended to the divinity, received its audible pronouncements, and interpreted their meanings for Maya military commanders and common people.

By the 1930s the cross had long since ceased to speak so openly, though, as patron, Pedro Pascual Barrera spent many hours alone with it and divined what it wanted said to its children—usually, it seems,

76

warnings of impending misfortune and commands for greater piety. Barrera also appointed subordinate Maya priests, who helped him marry Maya couples, baptize their children, and officiate at daily masses and special masses in the shrine center church. He sat in council with officers hearing accusations of misbehavior, judging guilt, and deciding upon punishments, and he advised them on still other matters both religious and civil. The Patron of the Cross was the most sacred and revered personage of the shrine village hierarchy, and his voice in religious matters was incontestable. He did not work to feed, clothe, or shelter himself, as did all other Maya men and women no matter what their rank, but instead was sustained by funds from church coffers (controlled, in turn, by Captain Cituk and Lieutenant Zuluub).[2]

The head priest addressed Sylvanus Morley and Alfonso Villa in what was likely a deliberate, chanting cadence as he dictated his letter:

> *Thus it is,*
> *There is the coming*
> *of Mr. Captain,*
> *Mr. Don Concepción Cituk,*
> *and Mr. Lieutenant,*
> *Mr. Don Evaristo Zuluub,*
> *and Mr. Sergeant,*
> *Mr. Don Miguel Chan,*
> *and Mr. Sergeant,*
> *Mr. Don Pedro Huuh,*
> *and Mr. Corporal,*
> *Don Marselino Ake,*
> *and two of their people,*
> *to visit you here in the town of Chichen,*
> *in order to see you,*
> *in order for you to see them, too,*
> *in order that you speak with them*
> *in order that they speak with you, too,*
> *with goodness*
> *and love.*

"It is very necessary you make accords with me through them," Barrera told Morley and Villa. "I would be very happy here, Messrs Don Chiefs, if what I say to you became so. May there be your getting out to us all the things I ask from you." The letter ended with a blessing and a reminder: "Very exceedingly Our Lord True God protect

77

Pedro Pascual Barrera, Patron of the Cross

your holy souls. He is eternal, He is infinite, there is none other than He."[3]

On December 5 two individuals from Xcacal Guardia arrived at Chichen Itza and reconnoitered the grounds, to see if it was safe for their superiors to approach. An hour and a half later the main group of officers and subordinates entered, on guard and "suspicious and mistrustful of everything. 'Who is that man?' 'Is he a Mexican?' 'Are there federal soldiers here?' " They were put up in the guest house of the Carnegie Institution project, where visiting dignitaries of Mexico and the United States were customarily sheltered, and in the afternoon four of the officers (and another man who had aspirations of becoming one) had their first session with Morley and Villa, Pedro Castillo acting as interpreter.[4]

Morley greeted them "in the name of the Institution" and said "that we had asked them up here to show them what we are doing here and to entertain them so that they might better understand what Alfonso was trying to do down there among them." Villa and Morley had planned to use the meeting to make the officers finally understand that no assistance of a "political nature" would be forthcoming, though medical assistance, help in the marketing of their chicle, and other aid would be offered. But as Captain Cituk began to speak, it soon became apparent he expected more. "I could see," Morley later noted, "what they really wanted was some sort of an assurance from me that the Mexican soldiers at Santa Cruz de Bravo would not molest them, forbidding them to hunt in this region or build milpas [cornfields] in that region or to bleed chicle in the other, but would permit them to live in peace as they used to do."[5]

Morley interrupted Cituk to stop this line of talk, only the dim outlines of which he could as yet have grasped. He instructed his interpreter to translate carefully what he was about to say, avoiding such words as "Teacher, Government, Mexicans, Federal Soldiers, Foreigners," which the officers found offensive, and otherwise taking care "not to make verbal slips which when dealing with those Indians tend to be of great consequence." Then Morley proceeded to tell the officers that "I was a stranger in Mexico working under the laws of the country and that no matter how friendly I was toward them, I could in no way take part in any political action, that that must be clear to them before we proceeded any further." Morley's translator repeated the message several times, Villa and Castillo then assuring Morley that "the Indians understood my position and indeed the Institution's position in Mexico." But Villa later noted in his diary, "Upon finishing our talks I was left with the impression of not having achieved good success. I believe the form could have been better."[6]

That first meeting did not go well in large part because the officers did not trust Morley's interpreter, Pedro Castillo. Earlier that day they had encountered him in the company of an employee of the Mexican National Agrarian Commission, who was by chance then touring the region. The Mexican attempted to interview and photograph them, using Castillo as his interpreter, which "caused [the officers] vexation that increased when they learned where he [the Mexican] had come from and what his job was. From that moment on Mr. Castillo was no longer for them a person to trust," and the officers could doubt that he was faithfully translating what Morley said to them.[7]

The next day Villa led the officers on a tour of the ruins, taking care to avoid any more untoward encounters with other visitors to the site. Chichen Itza had changed greatly in the dozen years since the Carnegie Institution began its work there. Numerous small shelters had been built to quarter its staff and laborers, and repairs had been made to the church and big house of the old hacienda. The Mexican government was also working there and had constructed offices for its research staff and for those monitoring all activities at the site.

As for the ruins, many of the ancient structures had been reinforced to prevent any further decay, while still others had been restored to something approaching their original condition. The effect of such restoration was remarkable. The Mexican Ministry of Education worked on the tallest pyramid at Chichen Itza, the Castillo, refacing two of its four sides with the cut stone that had for centuries lain strewn about its base, resetting two great serpent heads at the base of the pyramid's northern stairway and smaller ones flanking the portico of an entirely refurbished temple at its summit. The Mexicans had also restored the fallen walls of the Great Ball Court as well as the Temple of the Jaguars at its southeast corner.

The Carnegie Institution, in the meantime, had set first to work on a "plain and uninteresting mound" just northeast of the Castillo. They cut and burned the patch of forest that had grown on the mound since it was last cleared by an archeologist, Alfred Maudslay, more than thirty years before. Exploratory trenches were dug into the mound to reveal its interior and underlying structure. Fallen columns were set up again, walls were re-erected, sculptured elements were reassembled and put in place, including the temple's serpent-columns and the stone friezes, masks, and panels that had once adorned the exterior of the temple and the low pyramid on which it stood. Well over one hundred brightly

Morley, Cituk, Zuluub, and Villa at Chichen Itza, December 1935

painted blocks of stone were removed for safekeeping in the former church of the hacienda. After many seasons of such effort, what was once an amorphous pile of forest-covered rubble had been transformed into "the most elaborate and magnificent building in the city"—the Temple of the Warriors and the adjoining Court of the Thousand Columns.[8]

Other ruined structures received similar restorative treatment. The work was enormously painstaking, time-consuming, and sometimes dangerous, not to mention expensive. It had been undertaken by both the Mexican government and the Carnegie Institution (along with some private, individual backers in the United States) even though such restoration lacked almost any scientific merit. The science lay in the archeology, in what could be learned about each mound by stripping and tunneling it away piece by piece, layer by layer, until nothing was left but the disarticulated elements of its ancient structure scattered about on the ground or stored for safekeeping in warehouses and museums. The archeologist, of course, was expected to record meticulously the location, dimensions, and features of each piece of ancient edifice removed. Informative reconstruction of the ruin was less urgent: it could take place only on paper in the artist's rendition (and today, of course, with computer-aided graphic design). It was Morley's firm policy in directing restoration that no fallen stone be put in a place unless the restorers were certain it belonged there—unless they already knew, that is, just what the building, the frieze, the bands of carved stone around a temple were supposed to look like.

Destruction of great architectural remains—whether butchery or autopsy—was then, as now, entirely out of the question; some repair and restoration in the wake of excavation was required on ethical grounds—to preserve, unlike looters and vandals, the integrity of historic sites and national treasures.[9] Morley and his superior at the Carnegie Institution, Alfred Kidder, also advanced some scientific arguments in favor of preservation and limited restoration. (Complete restoration of all the ruins was not feasible.) First, though Morley and his staff were exceptionally skilled and meticulous researchers, they believed the ruins should be left in such a condition that future archeologists could return either to correct the original observations or to supplement them in the light of new problems being investigated. Second, the actual labor of reconstructing a Maya temple, from the ground up in at least one case, was itself a learning experience that might yield unexpected insights into the principles and techniques of Maya architecture and construction.

The Castillo at Chichen Itza

But those alone were not the driving motives behind years of exceptionally extensive restoration of Chichen Itza financed by the Carnegie Institution. Alfred Kidder felt that "when cleared all buildings should be both understandable and beautiful. . . . Subjective values must not be overlooked. Beauty, in detail and in mass, must be striven for." Not the beauty of pyramids, temples, ball courts, platforms, and so forth, restored to seemingly mint condition, but, rather, the beauty of *ruins* only partially restored and left visibly touched by the "genius of desolation" that had for centuries "presided over this awful solitude" (as a prior visitor, B. M. Norman, put it). Again Kidder: "Unintelligent [i.e., excessive] restoration, no matter how accurate, destroys beauty and so robs ancient structures of their most important psychological effect. The mere fact of ruin induces realization of the inevitable and relentless erosion of time and brings the beholder to the proper frame of mind for grasping the deeper significance of what he sees."[10]

So some fallen columns were stood upright again, others left just as they lay, though the brush around them was cleared and burned so that a visitor could have an unobstructed view of the decay. Temples were restored, but some reparable ruins were preserved as they were found. Was all the extraordinary effort invested in this project simply to put the beholder of Chichen Itza in "the proper frame of mind"? Not quite. As an investment, the work of restoration was calculated to yield very tangible dividends for many years to come, in the form of public and private funds for archeological and anthropological research. Once again, Kidder was delightfully explicit in this regard:

> If Chichen Itza can be kept both interesting and beautiful, it will without question become a Mecca of travel, and, incidentally, a most valuable asset for archeology which, like every other science, needs its "show-windows." Its more recondite aims the public can not, in the beginning, be expected to grasp; but public interest must be aroused and eventual public understanding must be achieved if archeology is to go forward; for from the public comes, in the last analysis, all support for scientific endeavor.[11]

Chichen Itza, it is fair to assume, was once erected at the direction of a Maya élite to impress upon its public the immanence of abstruse gods and the imperative of obedience to those holding the power of command. Chichen Itza was resurrected to impress a very different audience with the mystery of a lost civilization and the value of public expenditure to support those who promised to solve the mystery. When the restoration of several structures was completed, Morley received ever more frequent parties of visiting dignitaries — Mexican and North American — as pilgrims to his new New World Mecca, a trek that many tens of thousands of us more ordinary folk have made since then. As for Morley's Maya visitors from central Quintana Roo, they were impressed, too, though as usual in ways Morley was coming to find exasperatingly different.

Though at times Maya officers called Morley "the important man at Chichen," they believed another was far grander than he. Mayas had long pondered the obviously catastrophic fate of their ancient predecessors, those who built the great ruins that dot the land, who fought the Spaniards long ago, and who disappeared in defeat or disgust. In some Maya legends that ancient race still lives in a distant land to the east, or hidden underground, or immobilized as enchanted beings of the sort whose carved images abound amongst ruined temples and pyramids. Wherever they are, Mayas have believed, those predecessors *do* live and await the moment of their return. Chichen Itza has seemed a likely abode for such mysterious beings, and Mayas have long spoken of a dormant king who resides there to this day, his still loyal subordinates dwelling in the subsurface water passages that honeycomb the peninsula.[12] The enchanted king holds a bugle that inches closer to his lips with the passing of each new year, and eventually he will sound it in the Final Days, heralding Armageddon.

As Villa showed them about the site, the officers evinced great interest in everything they saw, particularly in the Great Ball Court, the largest pre-Hispanic ball court in Mesoamerica. Sound carries and echoes remarkably well within the broad channel of its two high walls, and Villa observed that

> the phenomenon interested them so much that for more than 15 minutes we remained under one of the [stone] rings [in its walls] repeating phrases and names that then multiplied themselves indefinitely. For them this was nothing less than palpable proof of the current version [of legends to the effect that] the ancient Maya cities are enchanted places inhabited underground by the souls of their old inhabitants. So, upon hearing the echo, they did not accept it as an acoustic effect, but rather as direct communication with their ancestors who thus demonstrated their real existence.

"Stimulated, perhaps, by this experience," Villa later wrote, "Captain Cituk right there told me the following story":

> In very ancient times, when the Whites arrived, a contest was held to see which of the two kings was more powerful, whether that of the Foreigners or that of the Indians. For this, it was agreed to name "victor" him who managed to carry a hot tortilla from Merida to Tulum, passing through Chichen Itza. The King of the Indians, racing on horseback along the "living rope" [kušaʼan sùum] that in those times linked in the air all the Maya cities, very quickly arrived at his destination, winning for himself the prize. The King of the Foreigners, racing through forest and stony terrain, could never do the same.[13]

Officers today recall that the delegation heard the voices of thousands of their ancient predecessors, čilankabob, coming from the Ball Court's walls covered with the bas-relief carvings of human form. They also say that Morley told them the temple at one end of the Great Ball

The Great Ball Court at Chichen Itza

Court was the office of the Maya king. Captain Cituk and Sergeant Chaac
are said to have enacted a dialogue with the monarch across the length
of the long playing field. "Well, hello!" said the captain.

> *Well, I, I came to visit you, Mr. King,*
> *here in the town of Chichen Itza.*
> *Because since long ago when the world was settled we*
> *   have known that you are here, your Majesty.*
> *We came to visit you. We came to greet you. We came to*
> *   do our duty, here in the town of Chichen, here where*
> *   your office is.*
> *Here we are conversing thus. God made you lord. We have*
> *   come to visit you.*

Sergeant Chaac spoke for the king:

Good.
You, Don Concepción Cituk,
if it is you, I am happy.
Come and visit me here in the heart of my town, here in
*   the town of Chichen Itza.*
I am very happy with all that is said
[about] how it happened that the revolution happened
here in the town of Chichen.

The king went on to point out the enormous proportions of his residence, reflections of the grandeur of his body and greatness of his power. The audience was brief, however.

With the King of the Maya and the hidden *čilankabob* speaking to them from beyond, the officers also made special note of the many feathered serpents adorning the temples of Chichen Itza—especially the great serpent heads at the base of the Castillo—beings which, though stone, also live and await the day they may stir again and feast on human flesh. This will come to pass, Mayas say, should they fail to defend themselves against the encroaching dominance of the foreigners; only if they fail to make human war will these creatures stir to make apocalyptic war. It was the mission of the officers to keep the enchanted beasts still.

After touring the ruins, the officers met again with Morley and Villa, without the interpreter Castillo present, and they repeated their persistent requests: annexation by the United States, delivery of a flag of the United States and the seal of its government, and of course "weapons sufficient for their defense." Morley and Villa tried "very carefully" to explain that the requests were impossible to fulfill and unnecessary, to boot, since "no one was presently trying to harm them" or seize the Mayas' forests and lands. Morley said he would speak to the military governor of the territory, General Rafael Melgar, asking him to curb the abuses committed by federal soldiers; and he would contact a chicle merchant he knew who might buy the officers' chicle at a good price. Finally, Morley promised to visit the shrine center of Xcacal Guardia sometime early next year.[14]

To make all this more palatable, Morley offered to send the officers sets of hand bells for the masses said in each of the principal villages of the Xcacal Guardia cluster, as well as twelve meters of silk in which to garb their crosses, while Villa promised to bring medicines, incense, mirrors of the sort that adorn the Mayas' altars and crosses, and "other cheap things of little worth." "The meeting," Villa felt, "concluded in the midst of general contentedness."[15]

During the next two days the officers were treated to a dance attended by some three hundred people from surrounding villages, and to silent films shown by an itinerant Syrian with an "antediluvian hand" projector. Among the films they saw was one of the first Charlie Chaplin ever made. Morley thought it simple enough for the officers to get the point and deemed the showing "an uproarious success," though it seemed to Villa that the officers had "practically paid no attention." At yet another meeting with Morley the officers agreed to build a house for Villa in Tuzik, and in a private session with both Villa and Morley, Lieutenant Zuluub recounted at length once again his personal trials over the previous several years, asking Morley for relief. (Morley and Villa, having "interrogated" him intensively, were half-convinced of his harmlessness and agreed to speak in Zuluub's favor, too, with General Melgar.)[16]

Upon parting the officers asked Villa to bring them various things when he returned to Tuzik: medicines to treat female sterility and menstrual irregularities, hair dye for one man concerned about his graying, and various schoolhouse supplies. (Though most of the officers adamantly refused to allow the federal government to set up primary schools in their villages—schools that would be staffed by Mexican teachers providing instruction in Spanish—they had long had their own secretaries teach a few children to read and write Yucatec Maya and so provide for the continuance of that skill so essential to Maya rulers.) The officers then carried away still other gifts from the Morleys and Villa: quinine, purgatives, antiseptics, bandages, adhesive tape, magazines, and "colored advertisements."[17] They also left with a letter addressed to the Patron of the Cross, Pedro Pascual Barrera, to whom Morley sought to make clear in writing what he had said to the delegation itself. Morley no longer avoided the matter of alliance and weapons (there being, in any event, no lingering confusion about just what the officers were seeking) but outright rejected such requests in what should have been unambiguous terms. From the "Ancient Town of Chichen Itza," Morley wrote:

> I have received your friends, those mentioned above, as well as the men who came with them, with all friendliness, and I have shown them my house here in Chichen Itza and how I live. They will tell you all they have seen and how I have for you and your people only friendliness. These men will tell you what we talked about and

how I want to help you in any way that is proper for me to help you.

You must know as I have told the men from your place that I am a stranger in this country and that I must obey the laws of this country just as you and your people must obey these same laws in order to live in peace and love. The good Lord desires that we all live in friendliness and peace with one another, and that is what I counsel you to do.[18]

In translation Morley's words to the Maya priest were anything but unambiguous, however. "I want to help you in any way that is proper" was rendered in Yucatec Maya as "I want to help you in any way I can." Where Morley wrote of the "country" in which he was a stranger and whose laws he felt obliged to obey, officers unsocialized in the abstractions of modern nationalism and citizenship would have instead read "village" or "town." Straining toward an overcorrect Maya rendition of the English word "law," Morley's translator wrote *almahthan,* a word that the officers would read as "divine commandments." (Unsure if they *would* read this correctly, the translator inserted a parenthetical Spanish gloss, *leyes.* But to these Mayas *ley* meant flogging or execution, the combination of that word with *almahthan* suggesting, therefore, divine commandments and a harsh punishment for their violation.) Similarly, the hoped-for peace of which Morley wrote was inexplicably rendered by an unusual compound word, *homanolal,* one of whose roots suggests "open roads" and the other, "spirit, will"; together they might be read as an openness of peoples to one another.[19] So, as the letter was read aloud back in Xcacal Guardia, what Barrera likely heard was that Morley would help the officers in any way he could; that Morley, like them, felt that people ought to obey the commandments of True God, which regulate town and village life, as it is God's will that they do; and that as a result there could be an openness of people toward one another (including the freedom of communication and commerce that the officers sought and that Mexicans were impeding). The officers would have been quite pleased.

Morley went on in that letter to say, however, that he considered the Mexican General Rafael Melgar, military governor of the territory of Quintana Roo, to be the "*nohoch jefe* [big chief] of all those lands in the places where you live." Morley's message in Maya was certainly mixed, then. However the officers took that and the rest of Morley's counsel, they did not take it as his final word. Efforts to persuade him would continue.

Morley accepted an invitation to attend a festival in Xcacal Guardia at the end of February 1936. The festival was one of two regularly staged there by Mayas of the surrounding region, one focusing on the day of the Virgin of the Conception in early December, and the other on the day of the Holy Cross in early May. Morley was going to attend the former, which had been postponed since December 1935 because a poor harvest had left Mayas without the wherewithal for such a grand affair. In anticipation of his upcoming visit to the shrine center, Morley reported to his sponsors at the Carnegie Institution that he and his wife were "very anxious to make a trip over there," in part, no doubt, to further advance Villa's standing in the region. The work Villa was doing, he also wrote, was first-class and of the utmost urgency: "It is only just in time. Customs are changing. Intrusions from the outside are increasing. The old order is passing and now or never is the time to record its manifestations."[20]

As for the officers, Morley's attendance and his bringing of gifts for the shrine would serve as signs of his sincerity. Today, Maya officers explain they told him just what to bring: money was not wanted, Morley was told; rather, he was to bring several cartons of candles, rockets, cloth for the altar, and two or three sets of bells for mass, all things for use in their ceremonies and churches. Though the men probably did not say so, these items, more than signs of his good intentions, would be ritual offerings for their divinity. If Morley did these things, they reckoned, then True God would see the virtue in his heart and would help Morley "with the thinking that he is going to do." He would help Morley help the officers, that is.

They were getting desperate for his help. Since their December meetings, and despite reassurances given about Mexican intentions, their fears of Mexican aggression had grown. In late January several officers visited Villa in Tuzik to relate rumors of an imminent offensive by federal troops against their villages. Only one Maya village in central Quintana Roo had allowed schoolteachers to set up shop, and tiring of the widespread defiance of their civil authority, the federal government was preparing to send in soldiers to accomplish that end. Furthermore, alarm had been raised among Mexicans in Santa Cruz by reports of an impending Maya insurrection stirred up by foreigners living among them; an itinerant merchant had apparently learned of Villa's presence in Tuzik. In response to this news, Villa went to Santa Cruz to convince authorities that his work among the Mayas was of positive value for the Mexican government. He was told he would still have to get General Melgar's permission for such research, and he was also told that the army would use force if necessary to ensure acceptance of federal schools, starting in March. Meanwhile, hundreds of federal soldiers were beginning construction of a highway connecting Peto, Yucatan, with Santa Cruz, a highway that would pass within five miles of Captain Cituk's village of Xmaben.[21]

Paulino Yama and Apolinario Itza again visited Villa in early February to urge that Americans quickly invade their territory, promising that if the *Americans* established schools in their villages all the children, and even adults, would attend. Villa again explained, as he had upon returning from Santa Cruz only a few days before, that Americans would not intervene in "political matters," that it was useless for the officers to resist Mexican authority, and that no one had any intention of seizing their lands or enslaving them. But Maya officers were still far from willing to accept the claim that, like it or not, they were now citizens of Mexico.[22]

On the morning of February 26 Sylvanus Morley left Chichen Itza bound for Xcacal Guardia, accompanied by his wife, Frances Rhoads Morley; his personal secretary, Helga Larsen; his interpreter, Pedro Castillo; and two mule drivers.[23] The first day they managed to travel south twenty-one miles to the small village of Chanchichimila, where they caught up with Alfonso Villa, then returning from a trip to Yucatan with his wife, Dolores Gómez; his field assistant, Edilberto Ceme, and Ceme's sister-in-law, who was to begin serving as the Villas' maid in Tuzik. The now rather large party passed the night there, and when they resumed their travels the next morning, they soon passed out of the state of Yucatan into the territory of Quintana Roo. The sun was "blazing hot," and the landscape eerie and desolate, "a phantom forest [in which] every leaf was burned to a crisp brown by the sun and the tangled branches were silver grey. . . . Not one green plant as far as one could see."[24]

After making another fourteen miles, they had had enough of traveling for the day as they arrived in Tihosuco, a frontier town located near what had been the epicenter of the most prolonged and desperate fighting of the War of the Castes. The town had long lain shattered and abandoned, though now more than a hundred Maya families had already settled down there again, and a new schoolhouse had been built by the government. A once great church, its front blasted off during wartime sieges, towered above the central plaza of the ghost town. "How much worse is the destruction of the hand of man than the slow erosion of time," Morley's secretary confided to her diary, surely with the ruins of Chichen Itza in mind, "and how much more sad is a ruin from our own time than the ancient ruins of vanished races." Most of Morley's party sought shelter in the new schoolhouse, while the Morleys themselves bedded down in the church, where they were plagued all night long by hundreds of bats and a few grunting pigs, with whom they shared the ruins.[25]

They left Tihosuco early the next morning, and as they headed farther south the forest grew taller and denser and the sun-baked trail they had followed changed into "a narrow green tunnel where a semi-twilight of soft light filtered through green leaves resting the eyes and making the journey cool and comfortable." So it was for miles until

> something told us that we were passing through what had been a town. At first we did not know what it was that told us so, but soon we noticed a line of stones along the path—an ancient stone wall now levelled to the ground. Shadowy forms detached themselves from the deeper shadows of the forest. Fragments of walls completely overgrown with vegetation—an entire town gone back to the bush. Not one building remained standing and still the undulating lines of walls under their burden of vegetation could be followed. Soon they stopped and the forest was unbroken again. We had passed through another ghost city from the War of the Castes and the forest had taken just a little under one hundred years to blot it out entirely.[26]

There were no inhabited villages between Tihosuco and the environs of Xcacal Guardia, which Morley and his party could not hope to reach that day, so after eighteen miles and the onset of heavy rain they put up for the night in a small camp used by chicle gatherers and itinerant merchants.

Again they set out at daybreak and continued on to find, about ten miles later, the trail grow alarmingly narrow, threatening to disappear entirely, until suddenly before them appeared the village of Tuzik. They could not linger there, however, as the festival in Xcacal Guardia was to begin the following morning. So they continued on the few remaining miles to the shrine center, now escorted by the ranking officer of Tuzik, Corporal Marselino Ake. After an hour and a half they began passing cornfields, the narrow trail they followed broadened to the width of a road, and with the crossing of a final, low ridge the shrine center came into view.

At the very heart of Xcacal Guardia the shrine itself was visible—a long, thatched-roof hut much improved by the addition of a cement floor and smooth, whitewashed clay packing on the outside and inside of its pole walls. A scant two steps from the front door of the church, crossing perpendicular to its long axis, was a similar, though more humbly finished, long-house that functioned as the community building, within which Maya officers and their troops held important meetings. These two buildings stood within a well-swept open square — the sacred precinct of the shrine center — whose corners were each marked by a pile of stones with a cross mounted on top. Just outside the perimeter of the square stood the long-house barracks, five in number at the time, many of them built upon small knolls, which sheltered men from the outlying villages who came to perform guard service there. Also in their midst stood the house of the Patron of the Cross, head priest of Xcacal Guardia. Further still from the sacred precinct were the village well, Lieutenant Zuluub's house, and the score or so houses of his fellow refugees, almost hidden amidst the trees and vegetation that had been allowed to intrude upon the less-sacred neighborhoods of the shrine village.[27]

Where trails leading to and from the outside world crossed the borders of the village, cruciform sentinels had been erected in small thatched-roof shrines. Beside one of those Corporal Ake halted the Morley party, asking them to dismount while awaiting permission to cross into Xcacal Guardia. Only a few minutes later Captain Cituk and his brother came out and warmly greeted Morley (with "double abrazos, etc."), inviting him to proceed to the center of the village, then crowded with hundreds of people from the surrounding territory.

The atmosphere was festive, "signs of merriment and activity were everywhere. The children ran about shouting crazily; the older people stood around in groups chatting and laughing . . . the women are the busiest, preparing the nixtamal [corn dough] for the morrow's feasting."[28] About a hundred men, including Lieutenant Zuluub, approached the new arrivals and, upon a signal from Captain Cituk, commenced a frenzy of handshakes and greetings. From there Morley and his companions were taken to a barracks that had been vacated for their use. Food was brought and they sat down to eat before a large and curious audience. A short time later, just as the tired travelers were about to stretch out in their hammocks and take a nap, a knock on the door signaled the arrival of a delegation of women:

> A long string of silent shy women filed into the room each one carrying a gift for us. They were dressed in snow-white huipiles [frocks] embroidered in cross-stitch in yellow, red and green. Long strings of blue glass-beads with heavy silver coins, large gold

earrings and gold rosarios [medallions] made a brilliant effect. . . . Conversation did not flow any too freely as we were without our interpreter and they were so shy that if we as much as looked at them they covered half of their faces with their hands in the characteristic movement of all Indian Mexico. One by one they presented us with their gifts. Fruits, eggs, flowers, tortillas, etc. They were much interested in all our things but too shy to venture more than a few steps away from the doorway, and presently with more handshaking they filed out again and at last we could settle down for a few minutes rest.[29]

Later that evening, with Captain Cituk's permission, Morley and his party went over to see the inside of the great church of Xcacal Guardia, and perhaps even the interior of the walled-off chamber at its eastern end, the "Gloria" or "Heaven," constantly guarded by an armed sentinel and within which upon a long altar stood those Mayas' greatest crosses. It was not a busy time at the church, and inside they found only Captain Cituk, Lieutenant Zuluub, several other officers who evidently did not then have pressing duties elsewhere, and an old man sleeping on a bench along the wall. A small orchestra filled the church with a constant stream of sacred notes produced on two homemade violins with pig-gut strings and henequen-fiber bows, two deerskin drums, and two cornets. Captain Cituk went over to the man on the bench — "the most neglected and abandoned and the dirtiest and filthiest" person they had yet seen[30] — announced the presence of the foreigners, and helped him slowly to his feet. It was the head priest, Pedro Pascual Barrera. Once introduced to Morley, Barrera launched into a long prayer in Maya, thanking True God for the arrival of Morley and his party, whose visit was harbinger of better times to come. "It was all very earnest and solemn."[31] Barrera went on to relate to his guests an abbreviated history of the trials of the Mayas of that region in their wars against the whites, especially against the Mexican general Ignacio Bravo, who had captured their capital in 1901.

The audience was cut short when Barrera was called into "Heaven" to begin the customary nocturnal praying of what they called the "Rosary." As the curtain covering a narrow doorway to the sanctum was pulled aside to let the head priest pass, Morley and Villa could but glimpse a colorfully decorated altar and a rack of steadily burning beeswax candles that briefly cast a warm glow out into the otherwise darkened church. They then retired to their hut to get some sleep before the onset of festivities early the next morning.

At 2 a.m. the Morley party was awakened and directed to a shelter in the middle of the village where a "roll call" and dance would soon officially open the festival. In that shelter they found all the Maya officers and many of their subordinates gathered around a table at which were seated the two scribes, Apolinario Itza and Antonio Xiu. The scribes were intently engaged in writing down the names of the men and women who would take charge of various aspects of the festivities soon to follow, functioning in official roles whose titles harked back to life on the haciendas of Yucatan that Maya rebels had abandoned decades before — the Lord of the Hacienda, the Mistress of the Hacienda, the Young Lord (their son), the Young Mistress (their daughter), the First Overseer, the Second Overseer (and his wife), the First Foreman (and his wife), the Second Foreman (and his wife), Cowboys (and their wives), Cowgirls, the First Swineherd (and his wife), the Second Swineherd (and his wife).[32]

When it was finally ready, Cituk's secretary, Apolinario Itza, stood up to read the document aloud. To Villa "the act seemed important, as everyone stood up to listen to it with the greatest attention." But as Itza read on,

> they began to laugh, becoming more hilarious as he went on, for the paper had been composed in a humorous vein and after the name of each person "elected" was a phrase satirizing some characteristic or mannerism of the individual. For example, one who was known to be heavy and awkward at dancing was entitled the "true master of the dance"; his wife, who had a very serious, grave countenance was designated as "she who laughs much"; another, somewhat inclined to avarice, was called "he who hands out cigarettes"; a man known to be henpecked was called "the seller of eggs," and his wife "she who keeps the money of the eggs," and so on with the rest of the characters.[33]

Immediately after the reading of the list, the Cowgirls and partners chosen for them danced the first round of the slow dance known as the *Vaquería,* in which a line of males and a line of females face one another and shuffle to the tune of violins, drums, and cornets, without touching or looking at each other. "The girls," it seemed to Helga Larsen, did not "enjoy it as diversion but rather as if they were performing some religious rite." Morley and his companions soon retired to Lieutenant Zuluub's barracks, where they were given hot tortillas and traditional hot chocolate spiked with chili peppers, and where they tarried watching dozens of women busily making tortillas. "Even though we could not speak to them, there was nothing but friendliness and good-will everywhere."[34]

At daybreak exploding rockets proclaimed the ritual "planting" of the "silk-cotton tree" (yaxče'), which had been felled and brought into the shrine village the day before. Despite their calling it a silk-cotton, like the tree which in Maya cosmology is rooted at the very center of the world and ascends through multiple celestial heavens, it was, in fact, a more prosaic, though economically important, sapodilla (ya'), from which chicle is bled and whose sweet fruits attract such edible prey as the coatimundi. Cowboys in procession carried the tree horizontally on their shoulders, while the Second Swineherd rode on top and posed as a cornered coatimundi. Two Maya priests followed them—each with a candle in one hand and a small bell in the other, which they rang while chanting prayers in harmony, the orchestra playing tunes to match. A motley crowd of excited, shouting men and boys brought up the rear. The procession twice circled the sacred precinct before entering a corral (where "bullfights" would later be held), in the center of which a small hole had been dug to receive the base of the tree. As the Cowboys raised the tree from their shoulders and tried to stand it upright, they deliberately let it fall abruptly this way and that while the "coatimundi" held on for dear life. The tree was finally "planted," after which the "coatimundi," still hanging on in its branches, threw handfuls of squash seeds out over the large crowd that had gathered about to hang yams and gourds on its branches, signifying that the tree had blossomed and borne fruit.

Later in the morning the first of the major ritual offerings of the festival were ready to be taken to the church for a ceremony known as *matan,* "offering, gift." To "make *matan,*" as they say, is the central activity of almost all religious celebrations among these Mayas. It involves preparing food offerings (special breads, corn gruels, dishes of pork or chicken, sweets, among others), arranging them on an altar in accordance with cosmological and numerological principles, and before them reciting prayers and invocations to invisible deities who, once called to present themselves, are supplicated and thanked, and allowed to feast on a similarly invisible aspect of the offerings. The food is then removed from the altar and distributed immediately among officiants, participants, their families and onlookers.

Matan is a consummately social form of worship, even when the goals of a supplicant are quite individual and private. It always entails feeding gods or the souls of the dead—to thank them for their beneficence during the agricultural season drawing to a close; to ensure continued cooperation during the upcoming farming cycle; to ward or remove illness, infestations, and evil apparitions; to revive dead gods (as during Easter) or appease the human dead, who are believed to return annually to their homes; to solicit divine assistance for myriad other tasks, hopes, and hardships of everyday life. *Matan* also always involves feeding *people,* whether it be the few children who gather around an individual supplicant praying for his own health, or the hundreds who participate in the elaborate series of great *matan* ceremonies that take place during shrine village festivals. The offerings of ritual foods both to insatiable deities and souls and to hungry children and adults are religious acts essential to the efficacy of the ceremony.

The scale of *matan* ceremonies—the amount and variety of foods offered and the number of people who participate—reflects rather directly the scale of the "good" that is sought. An individual makes a small *matan* to relieve his or her own suffering, or perhaps that of a child or spouse. A group of men farming in the same corner of the forest make a somewhat more elaborate ceremony to promote their own safety and an adequate amount of rainfall on their cornfields. An entire village offers a still more grand and elaborate *matan* so that their patron cross may live again after its annual demise on Good Friday, or to expel an accumulation of evil winds from within the marked perimeter of their settlement. Finally, the greatest of *matan* ceremonies have long been held before the supreme patron cross of all the villages for which Xcacal Guardia is the seat of religious and company authority.

During the shrine village festival of 1936 it fell to Captain Cituk's company to stage the first of the daily great *matan* ceremonies, the Offering of the Cracklings. In the early-morning hours before the planting of the silk-cotton tree, four pigs had been butchered and one hundred pounds of corn had been ground, after which dozens of women set to patting out hundreds of tortillas, boiling up cauldrons of a thin corn gruel called *sa'* (in Spanish, *atole*), and preparing seasoned fried pork, while the men cooked the cracklings. When the time came, a specialist in altar arrangements placed on a small table an appropriate sampling of the offerings: ten packets of thirteen tortillas each, wrapped in special napkins and adorned with sprigs of basil; three clay vessels of the fried pork, similarly adorned with sprigs of basil; eight gourds filled with the same; eleven gourds of cracklings; one gourd of chocolate; and two bundles of black candles wrapped in red napkins. All was now ready for the ceremony to commence.

In solemn procession, led by men carrying incense and by the

n the church were carried a small cross, the Beautiful
surrogate for the Most Holy One, which never leaves
' a small seat referred to as the "Chair of Beautiful
relics were borne to the door of Cituk's barracks,
:n and women chanted through their repertoire of
. Then the altar specialist handed the offerings to
..._.. and women outside who proceeded in a long line, followed by the
Lord and His Chair and priests singing to musical accompaniment, into
the main church and on to the inner sanctum at its eastern end. There
priests and officers took the offerings from outstretched hands and
arranged them on a long table before the altar, after which a high mass
began, led by the head priest Barrera and conducted amidst the playing
of the orchestra.

Back in the public space of the church men and women on their
knees recited once again, several times perhaps, their repertoire of
prayers, then retired to benches to wait out the summoning of deities
and the decent interval allowed for gods to take what part of the
offerings they would.[35] When the head priest signaled that it was proper
to do so—by now it was past noon—the offerings were once again
removed from the church back to Cituk's barracks. From there they
were disseminated in traditional order and amounts to all the officials
and companies then present in the shrine center, who, surely famished,
would have sat down at once to eat.

Later in the afternoon Morley and his companions went to the head
priest's house to deliver gifts they had promised to bring. Before all the
principal officers of Xcacal Guardia, Morley presented Barrera with
twelve yards of bright red satin with which to adorn the shrine village
crosses and altar, a dozen hand bells (at least one to go to each of the
principal villages affiliated with Xcacal Guardia) of the sort chimed
during the consecration of the Eucharist in Roman Catholic masses.
Morley had also brought tinsel and red tissue-paper bells, which he and
his wife had used to decorate their Christmas tree the year before. As
Morley's secretary later recalled:

> They simply gasped with astonishment when Dr. Morley unfolded
> the glossy folds of silk. The High Priest touched it and said: "Seda
> [Silk].—Is it red?" "Chac bey kike." "Red as blood," answered don
> Eb [Lieutenant Zuluub]. Then came the bells. . . . They were
> delighted and had to ring each one by itself and all of them
> together. Then one Christmas tree trimming—red paper bells and
> tinsel. Everything was hach malob—very good and hach hadzutz

—very beautiful, and they were as happy as children on Xmas morning.[36]

That same night a small *matan* ceremony was held and the Cowgirls and Cowboys danced again.

Though they had already been in the church a couple of times, Morley and Villa had not yet gotten a clear view of the inner sanctum and of the most important of all crosses, which reputedly resided there. They had asked Cituk for permission, but he kept evading them with various excuses. Finally, Villa persuaded him to ask Barrera himself, who, much to Villa's surprise, granted the request, in fact offered to stage a special prayer session on their behalf. So the next morning Morley, his wife, secretary, and interpreter, Villa, his wife, and their maid filed into the church, barefoot and with unlit candles in hand. Accompanied by Captain Cituk, Lieutenant Zuluub, the head priest Barrera, and one of his ritual assistants, they were not stopped at the doorway of the altar chamber, but instead passed unimpeded until they stood before the long altar, now decorated with the Morleys' tissue-paper bells and tinsel.

The guests' candles were taken by Cituk and Zuluub, lighted, and added to those already burning on the candle rack in front of the altar, after which all knelt as the head priest's assistant began to chant in Maya and ring two of the bells that Morley had brought. When he was done, Barrera himself began to pray, "asking blessings upon all of us." When the praying had concluded, "we all rose to our feet and the four Maya present turned to each one of us and bowed their heads and saluted us," as at such a moment they would customarily salute one another, with " 'Blessed words of God.' " With that, Captain Cituk "invited" them to return to the public area of the church, "without allowing us to examine the things on the altar," and as each of the sacred crosses was concealed within its own closed wooden tabernacle, the curious visitors had to leave without getting their coveted glimpse of the Most Holy One.[37]

That day another great *matan* ceremony was staged, followed later in the afternoon by more dancing. After that there was a banquet for officers only, before which the officers expiated their sins by performing acts of ritual groveling (*kat síipil*) in the church; during it, armed guards stood at the doors of the hut where the officers dined to keep out still-sin-burdened common people and foreigners alike, it seems. More dancing then ensued, as well as a mock bullfight (no real bulls were available), more dancing still, and a small evening *matan* ceremony.

The next two days saw much the same round of ceremony, banquets, dancing, and "bullfights." In spare moments Morley wrote down genealogies of principal officers, while his wife took hundreds of photos of the village and the events. On the last night of the festival the Dance of the Pig's Head took place — not a real pig's head this time, but an ornately decorated oblong mass of squash seeds pasted together with honey and set upon a tray. A groove cut into one end represented the pig's mouth, and into it was stuffed a thick tortilla of corn and honey; while on top rose several sticks from which hung home-made cigarettes, sweets of squash seed and honey, corn cakes fashioned in the form of crosses and birds, and small paper flags. The "pig's head" was carried in procession from the barracks of its confectioner to the altar of the church, and before it a round of prayers (a Rosary) were said, after which it was removed to the adjacent long-house in which the dance itself was to take place. Eleven men were to take part, each of them having performed some official function during the day. They lined up before the door of the long-house from which the altar of the adjacent church could be seen (the curtain shielding it having been pulled aside so the divinities could look out and watch the dance, too) and commenced to sing in Maya

> I adore thee Holy Cross,
> Because in thy Holy arms
> We are redeemed
> With the blood of our Lord Jesus Christ.[38]

With that the dance began. The eleven elect, led by one carrying the "pig's head" and another who shook a rattle, proceeded to dance nine times around a small table at which stood Captain Cituk and Lieutenant Zuluub. The two officers kept track of how many circuits the dancers had completed by placing on the table a single cigarette for each completed revolution, after each of which the dancers paused to sing again the hymn with which the dance had begun. After nine turns around in one direction, the dancers reversed their progress to dance nine times around in the other, after which the "pig's head" was returned to the altar, while preparations were made for yet another dance of the Cowgirls and Cowboys with which the night's festivities would conclude.

On the festival's final day "the village was crowded with men carrying rifles and cartridge belts," and to Morley's secretary it seemed as though "a revolution had broken out and our friends were on their way to join the army."³⁹ But of course they *were* the army, assembled in holy procession led by officers and divine images on a several-hour-long circumambulation of the sacred precinct of Xcacal Guardia, with long pauses for prayer cycles at each of its cruciform boundary markers. Such processions were usually scheduled for evening hours, but Cituk and Zuluub agreed to hold it earlier so that their visitors could take photographs, and it was for that same purpose that Cituk ordered frequent interruptions of its progress. Morley greatly appreciated such consideration.

> Never have I seen such courtesy, such friendly cooperation and such good-will. We were reaping a rich harvest for our friendly treatment of Captain Cituk's several delegations to Chichen Itza of the past 18 months. I could not help but contrast the actions of this group with those of our Pueblo Indians of the Southwest at their fiestas. Several times have I seen the Indians at the Pueblo of Santo Domingo between Santa Fe and Albuquerque smash cameras in the hands of tourists on the occasion of their Green Corn Dance on August 4 each year. And the Hopi go so far as to charge for the privilege of taking pictures—so debased and commercialized has the Snake Dance become.⁴⁰

The procession concluded with a high mass attended only by officers and women, while the remaining menfolk prayed in the longhouse adjacent to the church. After a small evening *matan* ceremony the celebrations ended quietly, without the usual "quarrels or any other disagreeable incidents to mar its festive and sacred spirit. The women had taken great pains to see that their husbands did not drink too much or roam drunkenly through the village."⁴¹ That evening, after Alfonso Villa, his wife and entourage, as well as most Mayas who had come from other villages, had already left, the Morleys and their aides went to bid farewell to Lieutenant Zuluub. Morley's personal secretary, Helga Larsen, had taken a special liking to Zuluub, whom she and Mrs. Morley had visited at home earlier during the festival. On that occasion Larsen spied a small cross on an altar in Zuluub's hut—"a darling cross in the gayest *huipil*"—and asked if she could buy it. Zuluub responded with a quite definite *no:* "it was his *cichcelem yum*—blessed cross guarding his hut and there it had to remain. I felt quite humiliated for having asked him, as our western mania for treasures was entirely unknown to him." Evidently Zuluub did not take offense, for on the eve of their departure, with the Morleys and Larsen once again guests in his home, Zuluub picked up the cross that Larsen so coveted, and

Armed Guard in holy procession, Xcacal Guardia, 1936

holding the *cichcelem yum* in one hand he made three crosses in front of it with the candle he held in the other, then he kissed it with great affection and placed it in my hand. '*Atial*,' he said very seriously, '*tiólal ma a túbzicen*,' 'For you—that you may not forget [me]'—and the kindness with which he spoke lent a solemn dignity to his words.

Larsen was "dumfounded." Not knowing what to say (and realizing an embrace would be improper), she gave Zuluub her hand and said "Adiós—until to-morrow." "'*Minaan zamal*' was all he said. 'There will be no tomorrow.' "[42]

Morley and his party left at daybreak for their long trek back to Chichen Itza. In having Maya officers come to visit him at Chichen Itza, Morley had hoped they would leave impressed by Villa's demonstrated association with the Carnegie Institution and the United States. He, in turn, now left Xcacal Guardia "greatly impressed with this last group of independent Maya in Yucatan," among whom he had been "royally received, royally entertained, royally treated."[43]

MAYA OFFICERS say it was not long after that they took the next, ultimate step in their ritual efforts to bend Morley's mind and heart in favor of their cause. They prepared for him a *juramento*. The *juramento* is both object and oath: a thing given, the knowing receipt of which binds one in a promise enforced by True God. Zuluub had sworn such an oath for Morley in his letter of September 20, 1935, drawing three cruciform representations that constituted the divine trinity. Morley's *juramento* took the sculpted form of the Most Holy Cross Three Persons, also called simply Our Lord—three crosses carved of wood, mounted jointly on a single wooden base, each cross garbed in its '*ipil* and varying in stature according to the person of the Trinity that it was (Our Lord the Father, Our Lord the Child, Our Lord the Holy Spirit). The carving was done on a Maundy Thursday, the day True God dies annually.

Still considered to be without life and power, the crosses were left on the altar of the shrine center church to pass all of Good Friday. No man or woman would have left the village that day, for, with the divinity dead, evil beings reign beyond the edge of the settlement. On Holy Saturday the divinity lives again; then the crosses were "resurrected," forever after endowed with "miracle," which is to say, power. The procedure was standard ritual for the creation of new crosses. But Morley's *juramento* was the most powerful possible, consisting as it did of the entire Trinity. The officers did not tell the common people of this, and even today they mention it only in subdued voices.

Endowed with miracle, the crosses were delivered to Morley at Chichen Itza. They say he knew full well the implications of their receipt. The oath to which Morley would thereafter be held was one of serious intent and resolve. "Prepare me the Holy Father . . . and give it miracle!" they say he told them, so that the officers would know he was not toying with them ("two-eye-balling-them" and "testing wills" as they say in Yucatec Maya) and that he would give them aid. His pledge was now not only to the officers, but also to their gods, under the threat of whose wrath Morley was to keep the crosses and fulfill the promises he had seemed to make—to help them protect themselves.[44]

In the meantime the Mayas' anxiety continued to grow. On April 3 at two in the morning, as the moon was about to set, it was seen to redden and fade. People emerged from their houses and fired off rifles for twenty minutes to frighten away the beings apparently then destroying the moon, who is the Virgin Mary herself. In Tuzik the gunfire startled Villa and his wife from their sleep, and they immediately threw themselves to the ground, supposing the long-expected attack by federal troops had come. People went to pray in the churches of their many villages, and in the shrine center, while they awaited the rising sun to know if it was also under supernatural assault. At dawn, though the sun itself rose red, the emergency passed. Had the sun and moon perished, the expected end of the world would have at last been upon them, when all domestic utensils—grinding stones, griddles, benches, and so on—would have come to life and slain their human users. Even though that did not happen, speculation continued concerning the import of that dire omen, which surely announced "war, epidemics, or other catastrophes."[45]

By mid-April consensus had it that the catastrophe foretold by the red moon included advances the Italian army was making in Ethiopia and a terrible flood said to have occurred in the United States. The events were not logically irrelevant to the Mayas' well-being in central Quintana Roo. Though they knew nothing of fascism, Mayas understood Mussolini to be an enemy of the British and Americans. Any victory for him was a defeat for their hoped-for benefactors, and it cast in severe doubt the invincibility of the Anglophone powers, in which Mayas so wanted to believe. Mayas also harbored distant sympathies for Ethiopians, whom they knew to be black like the people of Belize, whom, in turn, they understood to be a formerly enslaved and white-hating people like themselves.

Rumors of war grew, including suggestions of imminent hostilities between Russia and Japan, and Maya officers worried that failures of piety might have weakened them and their friends in such perilous times. Meanwhile, Villa still worried that an attack by the federal army on Maya villages in central Quintana Roo would come soon, and he rushed to complete his research.[46]

Several months after the visit to Xcacal Guardia, and perhaps after delivery of the *juramento,* the head priest Barrera wrote once again to Morley in Chichen Itza.

> On the fifth of June in the year of 1936 years, it is necessary the drafting of my letter here in the village of Xcacal, the drafting of my salutations, for me to ask mercy of you, Mr. Don Chief, you who are in the town of Chichen, Mr. Don Sylvanus Doctor Morley. In order that I hear how it will end, the agreement we seek. In order that I hear from you how it will end, then. Because I, the agreement that we made long ago, that is what I pursue even today. In order that I hear, then, whether it will be possible for you to give help to Our Lord True God here at Xcacal village, for the sake of the suffering of Our Lord True God who remains here. Because it is being heard said that all is going to be taken from us by the Mexicans. Therefore I make it clear to you, Mr. Don Sylvanus Doctor Morley, so that I hear from you whether it will be possible for you to help us here regarding the land that is all being taken from us here. So that we hear from you whether it will be possible for this land to be left within its former boundaries. So that we hear from you whether it will be possible for you to make the reckoning, so that it may be left to Our Lord True God, and to us. Because we, we wish to seek a union with you. How very truthful are my words. How very truthful are my thoughts from my heart.[47]

Barrera and other officers who signed the letter asked for a map of their lands to be drawn, for a flag to be delivered, for the merchant whom Morley had contacted to come finally and buy their chicle, and for further aid, unspecified but understood. Though Morley had hesitated to act upon their requests for military aid, perhaps by now his thoughts had changed. In any event, Barrera wrote Morley, there was "no one else with whom I can speak, only you."

It appears, however, that Morley sent no response.

VI

MENACE AND
COURTSHIP

To obtain what they needed from Americans Maya officers pursued
a strategy of words and deeds in which menace and the use of force had
no place. The absence is noteworthy, for in earlier years coercion *had*
been a prominent stimulus to trade and diplomacy between rebel Mayas
and the British Empire.

Nineteenth-century Maya armies fought Spanish-speaking enemies
to the north; for their munitions they turned to the south. Rebel Mayas
obtained weapons and gunpowder from British Hondurans, bartering
booty pillaged from the wasted towns of Yucatan and Campeche or
paying with cash garnered from the sale of farm and forest products or
from the "protection" sold to non-Maya settlers and woodcutters along
the margins of rebel territory. They also accepted gunpowder (and cash)
as ransom for prisoners of war and for people whom they had kidnapped
from settlements in British Honduras.

Though perhaps arming their own executioners, British Hondurans
had little choice but to trade with the rebels. In notes and letters to the
British, Mayas routinely framed their demands with paragraphs asserting
friendship and honorable intentions, but threats expressed or implied
were not to be dismissed. So when in 1856, in a letter to Young,
Toledo, and Company, the Maya leader Luciano Tzuc threatened to
burn all the firm's mahogany works if they did not start paying him four
dollars for each tree felled, the Superintendent of British Honduras
explained to superiors unfamiliar with rebel Maya epistolary rhetoric
that

Tzuc's own letter—half mandatory and threatening, and half fawning and conciliatory . . . would appear to carry little in their expressions that would create alarm, but they are written in the true Indian style in that respect, and when coupled with his own acts and demonstrations on the spot, there remains little doubt of his inclination to execute his threats in case of disappointment.[1]

While continually protesting their desire for good relations with the Mayas, British authorities attempted menacings of their own in order to stop rebel extortion and occasional incursions across the Rio Hondo. But these threats were ineffective. Mayas did not doubt their military superiority, knowing that there were only a meager number of British troops within the colony and believing that "the small garrison of Belize and Corozal represented the whole British army, a notion very generally fatal to our [British] interests in savage countries." British Honduras could receive land and naval reinforcements from the West Indies, but the British reckoned that responding with anything more than token displays of military force might draw them into a prolonged guerrilla war in Central America. Until the military balance on the Yucatan Peninsula had radically changed, the British would have to content themselves with occasional intimations of retaliation while providing rebel Mayas with the cash, guns, and powder demanded.[2]

In the nineteenth century, when thousands of Mayas still bore arms, the changes in the proportions of menace and friendship in exchanges with foreigners reflected military and political developments across the whole Yucatan Peninsula. By the 1920s and '30s, however, Maya powers of coercion were much diminished. The Mayas did still have their moments, as when the garrison of Chun Pom visited Sylvanus Morley at Tulum in 1922 and demanded to know what the foreigners were doing there. But the officer Caamal who greeted Gregory Mason at Tulum in 1926 was all too aware that the good old days of Maya military prowess were gone and, with them, the plausibility of threatening words and gestures.

The same was true for foreigners. Visitors to rebel territory had at times considered the option of coercion, like those archeologists at Tulum who recommended armed escorts to prevent Maya interference in their labors there. And when Thomas Gann visited Tulum village (near the Tulum ruins) in 1927, finding himself denied entry to a church in which he suspected a sacred relic of great interest was kept, he considered pursuing various tacks with the officer Canul, whom "we flattered, we cajoled, we promised offerings to the Santo [divinity], and might even have threatened, had we been in a position to do so." But Gann was in no such position, and Canul "simply refused to let us enter the church, his excuse being, 'I have no order to do so.' "[3]

In peacetime meetings and encounters, neither foreigners nor Mayas could plausibly invoke the menace of physical coercion. In pursuit of their respective ends, to one another they directed not harsh but, rather, "sweet" words (as Mayas would say) and other enticements as well. So a great many of the words exchanged between Maya officers and Sylvanus Morley were salutations and protestations of sincerity, friendship, even love.

In 1934 Morley initiated what would become an escalating rhetoric of friendliness with the officers of Xcacal Guardia, when he wrote to his "dear friends," whose "fine letter" he was "very happy" to have received, carried by one of the officers' "very good men."[4] He sent them gifts as a sign of his "friendliness and affection," and "with all my heart," he wrote, "I show you my friendliness." In translation, Morley's words emerged sweeter still, as his regard, esteem, respect, and affection were rendered in Maya as *yakunah,* "love," and officers thus read of themselves as "beloved companions," of "good-heartedness and love," of "love and respect," of "love," and of "desire."

In their earliest letters to Morley Maya officers were restrained, mentioning only that they were "very happy" to have received Morley's letter and hoped he would receive theirs with formulaic "goodness and love." They proffered no tender appellations or salutations for "Mr. Don Chief," and addressing Villa in those early days, they used only the term *winik,* "human being," a concession of sorts, considering still less pleasant things they might have called him.[5] Months passed before officers mentioned "love" again, even within that restrained formula that they occasionally deployed: "with goodness, with love, with propriety." They continued writing to "Mr. Don Chief" (and on one occasion to "Mr. Boss"[6]), and protested their "happiness" at times to some excess. Finally, they made a first request for "mercy" (which Morley's translator failed to render), and they offered blessings ("May Our Lord True God guard your soul and your body, Mr. Chief"[7]) and the promise of sustenance for Morley and his companions if they visited Xcacal Guardia. Amplifying their rhetoric, they once even called Morley "Great Mr. Don Chief," while they began addressing Villa as *nohoč ȼuul,* "great foreigner."[8]

Morley continued in much the same tone as before. To his "dear," "good," "true," "esteemed" "friends" he wrote with "all my affection" and thanked them "from the bottom of my heart" for their "kind and noble" letters and for the hospitality they were showing Alfonso Villa and his wife. He flattered the officers as "brave men" and their subordinates as "fine young men" for whom, he confessed, he had only "friendliness" and a "great desire" to see. And, while he rarely used the English word "love," officers continued reading in Maya about Morley's love for them. In translation Morley appeared to address them as "beloved and lovable friends," send his salutations "with all my love," protest for them only "friendliness and love" and a commitment to "remember with love" the favors they had done for him. Mayas also read time and again of Morley's "desires," *çibol,* toward them, *çibol* being the term Morley's translator used whenever Morley wrote of "wants," "hopes," "wishes," and "expectations."[9] When Maya officers wrote of *their* wants, hopes, requests, and so forth, they invariably chose other words to denote them, entirely avoiding that word *çibol.*

Eventually Maya officers warmed up to this exchange of courting words. By September 1935 "Mr. Don Chief" and his associates were addressed as "exceedingly beloved ones," whose letters the officers were "exceedingly happy" to receive. The officers claimed that among them there were "goodness, love, and propriety" toward Morley and Villa (the latter by then living in the village of Tuzik). The hour itself was deemed "exceedingly good, exceedingly loving," and officers assured Morley of the "truth" of their words while asking him for "favors" and "mercy." For the moment, they could offer Morley blessings in return.

Less than a year later, in 1936, after Morley had finally visited Xcacal Guardia, the officers' words reached the limits of propriety: "my exceedingly beloved, the great, venerable, respectable, my Mr. Don Sylvanus, Mr. Don Doctor Morley, my lord, my father."[10] Nowadays among those Mayas, a man may call himself your father to insult you, suggesting having had intercourse with your mother and asserting his authority over you. By calling Morley *their* father the officers seemed as if they were reversing the insult, making themselves its object, groveling rhetorically so they might have intercourse of another kind with foreigners. At first suspicious of him, they may well have taken their rhetorical cues from Morley's earliest letters. Once they grasped its potential, they deployed this flattering rhetoric to extremes; if they had gone farther, it would have become vulgarity, sarcasm, and self-parody. Still, not until their corresponding with Morley had nearly reached its end did officers reciprocate his own favorite form of address and deign to call him "friend."[11]

When Sylvanus Morley and Maya officers read the words of love they presumed the other had written, just how did they interpret them? Both the unadorned English word "love" and the Yucatec Maya word *"yakunah"* are ambiguous in their reference to emotions and sexuality. In both languages the love may be divine love, brotherly love, parental love, as well as heterosexual or homosexual love.[12] References to love between Morley and Maya officers would naturally have seemed unromantic and unsexual in import, since the fact of occurrence along with frequent mentions of divinities, mercy, propriety, the love of a father for his children, or that of a superior for his subordinates would deflect imagination from any sexual innuendoes. But, with Morley's "wants," "wishes," and "hopes" cast in Maya by his translator as "desires" (*çibol*), a sexual aspect was unwittingly suggested, for the term *çibol* strongly (if not exclusively, these days) refers to *sexual* desire.

Maya officers were unlikely to miss sexual suggestions in the foreigner's kind words. Sex, sexual desire, sexual exploits and escapades, and attendant mishaps and misfortunes are (after the weather and harvests, perhaps) the favorite conversational topics of Maya men in their gatherings (and of Maya women in theirs, as far as I can tell). They enjoy talking about sex, finding great humor in the follies of desire, and sensing, as they seem to, ambiguity in this domain of their language and their lives. Maya folklore explores such ambiguities as, for instance, in this story recorded by an American linguist in 1931:

> There was an unfortunate man whose erect penis was too small to please his wife. Because of that they quarreled often, and the fellow felt desperate and disgraced. He sought remedy from an old woman who, learning of the man's problem, gave him a ring to wear. She told him that if while wearing the ring he were to raise his hand his penis would grow one quarter in size. He wore the ring and followed her instructions. It worked. The wife was well pleased, and domestic tranquility was restored.
>
> One day, however, the man lost the magic ring while working in his cornfield. A priest chanced upon it and, not realizing it was a magic ring, donned it himself. Next Sunday while saying mass before assembled villagers, with churchbells ringing, standing in front of the altar, he raised his hands to offer the traditional blessing which begins "Dominos Obispo." Thereupon he had an erection, his penis growing by a quarter. Every time the priest raised his hands to bless the congregation, his penis grew by a quarter. It got so long it began to protrude from below the cuff of his pant leg. Unable to finish the mass, the priest withdrew to the sacristy. He called for a doctor and instructed him to sever his

penis, saying that with things as they were he could not perform benedictions. The doctor refused, as did a carpenter called in next. Then appeared the formerly afflicted fellow, who reclaimed his magic ring.[13]

If unlikely to miss apparent sexual allusions in Morley's words, Maya officers were inclined to exploit them. Evidenced in their exchange of sweet words was something that the philosopher Kenneth Burke has called the " 'principle of courtship' in rhetoric . . . the use of suasive devices for the transcending of social estrangement." For Burke estrangement is signaled by "any embarrassment or self-imposed constraint" in social intercourse, and its presence implies a "corresponding mystery in communication," language activity marked not simply for gradations of social differentiation between interlocutors, but for fundamental differences of *kind* between them.[14]

Morley and the Maya officers were thus estranged from one another, and the awkwardness in their dialogues was rooted in mutual fears and reciprocal ignorance. A long war of extermination against the Mayas had only recently subsided, and Mayas of the day still chafed at the consequences of their defeat. They expected lies and treachery from foreigners, even English-speaking ones. For their part, foreigners believed that rebel Mayas' hostility toward whites was intractable, that they thought little of killing, that their prowess as forest combatants was insuperable.

Estrangement derived not only from such harbored fears, but also from the limited means each side could use to address one another. It is a premise of much contemporary research into the nature of conversational interaction that its success depends upon interlocutors' sharing a "communicative competence." This includes knowledge of the rules of a language system that governs construction of intelligible messages and keys them to social contexts, and the conventions with which people judge whether what is said is appropriate and effective and in terms of which they interpret a speaker's intentions.

Just how much such competencies are shared even under conditions of the most ordinary conversational interactions (e.g., between members of a single community speaking the same language) is unclear and hence the focus of linguistic research. How conversations can proceed under more extraordinary conditions is still all the more questionable. The sharing of conversational conventions is a result of frequent contact among people along well-worn networks of communicative activity.[15] Mayas and foreigners — by no means members of a single community and only distantly connected by a single network of social (notably commercial) relations—interacted with minimal sharing of important communicative rules. And, though translators partially bridged that communicative gap, Morley and the Maya officers had to create other conditions for their dialogues, conditions not so much linguistic in nature as affective and economic. Given the kind and degree of their estrangement, a courting rhetoric, like that by means of which men and women establish viable domestic units, was a plausible strategy for interaction. For, while courting rhetoric may be rooted in the interactions of the two sexes, as Kenneth Burke asserts—between people biologically estranged, whose biological estrangement is aggravated by a sexual division of labor and life experiences—pronounced social distinctions of *any* variety may engender estrangement and so occasion use of "a corresponding rhetoric, in form quite analogous to sexual expression: for the relations between classes are like the ways of courtship, rape, seduction, jilting, prostitution, promiscuity, with variants of sadistic torture or masochistic invitation to mistreatment."[16]

We know unfortunately little about how Maya men and women converse and virtually nothing about how they court. From their 1930s study of Chan Kom, a Maya community in Yucatan, Redfield and Villa concluded that romance was not fundamental to Maya marriage, and that "relationships between the sexes are not in the least romantically conceived. There are no obvious conventional patterns of courtship, and many marriages take place without any courtship whatsoever. There are no lovesongs, no serenades, and no love stories. Caresses, either in word or act, between husband and wife are not to be observed."[17]

Yucatec Maya folktales then, however, told a different story—tales of the elopement of young lovers whose parents would not sanction their marriage, of a wayward woman who returns to her former husband's deathbed ("The conclusion of love, when she returned to serve him until he died . . . "), of a young man's search for his childhood love whom a king has taken away (upon reunion the young man "hugs her and kisses her, the conclusion of his love for her"). And, although perhaps quite rare, there *were* love songs and lyric poetry with romantic themes in Yucatec Maya, not to mention those in Spanish that Mayas could have heard and perhaps sung.[18]

Redfield and Villa's conclusion that romantic love was absent in Maya lives was certainly too categorical, dependent as it was on the public, visible occasions of male-female interactions—"there are no *obvious* . . . patterns of courtship," "caresses . . . are not to be *observed.*"

Captain Cituk with his wife and son

Romance, rather than entirely absent, was likely a matter of profound privacy. On only one occasion, from his vantage point in a chicken coop in the village of Señor, was Villa able to spy Maya romance.[19]

Still, it is true that romance is overshadowed in Yucatec Maya discourse, and in our ethnological observations, by three other themes pertaining to Maya male-female relationships. One is that of mutual, practical support. Of marriage in Chan Kom, Redfield and Villa noted:

> A man has a woman . . . and this woman is his wife because she lives with him and serves him, and also because, in many cases, she has been formally married to him. Mutual economic support is the essence of the relationship; in addition each spouse gives the other varying degrees of advice and sympathy.[20]

A second overshadowing theme, or rather configuration of themes, includes sexual desire and eroticism, seduction, and, alas, deception, infidelity, adultery, and separation. Folktales gathered in the 1930s suggest the currency of such topics among Mayas. Sexual desire, far more often than the emotion of love, was explicitly developed as the motive for unions between young men and women. Seduction, entailing above all else a man *saying* things to a woman, was often the means for effecting such union. Such means harbored the potential for deception, so the concept of seduction found expression in Yucatec Maya through such expressions as "to deceive a woman," "fit oneself inside [of women's intimacy or confidence] in order to speak to them," "to bore one's way into a woman's affections or trust."[21] Many Maya stories seem to say, If it happened once it can happen again; hence stories of double deceits, bigamy, and wife stealing.

Finally, a third theme that Mayas elaborated at the expense of romance is the idea that sacred and secular powers often intrude into the relations of men and women. So, for example, to talk of Maya courtship in Quintana Roo is to talk of how adult men speak to one another as they arrange the union of their offspring. The linguist Allan Burns reports that while courting words (čuhuk tàan) in a Yucatecan town are of romantic import, in a corresponding community in former rebel territory they are not romantic but, rather, sacred, "kinds of words from God."[22] In a related vein folktale after folktale recounts the intrusion into a pristine love or first seduction of obdurate parents, local and regional judges, non-Mayas, rich men, merchants, priests, celestial giants, and the like. Resolution of the attendant conflicts usually comes with the acceptance of loss, or with death, though sometimes the hapless man or woman does triumph, assisted by supernatural allies and/or suddenly bestowed personal powers that permit the reestablishment of a proper domestic relationship, or simple vengeance at the least.

Mayas' affect, sexuality, gender, and domesticity have not been much studied, and this discussion suffers accordingly.[23] Yet it seems safe to say there is such a thing as Maya loving, intimately connected in the minds and deeds of those involved with multiple other dimensions of their lives as subordinated, relatively powerless people. The dominant themes of mutual and practical support; sexuality, seduction, deceit, loss; and secular and sacred powers link Maya romance to intergender and interethnic or interclass discourse. In communication between the sexes *and* between interlocutors estranged on other bases, Mayas speak of love in usages made ambiguous and effective by the social contexts of their loving. Some Mayas have been adept at developing the ambiguities of such usages in their efforts to incline socially estranged others toward intercourse of various kinds.

An example drawn from wartime discourses reveals this well. Becalar (located in the southern part of what is now the state of Quintana Roo) was an isolated but strategically important town with some five thousand inhabitants on the eve of the War of the Castes.[24] A trading center in the forest, far from other populated centers of the Yucatan Peninsula, it sat astride a principal route of water- and land-borne commerce between English-speaking peoples of the Caribbean and Spanish- and Maya-speaking people of the mainland. During the war Indian rebels needed to control the town and its environs to secure their supply of British-made weapons and munitions, and their enemies needed to control it to choke off such trade. Success or failure for either side had military consequences in all other theaters of battle.

Bacalar fell to Indian rebels early in the war in 1848. It was recaptured from them a year later, and was besieged by rebels thereafter for months and years on end. The defenders of Bacalar were a miserable lot, suffering chronic shortages of food and medicine, and receiving no word from the outside world for long periods of time. Occasionally expeditions arrived to bring supplies and relieve the garrison. They would stay awhile and then depart, after which the Indian siege of the town would continue. A relief expedition had come and gone three months earlier when, in October 1852, the commander of the Indian siege, José María Tzuc, wrote this letter to the commander of the defenders of Bacalar:[25]

> My exceedingly beloved and revered Sir. This is the hour in which it is urgent for me to write to you, in order to show you the esteem which I have for you, thus in this world as before God. Do not think that I am only deceiving you, although you consider me an Indian. . . . I am not accustomed to deceiving my neighbor, however, even though I am an Indian. . . . Very well you know that one God alone has created us in this world.
>
> Thus it is that I love you very much, with all of my heart, as I do all the troops under your command in that town, even as I love all of your kind who are used to speaking with me. They should themselves tell you if I mistreat or harm any whites. Even as I love my fellow Indians, I thus also do love the whites.

Tzuc told the Bacalar commander that he had received written orders to begin a final assault, which would surely succeed, for Tzuc had been told "very many troops would be sent to enter that town once and for all."

Sometimes the defenders of Bacalar went for months without receiving supplies, correspondence, or relief; at times they felt they had been abandoned or were to be cruelly sacrificed.[26] And there was some problem with defections to the enemy. Tzuc pointed all that out to the commander, stressing the futility and waste of further resistance and death. "I sent you this letter," Tzuc continued:

> so that you know what is happening. Do not deceive yourselves. Your government will never win this war. I do not deceive you: Nothing which you do will ever succeed nor turn out as you plan. So do not worry about me. Try to have in your hearts the idea of presenting yourselves to me for good and for love, and thus no harm at all will happen in that town. Even with the weapons and munitions which you have in that town, if you try to resist you will suffer an infinity of misfortunes in these days which draw near. Better that you manage to turn over all the munitions and all the weapons which are there so that no harm occurs in that town. Because I would regret it very much if harm befell you for no reason.

Tzuc went on to assure the enemy commander that if they surrendered immediately the defenders of Bacalar would continue to enjoy their freedom and their property.

> Turn over all the weapons peacefully, do not think that any harm will happen to you! You will still stay in your houses. Do not think that your houses which are your property will be taken from you. Whether acquired by work or by purchase, they are still yours. And as for justice, it will be administered also as long ago. Nobody will prevent you or do harm to you. Therefore you may travel as merchants wherever you want. Nobody will prevent you. You can sell your things. You can also buy whatever things you need.

After again mentioning how the defenders of Bacalar had been wronged by their own government, which continued to deceive them, Tzuc implored the enemy while making the most naked of threats:

> For the better, put it in your hearts, this which I tell you. For God's sake think it over. You should not have to experience a thousand

deprivations for your government, because what they planned for the Indian will never turn out, since there should be none greater than God, because it is not God's order that the whites defeat the Indians in this war which is happening. The government of the whites must not think that we do not know what is God's command which he left on this sinful earth where we dwell or exist.

And so my beloved, friendly commander, if you do not believe what I tell you, if you do not wish to obey my friendly word directed to you, you will agree in time, because nothing will you salvage if I annihilate the town of Bacalar. If you begin to resist, you will lose everything you have. . . . If you deliver all the military supplies there are in that Bacalar, for good and love, without anger, this will be enough.

Tzuc went on to describe again the freedoms that all would enjoy when the war was finally over. And he excused himself for skirmishes that had already taken place with the defenders of Bacalar. Finally, he worked toward his conclusion:

If you suffered some harm, it is not my fault, because I had not come to fight, but rather peacefully I had come. Now, then, I send you this, my letter, with much affection, because I am not deceiving. I can even give you my word concerning this which I tell you. But see your way to turning over everything I tell you to! For if you do not wish to believe that which I tell you, you will all die in that little town of Bacalar, because I have many troops with which to close all the exits around Bacalar. The thing is, nowhere am I going to give you a road to leave on, not even one of you, no matter how many troops you may have there. There you will all perish. . . .

There is nothing more. May God give you health for many years. I love you with all [my heart].[27]

That the Indian commander would so profess his love for the defenders of Bacalar has at least two evident motives. First, though the Indian forces numbered in the thousands and the defenders of Bacalar only in the hundreds, the town was highly defensible, and failed assaults had cost many lives. As Tzuc had already been in charge of the siege for three years, he would have known well the likely costs of an all-out attack. So, despite his denials of deceit, we can assume that Tzuc might be lying to save the lives of his troops.[28] Second, Tzuc and his men were not professional soldiers: they were farmers, merchants, hunters, and family men besides, socialized in the Christian ethic against killing. So they might seek to absolve themselves in advance of the guilt of homicide.

But Tzuc's professions of love were also proposals for the future. The rebellion and prolonged war had reduced social relations between Mayas and non-Mayas to only a single element of their former complexity. The word *ɗùul* was and still is the common Maya term for the "Other," encompassing such an ambivalent set of meanings as "white men," "rich men," "foreigners," "respected ones," "enemy." The ambivalence of the term reflects the ambivalence of Mayas' many past relations with such people. In their written correspondence among themselves during the war Maya officers tended *not* to use this common and comprehensive term; rather, they wrote to each other about the movements and doings of the "enemy" (*enemigo*)—"the enemy is to the north," "the enemy attacked this town or that," "send me so many kegs of powder and so many troops because the enemy is operating in my district."

Those who had tired of the war, who were morally pained by the killing, and who saw both the necessity and opportunity of peaceful coexistence with those then known as the "enemy," searched for some basis upon which to recomplicate social relations rhetorically. With peace there would be a new social hierarchy and a new division of labor, some foresaw and even demanded. And some may have grasped that the social relations characteristic of that new order would need to be couched in a new rhetoric. The rhetoric of courtship and love was a plausible basis for reinterjecting "mystery" or "ambiguity" into social relations, which in war had been reduced to simple quantitative matters of so many guns, so much power. The rhetoric of courtship would cover the social relations of a new order with a eulogistic mantle so that people of different kinds could get on with living together in peace.

Mayas in various historical moments have deployed their particular rhetoric of romantic courtship to facilitate communication across profound social boundaries—with an Other who was a wartime enemy, with a foreigner with whom they sought alliance, or with God. This is not to suggest that Maya notions of romantic love are the same as ours. Nonetheless some allusions seem evident. When the Indian commander told his enemy that he loved him with all his heart, he developed the metaphor of courtship further by suggesting that the government had jilted the defenders of Bacalar, while assuring them the Indians would treat them much better, and he went on to exploit the metaphor by informing the enemy commander that other whites were already having at least social intercourse with Indians, so why not he and his troops, too?

He assured his enemies that after surrendering to his wishes they would continue to enjoy the security of a home, within which they could manage their own economic affairs—doing the buying and selling that are an important part of women's work and power in many Indian households. But, he told them, they would have to leave their weapons in the hands of Indians—even as guns are men's tools in the typical Indian household economy. Finally, he assured those whom he was courting that his intentions were entirely honorable; they should not worry about deceit in courtship (a common motif in Indian stories concerning the vagaries of male-female courtship), or about rape and pillage, either.

(In this rhetoric of courtship may lie yet another, concealed motive, one impossible to assess here. Only some eight months earlier enemy forces had captured and carried off Tzuc's own wife.[29])

Seldom before in their history had Mayas been in such an obviously superior position vis-à-vis those whom they called the Other. Capable then of annihilating the enemy, and with reason to believe they would never again be subject to the rule of foreigners, why would they propose to remystify their social relations with those defeated Others? Were they so dominated by the ideology of their original oppression that they could not clearly see the possibilities inherent in that exceptional historical moment? To use once again an idea from Kenneth Burke: it is likely that the profession of love in that Indian commander's letter obscured less at the time than it seems to today. The particular historical context in which the term *yakunah* or "love" was then used might well have made obvious to its users its multiple and ambivalent implications. That is to say, the mystifications that the text seems to construct result from our reading of it, so distant are we from the context of its original production and practical uses.[30]

If Indians and their enemies were to become lovers at that moment, it must have been clear to all of them that the relationship would be asymmetrical. The Indians would be "men" while the foreigners would be "women"—*not* men and women as they truly were, but "men" and "women" as social categories in the gender system of those times. What relations covered by such a powerful metaphor would actually entail in the day-to-day activities of production, exchange, and governance would have to be worked out after peace came, and most likely silently, as people continued to profess their love for one another on appropriate occasions. As long as Indians had the guns, they had reason to expect they would find happiness in such an admittedly open-ended relationship. In the meantime a rhetoric of courtship offered the prospect of peaceful union without precluding struggles to come.

I have found no record of a reply by the defenders of Bacalar to the Indian commander's friendly appeal. To maintain discipline after weeks and months of incessant Indian attacks, and with troops suffering from disease and hunger, the commander of the forces defending Bacalar had to have a "soul of iron," as the Caste War historian Baqueiro wrote regarding earlier episodes in the siege: "it was necessary to overcome all human feeling so as not to abandon that campaign."[31] The siege went on. José María Tzuc gave up the fight about a year later, as ongoing negotiations with the government of Yucatan finally bore some fruit, and he retired with his men to one of the more isolated parts of the peninsula, there to start new lives as best they could. Other Indian forces moved in to continue the siege of Bacalar under the command of officers less loving than Tzuc.

Six years after Tzuc wrote his letter to the commander of Bacalar, the town fell to a brief surprise attack. Many of its citizens were taken prisoners, and from British Honduras a party of Englishmen departed to obtain their release. A Mr. Blake had already gone to Bacalar and was told to leave and come back with cash and gunpowder. While returning to Bacalar, bringing the cash but still no powder, he met Captain Anderson of the 2nd West India Regiment, who bore a letter for the Maya general Venancio Puc, in which the superintendent of British Honduras asked for merciful treatment of the captives. In their response Mayas invoked the asymmetry of male-female relationships, not this time by reference to courtship and domesticity, but rather through demonstrations of a more violent kind. After the Englishmen arrived in the fallen town and presented the superintendent's letter to General Puc, they wandered about while waiting for a reply. They found

the main road parallel to the lake had been cleared and there were no human corpses in it, but even there the air was impregnated with the smell which came from the side streets where bodies stark naked, male and female, in every stage of decomposition were being devoured by the dogs and "John Crows" (Turkey buzzards). From the different degrees of decay it was evident that there had been successive massacres in detail. That many had been murdered when incapable of resistance, the marks of rope around the arms shewed. The majority of the corpses were female, and an

Indian explained, what might easily have been guessed—the cause of the deep nail scratches about the neck and other parts of the body; marks which were visible not only on the dead.

Captain Anderson spoke to some of the prisoners, including a girl of fourteen whom he recognized as the sister-in-law of the Mexican Consul in Belize. She,

> with deeply scarred neck, came forward and reminded Captain Anderson that they had met in Belize, whispered that she was to be released tomorrow, but was dragged away by the Guard . . . when she began to speak with dread of the intervening night of captivity from which, as he understood she was going, when interrupted, to entreat him to cause her to be freed.

Hours later there was still no reply to the Englishmen's letter, which had first to be translated into Spanish, then Yucatec Maya, before the Maya officers could read it and, they told the Englishmen, submit it for. "the consideration of the Santa Cruz—the idol and oracle of the tribe, consulted in every matter of importance, never seen by laymen and which in less exciting times goes up to Heaven for instructions." The Englishmen grew concerned as night approached, and even more so when

> Mr. Blake came with some alarm to enquire if it was true that General Windham had been beaten in India [during the recent Sepoy rebellion], for the Chiefs said so, and that the power of England was no longer to be feared. He had evidently had an unpleasant discussion with the Indians about the want of Gunpowder. They said that our Government is not impartial. . . . We allowed Perdomo [the defeated Mexican commander of Bacalar] to take Gunpowder out of English Vessels on the Hondo. The Sta. Cruz had only to give the word, and they would seize Perdomo in the middle of Corosal [to which he had fled].

"That night, as usual," the superintendent's report of the mission continues, "all the available Indians in Bacalar assembled in front of the house where the Sta. Cruz is kept. The Boy attendants of the idol, called Angels, sung in front of it, the drums and bugles sounded at recurring parts of the song." General Puc was inside with the Holy Cross, while his officers and troops remained kneeling outside until the mass concluded, at which time "they crossed themselves and rubbed their foreheads in the dust." It was eleven o'clock when the prisoners were brought out and lined up in front of the house harboring the visiting divinity, while many soldiers knelt along the road. "It was a perfectly clear night, and as the moon was only two days past the full, every face was visible. There was evidently considerable anxiety, and all the Englishmen kept close to the red Coats." The prisoners included about forty women and twelve or so men, along with children, too.

They were calm—except the children—although it was known that Sta. Cruz was pronouncing on their fate. Captain Anderson being close to the house where the oracle was, heard a "squeaking" noise, and when it ceased, it was announced that Sta. Cruz demanded a higher ransom for the prisoners. Mr. Blake jumped forward and offered to guarantee the payment of the 7,000 dollars. Had he got the amount with him? No—but he would forward it. Santa Cruz scouted the idea. Mr. Blake had deceived them about the powder— let the prisoners be killed. But Captain Anderson interfered and again called attention to my remonstrance. Puc was inside the house, and the question was referred to him. There was a pause, and the chattering of the teeth of one of the Englishmen was so distinctly audible that the Chiefs, to Captain Anderson's mortification, sent to tell him that the English need not be afraid.

From the sanctuary of the cross, a counterproposal finally emerged: If the English turned over the former Mexican commander of Bacalar, who had taken refuge in British Honduras, the prisoners would be freed. Captain Anderson refused, despite the pleading of his own men: "The thing was simply impossible."

Santa Cruz had nothing further to say. Matters must take their course. Two of the subordinate officers made a selection of four or five women and had them marched off under a Guard. The Soldiers commenced tying the women's elbows behind their backs, and then the children selected to be saved—little girls, eight in number— were separated from their mothers, and the only scene of violence which had been witnessed yet, was in the struggles and frantic screams of these little wretches, though adjured by one of the women not to make such a noise or they would be killed with their mothers. A procession was formed and marched off towards the East Gate. First came a strong body of troops, then alternately, in Indian file, a male prisoner, and his executioner driving him along with his *Machete* (Cutlass) and holding by the rope which confined his Arms. Next the women 35 in number driven and held in a similar manner passed on, and another body of Soldiers closed the rear. The Englishmen were not allowed to follow, but they saw the white dresses of the women, and of the procession generally, pass through the Gate and halt under a clump of Trees a hundred and fifty yards off. Captain Anderson returned home and soon the butchery seemed to begin. Shrieks were heard, but in ten minutes all was quiet again, and shortly afterwards the troops returned.

Not long after, the screams of a woman broke the silence again. The Englishmen guessed it was the fourteen-year-old girl with whom Captain Anderson had spoken and who had not appeared with the other prisoners taken out for slaughter earlier that evening. Her screams were "of the most violent description . . . more prolonged and piercing" than those of the earlier victims — "as if the prospect of escape had broken down the sullen strength of despair with which the others had met their fate." Later still, a messenger from General Puc paid a visit to Captain Anderson to say the general "hoped the Superintendent would not be offended by what had happened. The Spaniards always treated their Prisoners in that way. The Indians merely followed a lesson which had been taught them. Let not the English be afraid."

The next morning the only signs of the previous night's massacre were the buzzards on the killing ground and Indians washing their machetes in the lagoon. General Puc "called on Captain Anderson in the morning, but his manner was embarrassed and cold. He had no letter for the Superintendent. The englishmen might leave Bacalar when they pleased. All the Indians turned out as they embarked. There were awkwardness and silence on both sides."[32]

IT WAS NOT with sugar, a Maya once told me, that his people dispatched the defenders of Bacalar, but rather with the points of bullets. Yet for Mayas dealing with foreigners in the 1920s and '30s, sweet words would have to do, though neither Mayas nor foreigners expected words alone to have desired effects. Each side supplemented protestations of love and friendship with acts of gift giving, purchase, and sale.

As "an earnest of our good faith and future intentions" foreigners presented Maya interlocutors many gifts — usually things of little value, small amounts of cash and food, and medical supplies.[33] Mayas most appreciated the latter, and the longer Villa lived in Tuzik the more frequently adults and children came to be cured of their fevers, diarrhea, vomiting, night sweats, coughs, muscle aches, toothaches, skin conditions, menstrual irregularities, conjunctivitis, and for deworming. Such gifts and free services were eagerly accepted, unless would-be benefactors insulted the Mayas, as happened when the Yucatan Medical Expedition visited the village of Xiatil in 1929. They were welcomed there as itinerant merchants, having come accompanied by a jewelry vendor from Merida, and were allowed to dispense medicine free of charge, until one "member of the party, finding a dirty Indian in his hammock [and concerned about scabies], expelled him hastily. The impression created was unfortunate. Thereafter, most of the Indians held aloof, some gave us black looks, and few applied for treatment."[34]

Mayas occasionally gave gifts in return, usually food, if one was around at mealtime. While living in Tuzik, Villa was invited into Maya homes to partake of the fruits in season, or sometimes fresh corn on the cob or corn-based gruel beverages, and more rarely a cooked meal (especially during the public feasts of village and shrine center holidays). It was, however, more through their willingness to buy and sell, rather than give and receive gifts, that Mayas displayed their feelings toward outsiders in their midst. They had been known to set arbitrary prices for coerced sales from itinerant merchants, or sometimes simply to steal merchants' clothes and goods before whipping and sending them on their way. They not infrequently refused to give unwelcome intruders any food or water, even when offered "exorbitant prices."[35] On better days they might only intimidate merchants and rough-handle their wares, as Villa discovered while posing as a traveling merchant in 1932. Though he was well received in most Maya settlements, he found the people of Captain Cituk's village of Xmaben to be a "rough lot."

> Yesterday in the afternoon when I arrived here the news spread so rapidly that I had not even unloaded the horse when I was surrounded by more than twenty Indians. . . . Since they could not open the boxes as quickly as they wished because they were padlocked, they forced them open violently. Their rudeness increased when they found out that we had not brought *aguardiente* [a kind of rum], "which is the only thing we need," according to the exclamation of one of them. All this presaged an unpleasant time for us, for we could not find a friendly face among them.[36]

Even in the best of circumstances, selling to those Mayas was never easy, and they drove merchants to distraction. Villa described the technique at length:

Indians never buy things right off. First they look [at] the desired object a long time, considering the use to which they could put it. Then they approach it, touch it, study it by themselves, and finally, calling in others more experienced to help them, discuss the merchandise with the most complete thoroughness. Ordinarily they are not even satisfied then but take the merchandise to their homes in order to continue the discussion with their families. After all this, they must come and haggle about the price, in spite of the fact that this is already extremely low. If finally the matter is settled they take the article away with a promise to pay later. It is only fair to say, as to this, that they are very much people of their word.[37]

While Alfonso Villa was living in Tuzik a merchant from Valladolid arrived with goods to sell, including metal grinders of the sort that would eventually replace the stone grinding implements Maya women then used to prepare corn for tortillas. "They would have gone well," Villa thought. But of the villagers gathered about the merchant, one mused out loud that since the wares had been brought on the back of a visibly restless horse, it might well be that somewhere back on the trail the load had been thrown, damaging the merchandise. "Notwithstanding that this observation was a simple suggestion without any proof at all," Villa noted in his diary,

it sufficed to influence the others effectively, as immediately they set to checking the grinders, discovering scratches, damages, and dents visible only to them. The arguments of the merchant were useless, as everyone was completely convinced that the horse had thrown the grinders on the ground and, even more, perhaps it had even trampled them. Understandably, no one wanted to buy them.

The next day the merchant moved on without having sold anything in Tuzik, "as the distrust that in the beginning was limited to the grinders was extended, later, to all the other merchandise."[38]

With Morley and Villa, Mayas practiced neither forced exchange nor refusal to trade. On the contrary, amicable trade was a goal of their official communications with the Americans, as it had often been with the British. And trade of more limited and spontaneous sort was part of Mayas' strategy to create the understanding and sympathy that, they hoped, would result in their receiving the "wherewithal for war." Although trade with outsiders had at times been blocked by either official policy or public opinion, as long as Maya officers were speaking with distinguished visitors, common people could deal with them for the personal necessities of their individual households.

Alfonso Villa's cover as itinerant merchant was more appropriate than he could have imagined in 1932, and though he ceased to present himself so in the last year of his research in the territory—in favor of the more effective and prestigious pretext of middleman in Maya-American diplomacy—Mayas pressed him to continue playing the part. In the beginning they were seemingly content to accept the medicines he offered. Then they started requesting gifts he had not thought to bring—a bottle of hair dye, porous plaster for extracting harmful supernatural "winds" from the body, medicine for female sterility and menstrual irregularities, schoolhouse supplies, and so on.

Eventually, and in ever-increasing numbers, they placed orders with Villa for goods to be bought in Merida and brought with Villa's supply train every few months. Women seem to have been Villa's principal clients, ordering shawls, hats, kerchiefs, perfumes, gold-colored crepe, blue beads, "and other things of that sort that they will show off in the next fiesta." That next fiesta was never far off, and the volume of such requests burdened five or six mules with merchandise each trip.

That, along with the unceasing request for medical services, caused Villa to despair. "This day I have passed tremendously occupied attending to the crowds come from all the villages of this region. To leave each one pleased is something that requires infinite patience and tact in dealing with them. They are good people, but when they are all together they become a little foolish like impertinent children." And on another day he griped: "I am the focus of attention of the entire region; daily individuals come to me from all parts to order merchandise, for me to cure them, and even with the simple purpose of consulting me about meteorological, political, economic matters, etc. No less tiring are the women who do not want to leave here, inquiring about the most insignificant things."[39]

Despite the hassle, and sometimes futility, of attempting to be merchant, doctor, and adviser, Villa felt such efforts were vital to "overcome all unfriendliness or lack of sympathy for my ethnological labors" and deflect Mayas' attention from the political agenda behind their dealings with Americans.[40] As he explained to his mentor, Robert Redfield:

> Upon first arriving here I was considered a simple intermediary in
> the negotiations for annexation that they [officers] hoped to cele-

brate with said foreign Power [U.S.]. Immediately I realized how dangerous was this idea for the future of our labors, so I planned to go disabusing them slowly, without their coming to feel totally defrauded, of their hopes. That, without doubt, was difficult: to trust solely in the prestige of the Carnegie Institution and in little gifts made occasionally in Chichen Itza proved very ineffective; to tell them frankly that our only interest in them was to prepare an ethnographic monograph of purely scientific character would have been not only worse, but also unintelligible for them. What was lacking was a formula that would allow me to live among them [while] fulfilling a common need, that is to say, that the utility of my presence be palpable, felt immediately. The formula needed, to say it in the [anthropological] terminology presently in vogue, was that of having a social function in the group.

"To achieve that," he began speaking to Mayas of the need for medicines, "thinking that, with time, they would come to be a need that I could satisfy." So, too, with other consumer goods that Villa could order and obtain from Merida until "the utility of my presence thus becomes evident and undeniable."[41] That his "social functions" as gift giver, doctor, and friendly merchant might reinforce the Mayas' resolve for political union and war against Mexico, rather than deflect them from such conspiracies, did not occur to Villa. Minor in themselves, those medical and commercial transactions among Morley, Villa, and Maya interlocutors were good harbingers of future possibilities—for the conduct of research that foreigners hoped for, and for the conclusion of an alliance that Maya officers sought.

All the more so given the ongoing exchange of courting and sugges- tive words. Maya officers who corresponded with Morley said they wanted to be one with him and his people; they wanted there to be union between them. They wanted that "there be your opening of the roads for us, for us to speak with you, for you to bring us what we need here in Guardia, Mr. Don Chief." Love was spoken of, and sometimes even desire. The anthropologist Robert Redfield noted something of relevance here when he wrote that mutual economic support was the essence of the marital relationship among Mayas. Through minor trade Mayas and foreigners worked on creating such an essence between them while each got what they needed at the moment—Mayas, things with which to cure and adorn themselves, their divinities, and their altars; foreigners, labor and above all else, *information*.

In addition to courting foreigners with sweet words and acts of gift giving, purchase, and sale, Maya officers pursued alliance by willingly responding to the inquiries of strangers who asked to know about them, their history, and their way of life. Such openness was neither inadvertent nor customary. When in the late nineteenth century the British Surveyor General William Miller complained of the belligerently taciturn character of rebels, from whom it was "impossible to get any information . . . as they strongly object to being questioned," he might as well have been referring to late twentieth-century Mayas and those of Morley's day, too.

Early foreign explorers among the Maya most eagerly sought to learn the location of archeological ruins, and Mayas sometimes pointed the way, if there was something in it for them. As one explorer observed: "The eagerness of these primitive people for some of the mechanical advantages the white man has developed is pitiful to see. In return for our shotguns and radio sets they can give us light on the wonders of their past, as they have begun to give us their mahogany and their chicle."[42] Later visitors sought a much wider range of information — about social life, farming, hunting, language, religion, history — and Maya officers who obliged them went beyond anything they had permitted before. They revealed much of themselves, not just for immediate gain but as part of a more elaborate strategy that, they hoped, would result in alliance and union. If Morley and his kind (the "you" of the officers' letters to Morley was often plural) only understood certain things about the present conditions and recent history of Maya laboring, self-governance, and piety, then perhaps they would take pity and send the flag of their nation and the implements of war.

In their letters to Morley, Maya officers expended many words describing the plight of their people, of course, and making repeated requests for assistance. Beyond the words of love, the accounts of hardships, and the requests for aid, they described their current social practices in stretches of text often framed by such expressions as "it is necessary to write" or "we want to make clear to you." They gave lists of settlements under their rule and the names, ranks, and residences of living Maya officers. Even as earlier explorers were told of dissension within the ranks, so now the officers of Xcacal Guardia wrote Morley concerning who among them was in favor, who was out, who was with them and who was not.[43] (The "I" in Maya letters was collective but not all-inclusive.) They permitted copying of their most sacred papers — a Book of Chilam Balam and the revelatory manuscript known to them as "The Testament," to us as "The Proclamation of Juan de la Cruz."

In their letters to Morley officers continually stressed historical precedents for their acts. They told Morley that they had talked with the British in Corozal, in Belize City, and in other settlements to the south, and that the agreements reached were what they sought now with Morley. They said they wanted things "left like long ago, when our great fathers were speaking with the English gentlemen." Invoking the deeds of their "late, honorable fathers," the officers also invoked their names in several lists embedded in and appended to their correspondence — a list of those said to have negotiated with the British, a list of past secretaries, and one they titled "the ancient list of our kings." Forty-one names were given in all, including some known from published histories of the Caste War, and many others who were never so immortalized. These were the kings who ruled the territory, the officers told Morley, just as they sought to rule over that same territory restored. Listed thus, the dead served their purpose in the dialogues with Morley. No need to mention what the officers knew well — that the kings had slaughtered each other in a succession of coups in which peace talks were often a contended issue.[44]

The officers' key concession to foreign researchers was their decision to let Alfonso Villa live among them. From his renovated pigsty in Tuzik, Villa could observe the happenings and listen to the talk of this once-hidden Maya world as none before him had. Or at least he could observe the public happenings — the coming and going of visitors to various households in the village, the daily exodus of people heading to their labors in the forest, public rituals in the village church and small family chapels, and, of course, the changing seasons of those latitudes. Villa could talk with visitors who went out of their way to see him at his residence and chat with him about themselves, current events, recent history, and so on, among whom officers were prominent. In time they replaced Villa's pigsty with a grand thatched-roof hut, at nine by four meters the largest structure in their territory — apart from the shrine, village church, and barracks — in order the more comfortably to accommodate themselves, it seems, on their ever more frequent trips to speak with the Americans' representative.[45]

Villa stayed close to home in Tuzik, except for occasional trips to the shrine center, during most of his time in the region. Soon after his arrival he visited each of the villages associated with Xcacal Guardia and conducted a house-by-house census. Captain Cituk, Lieutenant Zuluub, and other officers made that otherwise impossible task successful as people usually loath to give their names or any other information to strangers ("so as not to be dominated by the whites") did so when company officers stood by the census taker and encouraged truthful answers. After their high-level visit to Chichen Itza and meetings with Morley in December 1935, Maya officers apparently became even more communicative, and Villa was able to collect such a wealth of information that his ethnography of the Mayas of central Quintana Roo has not been surpassed in thoroughness by any subsequent research.[46]

Though they had encouraged it, the officers were never fully comfortable with that new loquacity. The extraordinary measures Villa had employed to conceal his note taking while he was posing as a simple merchant were no longer necessary, but still,

> I soon had to give up the use of pencil and paper when talking with the natives for it appeared to arouse distrust. Instead, I made my house a sort of general meeting place, and there chatted with the people as would any friend. In these gatherings it was I who would suggest the subjects, discussion of which would often develop with warm interest. Later in the day, when I was alone, I would write down what I had heard and learned.[47]

In trying to construct an alliance with the Americans through Villa, Maya officers and common people constructed an image of themselves for the foreigners to write down and take home with them. Foreign authors subsequently revised that image greatly, in accordance with current anthropological theory and the conventions of ethnographic writing. Meanwhile, Mayas, in part through their interactions with the Americans, were changing themselves and the conditions of their lives in ways they could hardly have foreseen. Could they have glimpsed the future, they might well have resisted the advances of the anthropologist, applying to him the same well-founded skepticism customarily directed at schoolteachers. "We know their tricks," Paulino Yama of Señor had told Villa back in 1932:

> First they come with flattery and kindness in order later on to manage us like children. El Maestro [teacher] . . . when he comes here, brings us cigarettes, medicines, and other things as presents. Why does he act that way? Does he think we are girls (to be courted)? Without any doubt he is plotting something.[48]

VII

BETRAYAL AND
RECONCILIATION

AFTER TWO and a half years of exchanging letters and visits, and despite the courting words, gift giving, and mutual enlightening, the dialogues between Maya officers and Morley were shortly to engender bizarre calumny. Morley had written and spoken of peace and love; Maya officers had written and spoken of war and love. Morley had cited the respect due the laws of Mexico, a nation in which he was only a visitor; Maya officers had cited the respect due their heritage of self-governance within the boundaries of their homeland. Morley, an Episcopalian, had invoked Our Lord, the God of Christianity, who desired peace and brotherhood among all men; the officers had spoken, in turn, of Our Lord True God, who suffered for *them* and in whose forest they lived and labored. Once Maya officers began to realize that Morley would not help to bring about the war they wanted, some of them, even as stridently an anti-Mexican as Lieutenant Zuluub, broke ranks and turned with slanderous lies to long-time enemies.

In the summer of 1936 Lieutenant Zuluub sent his son to tell the Mexican authorities in Santa Cruz that Captain Cituk was a subversive, who with Americans had planned a Maya secession from Mexico, and that one of the Americans, a fellow named "Silvano," was supplying Cituk with weapons through an intermediary, Alfonso Villa. The following spring Zuluub himself, together with his estranged colleague Francisco May, publicly repeated the charges at a regional "Indian Congress" in the village of Chunhuas organized by Mexican schoolteachers and the federal official responsible for local Indian affairs. Amidst other speeches denouncing imperialism, fascism, and Yankee capitalism, Zuluub and

May accused Morley and Villa of arming Mayas around Xcacal Guardia so they would renounce the authority of the Mexican government, and of having photographed people "naked and in humiliating poses" during the Xcacal Guardia festival in February 1936. The charges were transmitted in a lengthy report to the President of Mexico, Lázaro Cárdenas, who in turn sent a representative to investigate.[1]

Morley had offered sound counsel in his last letter to the head priest, Barrera, of Xcacal Guardia, suggesting "that we all live in friendliness and peace with one another." For it was certainly true that even with the most powerful allies, Mayas would suffer terribly were war to resume. The would-be rebels were not nearly so numerous as their Caste War predecessors had been, nor was war waged as in the time of their late fathers, when they had an understanding with the Englishmen. The technology of nineteenth-century warfare had grown obsolete, and Mayas understood little of what the new century had spawned — machine guns, land mines, poison gases, aerial bombardment, and so on. However sound, Morley's counsel was disingenuous, as well. He had said that as a stranger in another's land he felt bound to respect its laws, yet that principle was not so inviolable as he seemed to claim: it was honored selectively and judged pragmatically, depending on the shifting realities of international relations.

During 1917 and 1918, for example, while traveling extensively in Central America — including visits to Santa Cruz, Tulum, and other points along the east coast of the Yucatan Peninsula — and posing as one engaged in archeological research for the Carnegie Institution, in fact Morley had been conducting espionage as an officer in United States Naval Intelligence. (The Carnegie Institution had known that and continued to pay him the difference between his government wages and his former salary as a regular employee of the Institution.[2]) A number of Morley's archeological colleagues had similarly engaged in spying for the United States and Great Britain — Thomas Gann, Joe Spinden, John Held, Samuel Lothrop, Arthur Carpenter, and others. The United States had entered the First World War, and while Mexico had yet to choose its side, the great powers actively pursued competing interests there through acts of public and private diplomacy, espionage, sabotage, subversion, and direct military intervention.[3]

Morley's espionage in Mexico and Central America had several objectives. He conducted coastal reconnaissance to determine which sites Germany might use or was using to resupply submarines that preyed upon Allied shipping in the Caribbean and along the Atlantic Coast of the United States. He informed on foreign residents who he thought might be spying for the Germans or promoting pro-German sentiments among the local populace, and he seems to have recruited "active volunteer helpers," locals who would keep an eye on things and report suspicious developments all along the coasts he traveled. For his superiors in Naval Intelligence, he described transportation and communication facilities, political developments, and the disposition of the indigenous population on the Yucatan Peninsula, all information possibly relevant to American economic interests and military action.[4]

And Morley worked in his way to counter the effects of anti-American sentiments where he found them. He deployed good will and his reputation as a scholar and scientist, for example, to assure the Governor of Quintana Roo that President Woodrow Wilson would not yield to those influential Americans who openly advocated seizing the Mexican oil fields around Tampico and sisal-growing plantations in Yucatan, whose products were strategically important to the United States. Morley did such a good job of it, in fact, that the governor provided him with a letter of introduction to assist in his further travels through the territory.[5] But President Wilson may still have been considering military moves on the peninsula, and based upon his reconnaissances Morley could secretly report that

> the almost universal feeling is that Yucatan is being exploited, milked dry, ruined for the benefit of the rest of the republic which they hate. Indeed so strong is this feeling that I believe it is not going too far to say that in so far as the Yucatecans themselves are concerned American intervention and An American Protectorate for the peninsula would be preferred to their present intolerable situation.
>
> I have not reached this conclusion off hand but after much thought and conversation with all kinds of people: planters, mestizos, Indians and foreigners. In this connection I may mention that Mr. Arthur Pierce the British Consul here in Merida told me that he had been approached several times within the past two years by Yucatecans with the proposal that he go to Washington to urge upon the British Ambassador there that Great Britain take over Yucatan as a British Protectorate. And you will recall that the Santa Cruz Indians made a similar proposal to the Governor of British Honduras two years ago at Belize. . . . [6]
>
> Those of course are only trifling matters, but after all they are the straws that show which way the wind is blowing, and I believe that with any sort of encouragement from us the Yucatecans would

throw off the Mexican yoke, separate themselves from the rest of the republic and declare themselves an independent state.

If Mexico should force our hand by allying herself with Germany and declaring war on us I am confident that such a separation could be easily effected.

Morley went on to note that the situation in Mexico was like that which earlier had prompted U.S. covert action in Panama to effect its secession from Colombia. In Panama U.S. strategic interests were linked to the canal, while in Yucatan, "if the supply of sisal is cut off altogether our hand may be similarly forced. We have got to have binder-twine and any step necessary to enforce the permanence of the supply can only be regarded as a measure of self-preservation." Morley was addressing an important point here, for sisal from Yucatan was vital to the North American cordage industry and to the various clients served by that industry, foremost among them midwestern farmers. The Mexicans dramatically increased the price of sisal during the war, and wanted import concessions from the United States in return for not raising the price still higher. In response, some in the Wilson administration advocated military intervention, an option that Wilson himself was very reluctant to invoke.[7]

In a memo concerning "cloaks" for agents operating in Central America, the Aide for Information to the Commandant of the Fifteenth Naval District bemoaned the obvious inadequacy of some agents' cover: "There are three 'cloaks' which are worn threadbare, i.e., mining-man, cattle-man, and timber-man. The only possible way for any of these to really serve their purpose is for the Agent employing the 'cloak' to actually have one of the above professions—on top of which he should be connected with some house in the United States to color his story." To U.S. Naval Intelligence it was, therefore, invaluable to have someone like Morley, whose work superiors praised as "excellent" and "thorough," who actually *was* an archeologist and *was* affiliated with an American foundation, and who would have ample reason to travel throughout Central America. His was the perfect "cloak," regarding which Morley had occasion to note that "ever since taking up my work with you [in Naval Intelligence], I have maintained at the same time my connections with the Carnegie Institution and indeed I have had to carry on numerous archaeological investigations during this period in order to better facilitate the other work [i.e., espionage]."[8]

However enthusiastic Naval Intelligence was about the work Morley was doing, some of Morley's anthropological colleagues, including the preeminent figure in the field, Franz Boas, felt very different about such spying. For two decades already Boas, a German immigrant, had fostered the growth and institutionalization of an American professional anthropology that would, armed with the concept of culture and the methodology of fieldwork, dethrone racist evolutionary dogmas of his predecessors (and some contemporaries). He was, before all else, a critical scientist, once repelled by the conservatism, militarism, materialism, and anti-Semitism of his former homeland, and thereafter avowedly unwilling to sacrifice truth to any allegiance more parochial than that which he pledged to humanity as a whole.

Boas denounced the imperialism of America after the Spanish-American War — "a young giant, eager to grow at the expense of others, and dominated by the same desire of aggrandizement that sways the narrowly confined European states." He denounced an ever more virulent arrogance and intolerance of human diversity that was making of Americans the would-be "dispenser of happiness to mankind," each unreflectively confident that "his own Government is the best, not for himself only, but also for the rest of mankind [and] that his interpretation of ethics, of religion, of standards of living, is right." Boas openly opposed America's entry into the First World War and sympathized with Germany, with whom, it seemed to him, the right at that moment lay.[9] Finally, acting less as a German-American than as the scientist who had once written, "All that man can do for humanity is to further the *truth*, whether it be sweet or bitter," Boas exposed the wartime espionage of misguided patriots within his professional community.[10]

In an October 1919 letter to the editor of *The Nation*, without naming any of the individuals involved, he angrily protested

that a number of men who follow science as their profession, men whom I refuse to designate any longer as scientists, have prostituted science by using it as a cover for their activities as spies.

A soldier whose business is murder as a fine art, a diplomat whose calling is based on deception and secretiveness, a politician whose very life consists in compromises with his conscience, a business man whose aim is personal profit within the limits allowed by a lenient law — such may be excused if they set patriotic devotion above common everyday decency and perform services as spies. They merely accept the code of morality to which modern society still conforms. Not so the scientist. The very essence of his life is the service of truth. . . . A person, however, who uses science as a cover for political spying, who demeans himself to pose before a foreign government as an investigator and asks for assistance in his alleged researches in order to carry on, under this cloak, his political machinations, prostitutes science in an unpardonable way and forfeits the right to be classed as a scientist. . . . In consequence of their acts every nation will look with distrust upon the visiting foreign investigator who wants to do honest work, suspecting sinister designs. Such action has raised a new barrier against the development of international friendly cooperation.[11]

Other American anthropologists found more fault with Boas, his denunciation of colleagues, and his evident lack of patriotism than they did with the spying he exposed. Shortly after the letter to *The Nation* was published, the Council of the American Anthropological Association voted twenty to ten to censure him! Voting in the majority were Morley, four others who had served in U.S. military intelligence during the war, former school buddies and instructors of the archeologists-turned-spies, and, by and large, men who harbored long-standing personal and professional animosities against the very influential Boas, from whom they thus plotted to wrest power. So Boas was removed from the governing council of the association he had helped to found. Meanwhile, Morley continued on in the employ of the Carnegie Institution.[12]

Not until 1967, after revelations concerning plans for U.S. Army-sponsored social-science research on insurgency and counterinsurgency, did American anthropologists awaken from "their own failure and sloth in identifying the ethics of scholarship as something distinct from the ethics of nationalism," as one of them put it, to enjoin each other from the conduct of espionage under scholarly cover. "Constraint, deception, and secrecy have no place in science," the American Anthropological Association finally concluded, concerned that "actions which compromise the intellectual integrity and autonomy of research scholars and institutions not only weaken those international understandings essential to our discipline, but in so doing they also threaten any contribution anthropology might make to our own society and to the general interests of human welfare."[13] Boas had, of course, said much the same thing, only better, half a century before.

In the same year as Morley's wartime reconnaissance along the coast of the Yucatan Peninsula, the U.S.S. *Salem* landed men at Isla Mujeres and Cancun Island to investigate possible stockpiling of supplies for German submarines, and briefly listened under cover of darkness for enemy activity in Ascension Bay. In the late 1930s intelligence officers again scouted those waters for crafts of suspicious origin and purpose, while in 1939 Lieutenant Colonel D. J. Kendall of the U.S. Special Service Squadron gathered intelligence from knowledgeable foreign residents on the peninsula. As had Morley before him, he reported that local residents were likely to be friendly to American interests in the event of hostilities: "The most logical place for submarines or seaplanes to use is Mujeres Bay, between Mujeres Island and the mainland. . . . Even if planes landed at those lagoons south of Carrillo Puerto or in Laguna de Bacalar the Indians would carry the word outside in a few hours and it would go out on the radio unless the governor prevented it. The government of Quintana Roo is rather unfriendly to Americans, although the people are very friendly as they have worked with us so much in business."[14]

Whether or not Mayas who spoke with foreign explorers, archeologists, and anthropologists could sense the potential of the tumultuous years of the Mexican Revolution, the First World War, and the Great Depression, their hopes for an alliance with the North Americans against Mexico were not all so fantastic as time has made them seem. During the interwar years, however, Morley and his people were once again legitimate archeologists working under the exclusive auspices of the Carnegie Institution and concerned to maintain the appearance of propriety and foster good relations with the host government. While one goal of the Chichen Itza project was to make those ruins an "enduring monument to the genius of the ancient Maya," it was also hoped that the very manner in which the project was handled would "not fail to produce a feeling on the part of the Mexican government and the Mexican people that American agencies can be trusted within their borders."[15] It must have seemed to Morley that his worst fears were coming true, then, when his flirtations with conspiring Maya officers were publicly exposed by the denunciations of Lieutenant Zuluub and General May.

To help Villa's research in central Quintana Roo, Morley had fostered the illusion of a close personal relationship with him, graciously received Maya visitors to Chichen Itza, and encouraged Maya officers to return such friendly gestures by permitting Villa to study among them for a book that he, Morley, was preparing. But, as time passed and officers continued to press for "political assistance," Morley thought it best to discard the fabric of casual friendships, illusions, and lies with which— partly inadvertently, partly by design—he, Redfield, and Villa had cloaked their involvement with the Mayas. Since Morley and Villa disagreed on just how and when to do that, it took as long to jettison those increasingly awkward relationships as it had taken to create them in the first place.

In the spring of 1936 Villa pursued his field research with a sense of urgency, believing that the federal army would soon intervene in the region. He thought he could ease local tensions and avert armed conflict by helping resolve Maya grievances over the gathering and marketing of chicle. So Villa suggested to Morley that they get General Melgar, Governor of the Territory of Quintana Roo, to guarantee local Mayas full rights to gather chicle in their own forests, and that Morley ask the Mexican Exploitation Company (with an office in Santa Cruz) to station a chicle buyer right in Xcacal Guardia. Morley, on the other hand, seems to have preferred just pulling out altogether before he, Villa, and, by implication, the Carnegie Institution got more involved than they already were in these internal political affairs. Better, Morley thought, that the officers themselves go to the territorial capital at Payo Obispo and deal directly with General Melgar.[16]

Villa responded angrily to Morley's suggestion. The idea of the officers' going to Payo Obispo to talk to General Melgar "is simply impractical. To think that these Indians could voluntarily present themselves before the government, without prior efforts of approach on its part, is something which places the facts beyond reality." Second, Villa reminded Morley, "my involvement in this matter has not been for pleasure, as you can imagine, but obligated by the circumstances. To live among these Indians without demonstrating interest in their vital problems is a thing impossible to achieve." And, after all, it was Morley who had "offered them, spontaneously, to intercede on behalf of the whole group and also in favor of Zuluub, before General Melgar who, according to what you told them, was a friend of yours."

Villa assured Morley that helping the officers now would not produce the "catastrophes and crimes" that Morley imagined but, rather, would "increase the prestige of the Carnegie Institution" and leave the door open to future field research. In any event, Morley could expect more Maya visitors soon, and Villa asked him not to say anything that would force Villa to abandon the field during the next two months.[17] Meanwhile, Villa continued to encourage Maya officers to solicit application of federal agrarian-reform laws as the best way to secure their livelihood in the territory.

While Maya officers pursued alliance with Americans to the seemingly bitter end and hoped for war against the Mexicans, at the same time they gradually developed a separate set of conversations—a counterpoint to their bold and angry rhetoric of rebellion—concerning those agrarian laws. When the head priest Barrera told Morley there was "no one else with whom I can speak, only you," that simply was not true. In February 1935 General Melgar, then newly appointed governor, had toured central Quintana Roo in the company of General Rafael Cházaro Pérez (former Chief of Staff to President Cárdenas), other military officers, journalists, and the discredited Maya general Francisco May. They skirted Xcacal Guardia, where their presence was unwelcome, and arrived on February 18 in Santa Cruz (recently renamed Felipe Carrillo Puerto in memory of the assassinated socialist governor of Yucatan), where General Melgar interviewed Maya officers. Officers from Xcacal Guardia declined to attend, but those from other villages with similar grievances told Melgar about chicle contractors from Yucatan who worked their forest and who " 'bought' chicle, corn and pigs in exchange for worthless trinkets and, in some cases, [paid] for them with fake coins." Melgar offered to put an end to the abuses, principally by providing Maya communities with legal titles to the forest through action of the agrarian reform. And Melgar spoke of extending the railroad from the southernmost terminal at Peto, Yucatan, straight through to Santa Cruz. Journalists photographed the Maya officers in assembly before the general, the Mayas dressed in their white shirts and trousers, bare-headed and looking frankly humble under large posters of President Cárdenas.[18]

The Mayas from around Santa Cruz apparently found what Melgar said acceptable, and petitions for land grants followed quickly.[19] But they may not have fully understood Melgar's offer to extend the railroads. Elsewhere in Mexico agrarian reform was restoring to peasant communities lands grabbed from them by rapacious haciendas and plantations before the revolution. In central Quintana Roo, which had never had large landed estates to prey on independent agriculturalists, implementation of the reform was not a return to an earlier, more equitable distribution of land but rather, in combination with railroad development, part of a program to open sparsely settled forests to colonization by non-Mayas. General Cházaro thought expatriate Mexicans recently returned from the United States (driven out by the Great Depression, perhaps) would be particularly suitable colonists, since "the vicissitudes of a foreign land have formed in them a broader concept of the nation, and their observations and experiences of very difficult work to which they were subject on the other side of the Bravo [i.e., Rio Grande], has equipped them better for the daily struggle in this part of the country."[20]

The Maya officers in Xcacal Guardia would have nothing to do with the Mexican generals and their plans for pacification and colonization of the territory. They told Alfonso Villa:

We do not need anyone to grant lands to us since all these forests are ours. Besides . . . if it were necessary to distribute these lands, surely it would not be the Government that would be in charge of doing it. Rather, True God is the one who did it. We do not want to negotiate anything with the President of Mexico or with the Mexicans. Let them stay in their towns, leaving us in ours, and thus we will live in peace.[21]

And to Morley they wrote:

And another thing there is my letting you know, regarding the Mexicans who are there in Noh Cah Santa Cruz. They are really going to go about harming us, they said. I have learned that on the 20th of November they are saying they will come here to Guardia to measure my land and my forest. If they do not come on the 20th of November, [then they will do so] on the first day of January. Therefore there is no way they will not come, they say, whether for better or for worse, they say. That then I let you know. May you do me a favor—make good reckoning for me, Mr. Chiefs, because I am in my village, I am on my land here in Guardia, Mr. Don Chief. I am not happy. That I let you know, also, what these people are planning here over Our Lord True God.[22]

It was with "great happiness" that the Mayas of Xcacal Guardia later received news of the death of General Cházaro, whose plane crashed during a training flight near Mexico City. They counted that as the fourth time military aircraft attempting to fly into Santa Cruz (or so they believed) had crashed, and "as is to be expected," Villa noted, "all this is attributed to the power of the Most Holy One which is worshiped in the Sanctuary [of Xcacal Guardia]."[23]

While senior Maya officers vigorously rejected suggestions that they deal with the government, some of their subordinates did not. Young men of the village of San Jose had petitioned the federal government for a land grant in 1935, complaining to federal authorities that "the forests which surround the village are being exploited by contractors from the state of Yucatan . . . [and] we find ourselves obliged to work with them and to sell our products, sometimes at very low prices and always at *their* convenience." But the petitioners were men of little consequence, whose village of some forty-five inhabitants living in seven houses "presents a quite miserable picture. . . . In speaking of San Jose, a village where no chief lives, the natives will say, 'There nobody lives, only *gente* [common people].' "[24]

The federal government took no action on that petition, while officers of Xcacal Guardia gradually concluded that they should explore such a new dialogue with their enemies. The officers had come to understand—after speaking with Morley and Villa, feeling the pressure of annual invasions of their forest by chicle gatherers, and hearing of similar actions already taken by other villages in neighboring parts of the forest—that they might yet preserve their domain through the peaceful alternative of reconciliation and reform. Their inquiries about the government's economic and agrarian policies in Quintana Roo still produced tense conversations at times. "To explain the situation such as it is," Villa noted in his diary, "will give rise to suspicions unfavorable and even dangerous for our stay here [in Tuzik]. . . . It will be necessary to find a formula that permits me to explain the truth to them without being taken for a spy of the government."[25]

In May 1936 Villa summoned the officers of Xcacal Guardia and their subordinates to his residence in Tuzik, where he spoke to them for two hours. He explained that in political matters he and Morley could help only as intermediaries between them and the federal authorities. He described the Mayas' situation "with respect to the rest of the world, seeing to it that by themselves they would discover the reality which surrounds them," and he spoke of the advantages of having a government surveyor come to chart the boundaries of a future grant of forest that they alone would exploit.[26] More than thirty years later Villa still vividly recalled the officers' reaction:

> The impact of this startling news on the leaders of the tribe who had gathered in my hut was one of incredulity, and at first they showed disbelief. How was it possible that I, who had always been on their side, could now propose to them that they come to terms with their natural enemy, the Mexican government? Could it be that I was a spy of that government who had penetrated their ranks to "sell them" later? Some said, in an angry tone, that they were the ones who could grant lands to that government and not the reverse; others blamed me for my supposed false loyalty; and still others asked for more information. The whole time I remained calm, willing to give them all the explanations they requested. I emphasized that I had always been unarmed, even though they all boasted of their good shotguns and machetes.[27]

Having said what he wanted, Villa left the officers to discuss the matter alone, and when he returned, they announced that they had agreed to have their lands mapped; Villa said he would relay that decision to General Melgar. At the time only one man present, Paulino Yama of Señor, still openly insisted that they continue to pursue alliance with the Americans.

Only a week later, before Villa could write to General Melgar, some of the officers changed their minds. Lieutenant Zuluub and members of his company presented Villa with three new conditions upon which their cooperation would depend. Within the territory between Tihosuco, Tulum, Ascension Bay and Chichankanab Lagoon there was to be: (1) Maya self-governance; (2) performance of guard service at Xcacal Guardia by all residents of all villages; (3) a prohibition on the gathering of chicle and the exercise of any governmental functions by outsiders. Zuluub thus abandoned an earlier claim to the rest of Quintana Roo south to the border with British Honduras, but in other regards he upped the ante, seeming to demand the subservience of the shrine centers of Chun Pom, Chan Cah Veracruz, and Tulum to Xcacal Guardia, as well as the subordination to their rule of any new settlements in the territory.[28]

Villa tried to explain the impossibility of meeting those demands, but his visitors were unyielding and left dissatisfied. Two days later other officers and Cituk's secretary, Apolinario Itza, came to Villa in Tuzik to denounce Zuluub's intransigence and reaffirm their desire that a land surveyor come, immediately if possible. Another meeting of all officers of Xcacal Guardia again ratified that decision, and a commission was dispatched to Chichen Itza to solicit Morley's help in implementing it. The men returned dissatisfied, however, as in Chichen Itza they finally grasped that they would not receive one undivided grant for all the territory around Xcacal Guardia and its affiliated villages. The federal agrarian reform did not work that way. Rather, each settlement separately would have to petition for an individual grant, to be administered locally by representatives they chose in free elections. To proceed that way would shatter the unity of the villages around Xcacal Guardia and certainly undermine the company system and authority of its officers, who told Villa that in that case they would prefer not to have anything to do "with the Government or anyone else."[29]

General Melgar's response to Villa's letter on behalf of the officers was similarly discouraging. Villa had written to the general in Payo Obispo of his desire to provide "some data that might be useful in the task of incorporating the Indians of this territory into our civilization." He reminded Melgar that Morley had already explained to him Villa's residence in Tuzik and research in the region, and he noted that communities of the area refused to accept schools or deal with any outside authorities, living in constant fear of attack by the federal army stationed in Santa Cruz. Because of this, Villa suggested, Mayas of the region avoided making certain "material improvements" that they otherwise would—raising cattle, improving their homes, and so on. While that fear was a legacy of the years of terror when Mexican general Ignacio Bravo ruled the territory, it was annually renewed when outside chicle gatherers invaded the forest at the instigation of a malevolent government, local Mayas believed. The solution, Villa wrote, lay in applying the agrarian reform to the disputed forest. The Maya officers of Xcacal Guardia had already agreed to receive an official land surveyor, and Villa urged Melgar to send one quickly. Once the "natives" were convinced of the federal government's good intentions toward them, the "installation of schools, authorities, cooperatives and other institutions necessary for the achievement of their betterment" could proceed.[30]

In his response Melgar thanked Villa for his work among the Maya, acknowledged that his administration considered the lands in question to be "property of that Indian race," and instructed Villa to have a delegation of officers come to speak with him directly in Payo Obispo, perhaps even bearing in hand the requisite petition for an official land grant. "To think that these Indians could present themselves of their own free will before the Governor," Villa mused to his mentor Redfield, "is something positively naive. . . . I am not going to waste time trying to solve one of the most difficult problems which faces the government of this region." Yet, once enticed by Villa's proposed solutions to their problems, Maya officers would not let him drop the matter so easily. As word spread that outside chicle gatherers intended to establish a base camp and exploit the forest very close to the village of Señor, officers planned an assault against them; then, changing their minds once again, asked Villa to get them a land grant quickly.[31]

Villa's efforts were greatly complicated when a dispute over the right to bleed chicle from trees around Señor spawned sharp, open conflict between Lieutenant Zuluub's company in Xcacal Guardia and residents of Señor. Tensions between Zuluub and his colleagues in Xcacal Guardia had already been growing since he and a colonel engaged in a public exchange of insults earlier that spring, each accusing the other of having maliciously opened visible paths to the other's cornfield, hoping that federal soldiers would find and destroy them.

Captain Cituk, angered by the breach of official etiquette by colleagues "who are deviating from the norms of love and of harmony that must always reign among the children of God," convened a meeting of officers and soldiers in the shrine center church to discuss the accusations and the conduct of the two officers, and to consider appropriate punishments. A heated debate ensued, and Zuluub, for whom it seemed to be going badly, accused Captain Cituk of having set the colonel against him. The meeting grew so acrimonious that the head priest came out of the altar chamber—the "Gloria" or "Heaven" of the church—where he had been praying, and expelled the officers from the temple. Thereupon the meeting broke up inconclusively, and neither the colonel nor Lieutenant Zuluub was punished, though public opinion ran strongly against the lieutenant.[32]

When Zuluub and the people of Señor started arguing over chicle, officers ran to Villa asking him to intervene. Zuluub told Villa that he and his company would "punish" the men of Señor who continued to accost his people bleeding chicle in a patch of sapodilla near Señor. Other officers said they were inclined to expel Zuluub's company from Xcacal Guardia if he continued acting on his own "without taking into consideration the opinion of the others" and abusing the hospitality they had extended his people in their exile. Opinion was passionate and divided, as most people did not much like Zuluub but neither could they tolerate the claim of the Señor men to exclusive rights over any part of the holy forest.[33]

Villa recommended "prudence and harmony" and called all interested parties to a meeting in Tuzik. They came from every village in the region and brought their rifles with them. Villa opened the meeting in the main church by explaining that he had assembled them to resolve the dispute, and as they were gathered in the "House of God" they should all refrain from insults and fighting. His counsel had little effect, though, for when they got down to discussing disputed details, insults began flying back and forth—"Hypocrite!" "Coward!" "Liar!" "Lackey!" —with Zuluub and Cituk pitted against one another. Villa interrupted the verbal brawl to remind them that, if they could not resolve the matter, federal authorities in Santa Cruz might have to intervene. "This last [advice] was very effective," Villa noted in his diary, "since the memory of a common enemy made the group solidarity appear again." With calm restored it was finally decided that people of Señor did have greater claim to the patch of sapodilla in question, but the men of Xcacal Guardia, including Zuluub and his people, also had a right to tap the trees if they could not find adequate unworked stands elsewhere.

Though Zuluub and Cituk seemed to have reconciled, Villa feared that after the bitter exchanges of the last few days "friendship may never return to exist between them."[34]

Since receiving Melgar's response instructing the officers to present their requests before him in Payo Obispo, Villa had delayed passing on the message to them, fearing it would bring an abrupt end to his field research. But he could not stall them much longer, and with the disputes between Zuluub and others Villa's exasperation grew daily:

> All these intrigues make me lose, with great sadness, no few hours of my time. For example, the writing of this letter has taken five hours, since I have had to interrupt it twice to attend to diverse commissions, among them one from Xcacal headed by Zuluub himself who does not want to permit under any circumstances the presence of outside chicle gatherers in those forests.[35]

He prepared to vacate Tuzik in two weeks and called a meeting of officers for three days thence. On that day Zuluub showed up early to let Villa know that because of his bad relations with fellow officers he would not attend, though that did not mean he was unwilling to join in any agreement they might reach. When the other officers and their escorts arrived, Villa finally explained the gist of Melgar's recent letter — that they would have to go and speak with Melgar personally in Payo Obispo. They reminded Villa of past Mexican efforts to exterminate them and suggested this was just another trap, but Captain Cituk's voice again carried the day, saying

> Ok, Don Alfonso, since we do not want to fight with anyone, but on the contrary, only want to have lands on which to work and guarantees of life, we will do what you tell us. But if, in spite of our good intentions, the *Mexicans* try to enslave us as in other times, then we will emigrate to another place where we can live in peace; perhaps Belize or also Guatemala.

With that a delegation was selected to journey south for an audience with General Melgar. Villa announced that he would soon be leaving Tuzik, earlier than he had planned, as his wife was ailing from a painfully swollen breast. The Mayas were not pleased and asked that Villa spend at least another month among them. Though it pained him to leave, Villa told them, it simply was not possible. So they said their goodbyes then and there, one by one: "May God be with you always, and may you manage to return soon."[36]

Three short days later the Maya delegation to Melgar was back, having aborted the mission because, they said, torrential rains had made the trails impassable. Perhaps before he left, Captain Cituk asked, Villa could help them draft a letter to Melgar explaining what they wanted from him. While Villa was in the midst of drafting the letter, his wife's pains worsened, and she showed signs of growing gravely ill. She clearly needed medical attention, and Villa decided they must leave that very day.

It took several hours of pleading to persuade the corporal in Tuzik and a number of other men to help bear Mrs. Villa out to Chichen Itza. The offer of two-pesos-a-day pay and the prospect of an audience with General Melgar in Merida (where he maintained a second residence and office) did the trick, and the party left Tuzik at 8 p.m. under continuing downpours. By midnight they had advanced only half a mile, and had to spend the rest of the night camped under the trees along the trail. At daybreak they continued, walking ten more miles to reach the muleteers' camp at San Jose where they could pass the night. The next day—with Villa urging the bearers to move more quickly—they made fourteen more miles and found some shelter from the rain in the ruins of the church of a long-abandoned town. Villa's wife seemed to worsen markedly, with vomiting and fever, and he had nothing with which to treat her but aspirin and antiseptic cream. The next day, however, they reached Tihosuco, where Villa relieved the exhausted litter bearers and the party hurried on. After two more days' travel, they arrived in Chichen Itza. In Merida, Villa's wife recovered rapidly. Three men from Xcacal Guardia had followed Villa all the way there to see if they could have that meeting with Melgar, but the general was not in town, and after waiting several days for him to appear, the would-be petitioners left again for the south. Thus ended Villa's sojourn among the Maya of central Quintana Roo.[37]

IN EARLY AUGUST the scribe Apolinario Itza and two other men sought out Villa in Merida to inform him of recent developments back home, especially of a sudden worsening in their relations with Lieutenant Zuluub. In a letter to Morley the officers wrote that Zuluub's "thoughts had gone bad" toward both them and Morley; that Zuluub was saying Morley was lying to them; and that Zuluub had separated himself from them and from Morley. (In yet one last failure of translation, the English version of that letter mentioned only Zuluub's anger toward his former comrades, not his comments on Morley.[38]) Someone in Señor had apparently stolen several bags of chicle resin from trees that Zuluub had tapped, and since Captain Cituk had not punished the thieves, Zuluub sent a delegation headed by his son to Santa Cruz to seek redress from authorities there. To get the federal authorities to act against Cituk, the delegation denounced him as a subversive who conspired with Americans against Mexico. Then, when federal authorities summoned the other officers of Xcacal Guardia to an inquiry in Santa Cruz, they dispatched Apolinario Itza to seek Villa's and Morley's intervention. Meanwhile, they removed the Most Holy One from the shrine center to a hiding place in the forest, fearing that Zuluub might steal it, even as he and Cituk had once stolen it from the discredited General May's church in Santa Cruz.[39]

Villa found Itza's presence in Merida very fortunate, for as a scribe and shaman he was the "depository of the sacred knowledge of the group" and could add greatly to what esoteric lore Villa had been able to record while in Tuzik. He sent Itza to speak with General Melgar's representative and, since Itza could stay in Merida only two days, arranged to have him return again in a month, all expenses paid.[40] When a Maya delegation returned to Merida on August 19, General Melgar was notified by telegram, and that Saturday the long-frustrated attempt to bring them together finally succeeded. At his private residence the first thing Melgar asked the assembled officers was whether they were "true Cardenistas" — supporters, that is, of the popular president of Mexico responsible for widespread application of the agrarian reform and the expropriation of American-owned oil companies in Mexico. The Maya officers knew little about national-level Mexican politics and international relations, but "fortunately," Villa noted, "our friends did not clam up and they responded with a categorical affirmation." The officers found General Melgar sympathetic to their plight and petition, though at the conclusion of that first meeting Villa was not confident, for "neither did General Melgar come to grasp the true desires and aspirations of the Indians, nor did they, the proposals and intentions of him. In summary, the interview, although cordial and full of promises, did not have the result of mutual understanding that I had desired."[41]

The next day General Melgar and his Maya visitors went to Chichen Itza to continue their talks in the presence of Sylvanus Morley. Villa noted, "I think our friends must have left very pleased, since General Melgar offered to give them not only *ejidos* [land grants] but also farm tools, musical instruments, and means for the exploitation of their chicle."[42] How fitting it was that the Mayas chose Chichen Itza as the place to draft a formal petition to the Mexican government and affix their signatures to it:

> All of us, residents and natives of Chunculche, Tuzik, Xcacal, Señor, Xmaben, Yaxkax, San Jose, Chacchan, and Chanchen Laz [villages of the Xcacal group], we form a community, that since the time of our ancestors has been living on lands within the jurisdiction of the Territory. And though the Governments of the Republic have not bothered us in the least, those same lands are legally considered as property of the Nation, because of our lack of titles, though [our] ownership has practically been acquired. . . .
>
> The authorities who rule the community formed by said villages include a chief and a commander as the principal ones, who have been designated such by the will of the residents, since the authorities of the Government who are responsible for caring for and maintaining the order and lives of the same are located very far from said villages. But the present situation will serve to demonstrate that we have always recognized the Government of the Territory.[43]

Disingenuousness gave way to outright dissimulation in this new discourse with other powerful men, and all in Spanish at that. (The petition seems to have been drafted by Morley's translator, Pedro Castillo, who also signed it.) The petition went on to name the principal places that encompassed the territory which the Mayas considered rightfully theirs and to which they now wished to establish legal, not just customary, claim. It included a vast expanse of central Quintana Roo. The first to sign that letter was Francisco Chaac of Chunkulche, the sergeant of Xcacal Guardia, who was among the officers who had opened the Maya-Morley dialogues only a few years earlier, and who spoke the part of the king of the Maya at Chichen Itza. A definitive step had now been taken in a new round of dialogues and negotiations.

Officers returned for further talks with General Melgar in late September. Captain Cituk headed the delegation of fourteen, who concluded their meeting with Melgar apparently pleased by further promises made. Meanwhile, during their three days in the capital city of Yucatan they were escorted about town by an assistant to the general. "By their clothing, mannerisms, etc.," Villa observed, the Maya visitors from central Quintana Roo "came powerfully to the attention of the public." Cituk went on radio to speak for fifteen minutes, telling, among other things, of his friendship with Alfonso Villa and the reasons for their presence in Merida.[44]

Men from Xcacal Guardia returned again in early December with word of continuing bad relations with Lieutenant Zuluub, who, they said, was still trying to impose his will upon all the companies of Xcacal Guardia. Zuluub had joined up with General Francisco May, who had taken up residence next to him in Xcacal Guardia. And apparently a well-known itinerant merchant of the region was in league with them, as well, spreading rumors and raising tensions in the villages he passed through. This most recent Maya delegation asked of General Melgar's representative in Merida that Zuluub be given his own village so that he would leave them alone in Xcacal Guardia. Still another Maya delegation arrived at Villa's Merida residence in late January 1937. A land surveyor had finally gone out to Xcacal Guardia, but officers there rejected his draft plan for a proposed land grant, since the area seemed too small—only 260 square miles, instead of the well over 1,000 they had requested. In any event, it did not even include the shrine center itself! General Melgar was too busy this time, however, to speak with the delegation, and after having waited a week to see him they returned to Quintana Roo.[45]

Tensions among Maya officers continued to worsen in the spring, culminating in Zuluub and May's public denunciations of Villa and Morley at the Indian Congress in central Quintana Roo. Villa quickly sought out General Melgar and got him to reaffirm his support for Villa's research activities. Melgar even invited Villa to accompany him on an upcoming tour during which he would visit Xcacal Guardia and present petitioners there with their long-awaited land grant or *ejido*. Villa seems to have been reluctant to take the time for such a trip, but decided he should go so that Melgar would truly understand the "nature of our labor as well as the rectitude and honesty that have always been the norm of our actions." Meanwhile Morley was very upset with the news of Zuluub's back-stabbing lies and their possible consequences for the Carnegie Institution's operations in Mexico. A presidential envoy had already passed through Chichen Itza on his way to Xcacal Guardia to study the situation and make recommendations to President Cárdenas— Morley provided him with a letter of introduction to Captain Cituk.[46]

In May 1937 General Melgar journeyed north from Santa Cruz accompanied by his Chief of Staff and a suitable armed escort, heading for Captain Cituk's village, where he intended to deliver documents officially establishing the "*Ejido* of Xmaben." Unfortunately, Cituk was unaware of Melgar's approach and purpose, and the arrival of Mexican soldiers in Xmaben acutely alarmed the Mayas there. Alfonso Villa and a Yucatecan linguist, Alfredo Barrera Vásquez, were then in Tuzik, where they had stopped on their way to join what were supposed to be happy ceremonies in Xmaben. At ten that night they received an urgent message from Melgar to come immediately to Xmaben. Villa arrived there at dawn to find Melgar and his escort holed up in a small chapel and surrounded by "a great number of Indians armed with their 30×30 carbines, ready for anything." He quickly explained to Cituk the purpose of Melgar's coming, and immediately, Villa recalls, Maya hostility changed to hospitality and the Mexicans were served breakfast.[47]

Maya officers asked that the ceremonial establishment of the *ejido* take place in front of the main church in Xcacal Guardia. So Melgar, his escort, Villa, Alfredo Barrera, and the Maya officers and their subordinates walked the short distance to Xcacal Guardia, where after a brief ceremony legal documents establishing the *ejido* were transferred to Cituk and his colleagues. On a table outside the church the official map of the *ejido* was spread out for the officers to view. They inspected it with "extreme caution," Villa recalls, and they were angered by what they saw. Cituk and others had agreed to petition for lands on the condition that, contrary to common practice elsewhere in Mexico, a single enormous grant would be made encompassing all the settlements of the Xcacal Guardia group. The officers had already chosen from among their ranks two slates of agrarian representatives, and the government surveyor presumably had explained to them just what the grant was to include. But now, as they scrutinized the map, they found that Xcacal Guardia did not appear on it. The shrine center had been cut out of the picture altogether yet a second time! The official report of the incident noted in bland bureaucratese that "Citizen J. Concepción Quituk [i.e., Cituk], President of the Ejido Commissariat and representing all the residents recipient, indicated non-conformity with the grant." But Villa recalled that the omission "alarmed the Indians greatly," and "initiated a violent discussion." They presumed the omission was intentional. When the governor immediately ordered that the grant of 260 square miles of forest be corrected to include the shrine center, that seemed to calm the Maya officers, but Melgar himself was by now so "fed-up" that he departed without partaking of a banquet the officers had prepared. Besides, Villa noted, Melgar and his escort "did not feel entirely safe" there.[48]

Despite General Melgar's last-minute modifications, officers remained deeply dissatisfied with the results of their cooperation with the government. In late June a delegation of twenty-eight officers and their subordinates came seeking Villa's and Morley's help once again. They spoke with Villa first in Chan Kom, Yucatan, the officers now insisting that the grant must be increased to include a total of 364 square miles of forest; that chicle be bought from them for no less than seventy pesos per hundredweight; that a sacred cross currently sheltered in the shrine center of Chun Pom be returned to the village of Balche from which it had been removed; and that, since they could not "sympathize" with the Mexicans at all, Morley should give them nine American flags to be raised in each of the nine villages of the Xcacal Guardia group. The flags would serve to signal their definitive separation from Mexico.

Villa felt it was finally time to "speak to them forcefully, not only for their own good, but also for ours," but he thought it would be more effective to talk to them with Morley in Chichen Itza. So the next day Villa and the delegation went over to Chichen Itza, where during a four-hour conference he and Morley reiterated that they could not meddle in political matters and said if the officers and their subordinates wanted to continue visiting them they must do so as simple friends, "soliciting no assistance of any kind." "Notwithstanding the severity of our admonition," Villa later observed, "the Indians knew to hide their displeasure, remaining on friendly terms in Chichen Itza all the following day." After this last encounter Villa wrote to his mentor, Robert Redfield: "I consider our efforts as intermediaries between the Government and the Indians to have terminated definitively."[49]

Several months later an article appeared in a local newspaper with the headline "Demarcations of Ejidos in the Maya Zones." Beside two photos of Captain Cituk standing with his former superior, General May, and the federal Attorney for Indian Affairs in the Territory, the article reported:

General May delivered to the President [Cárdenas] a letter, written in Maya, from Captain José Concepción Cituk, in which he expresses his gratitude to the federal government for the guarantees that he and his tribe have been enjoying in recent months.

Captain Cituk was until recently withdrawn from the activities of [Mexican] authorities and it was rumored about him that he was in connivance with a foreign government because of his frequent trips to Chichen Itza.

Cituk, called before the Attorney for Indian Affairs in the Territory, . . . declared that the object of his visits to Chichen Itza was due to the fact that he was denied justice in Carrillo Puerto [Santa Cruz].

In the meeting which took place on the sixth of August and which was attended by all the other Maya chiefs, Cituk arrived at an agreement with the other chiefs, ending their old grudges.[50]

ALMOST TWO YEARS after the suspension of their contacts with Morley and Villa, Maya officers once again tried to renew their search for weapons and allies. A delegation of five Mayas from Xcacal Guardia headed by Captain Cituk's oldest son came seeking Morley at Chichen Itza in March 1939. Cituk's son brought letters from his father for Morley and Villa, in which he denounced the lies of General Melgar and the evil intentions of government employees, and referred to continuing difficulties in getting chicle to market. The officers told Morley and Villa they wanted to sell chicle directly to them. The letter apparently referred to other "desires" as well, but in his translation Villa seems not to have specified just what they were. In any event, Villa—then already engaged in research elsewhere in Mexico and Guatemala—lamented, "I will not be able to do anything to help those Indians who were so good with me."[51]

By the time Maya officers renewed their efforts to speak again with Morley, Morley's days at Chichen Itza were coming to a close. With the outbreak of the Second World War, Morley's staff departed one by one—for North Africa, Burma, India, France, and elsewhere—to fight on behalf of the allied powers, while the Carnegie Institution began to scale down its support of ethnological, historical, and archeological research. The chairman of the Historical Division of that foundation, Alfred Kidder, acknowledged in the foundation's annual yearbook that "in these cataclysmic days" the trustees might doubt the value of the "study of an Indian people whose glory had faded some centuries before Columbus landed and who today are but humble soil-tillers ruled by the descendants of their European conquerors." "Nevertheless," he continued, in defense of such research, "if civilization is to persist, it seems essential that the study of man should go forward and should be broadened and deepened and rendered more precise." We who to solve our problems have made "repeated resorts to the brutalizing and cruelly wasteful expedients of war," Kidder argued, might learn something from the experience of the Mayas—"the dominance of absolute rulers, political rivalries and civil wars, the decline and eventual fall of a virile civilization, submission to foreign military conquest." Topics of the day, they must have seemed to him. But in the end even he had to acknowledge that "one does not, of course, pursue researches upon the nature of combustion while the house is burning over one's head."[52] In 1940 Morley vacated Chichen Itza.

IN 1940 Lawrence Dame, who was art editor for the Boston *Herald,* visited central Quintano Roo in the company of a North American Presbyterian missionary named David Letger. Letger and his wife had several years before established themselves in the village of Xocempich, Yucatan, from which they undertook to evangelize the Mayas of Yucatan and Quintana Roo (a task they were still engaged in, quite successfully, several decades later). Dame, Letger, and another companion found their way to Tuzik—"a primitive haunt of the most aboriginal of the Maya bush tribes"—and after a couple of days there were escorted, as Villa had been in his day, to the shrine center of Xcacal Guardia. "You may wonder why we allowed you to come here," said the "chief" of Xcacal Guardia, who from Dame's description—pockmarked face, about sixty years of age, holding the rank of captain—we can be sure was Concepción Cituk:

> Well, we have been informed, never mind how, that you, Señor [the missionary], live in Xocempich, and we know that is near Doctor Morley's headquarters. For a long while we have needed a more powerful leader. We have already sent a delegation to Señor Morley, asking him to become our white chief. It was only a short time ago that we learned our old friend, Queen Victoria, who let arms slip over the border when our grandfathers were alive, had died. We believe, and the Cross has told us this, that only the American doctor can guide us in our independence. Now, we want you to take a message to him. Tell him we are friendly, that we await his coming again. Tell him that we want nothing of Mexico, but want to become part of his country, under American protection. We want him as chief.

The language attributed to Cituk, or whomever, smacks of journalistic concoction, but that there would be a message like that for Morley is plausible. In any event, according to Dame, he delivered the message to Morley, who asked him not to write about what the Maya officer had said.[53]

Alfonso Villa and Robert Redfield also "buried the story," in a way, as they wrote two books from the data Villa had gathered in the villages around Xcacal Guardia—Villa's own *The Maya of East Central Quintana Roo*

(1945) and Redfield's *The Folk Culture of Yucatan* (1941). In his book Villa mentioned that those Mayas sought friendly relations with Americans, who they believed possessed "extraordinary and magical powers"; that, promising to help them in all matters "non-political," Morley had won their respect and sympathy, greatly facilitating Villa's research among them; and that Captain Cituk believed that hieroglyphics engraved in the ruins of Tulum foretold an alliance of Americans and Mayas in common war against Mexico. Villa also wrote that "during the course of these investigations a principal objective of the people was the formation of an alliance with the Americans."

Yet Villa omitted so much—the officers' persistent courting and efforts to conspire with Sylvanus Morley; the tensions, doubts, and fears both on his side and theirs; the very substance of Villa's everyday interactions with Maya officers. The officers' repeated requests for arms from America appears in Villa's book only once, and there seemingly as something but "one man said."[54] In Redfield's book—incorporating data not only from Quintana Roo but also from research conducted in a village, a town, and a city in Yucatan—there is mention that the Maya of Quintana Roo had been friendly toward the British and, later, the Americans; that at one time it was "not uncommon" for them to go to British Honduras; and that "in 1935 the natives sought the aid of the Americans at Chichen [and] in 1936 negotiations were opened between the people of the X-Cacal subtribe and the Mexican government for a grant of ejidos and acceptance of the federal government; an agreement on these points was later reached."[55]

Villa had once thought to include in his book an appendix consisting entirely of the many letters that Maya officers had sent to him and Morley over the years. That appendix, to be entitled "The Native and His Problems, Expressed by Himself," would reveal "the vision that the Indians have of the things and problems that surround them." It never, however, got written.[56] Perhaps the story was politically too sensitive for any fuller telling, raising as it might the specter of subversion at a time when foreign researchers looked forward to much fieldwork still to be done, presumably with Mexican government permission and the collaboration of Mexican scholars, both on the Yucatan Peninsula and among Indians elsewhere in Mexico. I doubt that was the reason, however. Rather, Villa and Redfield had other stories to tell about the Mayas of central Quintana Roo. As each author related his understanding of the facts about Maya lives in the present, he also cast Mayas as protagonists in history, history the two authors portrayed in quite different ways, and in both of which the Mayas' search for arms from America could be, at most, a minor and discordant note.[57]

Villa saw in the recent history of Quintana Roo evidence of the triumph of justice and reason over exploitation and violence. His Mayas are protagonists in a romantic history, people in difficult transit through centuries of victimization at the hands of their conquerors, colonial overlords, and pre-revolutionary Mexican officials, on to the era of social justice and progress heralded by the Mexican Revolution and furthered in Quintana Roo by the efforts of beneficent military governors, dedicated rural schoolteachers, Sylvanus Morley, and Villa himself. To achieve such a historical, moral, and political coloring of the bare ethnographic facts he subsequently reported, in Part One of his book Villa emphasized the marginal character of the territory of Quintana Roo during both the prehistory of Maya civilization and the Spanish colonial period. With the War of the Castes, "sequel to three centuries of native rancor against the conquerors," the isolation of Mayas in the territory became even more pronounced. But, with the Mexican conquest of Santa Cruz in 1901, it began to slowly erode, as these latter-day conquerors turned the territory into a penal colony and systematically persecuted the Indians. Finally, however, the success of the Mexican Revolution replaced force with persuasion in the Mexican way of dealing with the Mayas, the trade in chicle brought wealth to them, and schools were established. Those successes were consolidated, according to Villa, only during the years of his presence in central Quintana Roo.[58]

Those years are the "ethnographic present" of Villa's account, the "now" and "today" of his description of Maya lives. But the short historical narrative with which he prefaced his report also related events several years still further down the road (making use of the usual time lag between an anthropologist's field research and the appearance of his major publication) to establish more definitively the arrival of reason and progress in the territory. By 1940 problems of land and persecution had been amicably resolved, Villa thought he could report, and in a second present moment "the natives of the central region now feel themselves less isolated and less 'different' from those of other sections."[59]

Part Two, the longer part, of Villa's book proceeded with the ethnographic description of these Maya people — the number, size, and location of their villages; how they built and furnished their houses; the techniques and economics of farming, chicle gathering, hunting, apiculture; matters of property, inheritance, and money; how they divided tasks and social positions among themselves and scheduled the round of an average year's activities; how they were organized into households and families, got married, addressed and behaved toward their kin; how they governed themselves; and, at greatest length, who and how they worshiped. The subject of such description was somewhat elusive, being neither Caste War Mayas, "characterized by seclusiveness, by a hostility toward civilization, and especially by their dislike of the Mexican Government," nor those less-isolated Mayas of circa 1940. But at least the subject had been corraled, fenced in by the termini—between very closed and very open—of a changing Maya orientation toward the world, within which the anthropologist could describe the subject's seemingly fixed and common characteristics. To raise still-unresolved issues so central to who these people were, how they viewed the world, and what the future had in store for them—all the issues about guns, conspiracies, hoped-for alliances, and prophecies—would have been a very difficult and novel gesture in the scientific genre in which Villa wrote.

While Villa plotted his mini-history in somewhat romantic mode, Redfield chose to write in a decidedly more tragic tone. Throughout his very distinguished anthropological career Robert Redfield returned again and again to a single dominant, evidently quite personal, concern—the contrast between primitive or folk societies on the one hand, and modern, urban societies on the other. He made it a lifelong anthropological mission to depict repeatedly in high relief the contrast between the life circumstances of people like himself and the life ways of man before cities, industry, and capitalism had forever altered them. The earlier, folk society that Redfield envisioned was a "small society [with] . . . no more people in it than can come to know each other well and . . . remain in long association with each other." Its members had little communication with outsiders (even though there might be knowledge of and contact with them) and correspondingly intimate communication among themselves. The insiders were illiterate, so their knowledge of the past was greatly limited—"there can be no historical sense, such as civilized people have"—and oral communication bore the burden of transmitting tradition to each new generation.

"The people who make up a folk society are much alike," in Redfield's imagination. They were physically homogeneous, and there was little specialization or division of labor, so that "what one person does is what another does," and "what one man knows and believes is the same as what all men know and believe." From their isolation and homogeneity, it followed that members of such a society would have a strong sense of group solidarity—"they say of themselves 'we' as against all others, who are 'they' "—a sense of the group perhaps reinforced by their economic independence, the fact that they produce what they need and consume only what they produce. Roughly speaking, wrote Redfield, "the folk society is a little world off by itself, a world in which the recurrent problems of life are met by all its members in much the same ways." Ways, he was careful to emphasize, fashioned not through conscious innovation and experimentation, but rather established by tradition. Those conventionalized life ways made up an internally coherent, well-knit fabric of beliefs and practices without troubling gaps, pattern changes, or inconsistencies, and not subject to objective examination or criticism. Where people had grown up living in intimate association with one another and were accustomed to treating one another as persons, rather than as objects or instruments, the social order, social relationships and actions were grounded in intuitive, tacit, and natural principles, rather than in contracts, formal agreements, legislation, litigation, and force. Family and kin were central, and the boundaries of both extended outward to embrace an entire society. Furthermore, folk society was sacred society — traditional ways of doing things were charged with the moral imperative of divine commandments. All told, the folk society of Redfield's imagination was a quaint and homy place to live in.[60]

In Redfield's conception of human history, the path from primitive or folk to urban society entailed the loss or inversion of those properties of social life, belief, and action through processes he pejoratively labeled "disorganization," "individualization," and "secularization." Redfield conceived of the Yucatan Peninsula as a human arena where social history well reflected that universal, human experience of the loss of primitive innocence and harmonies on the inexorable road to modernity. The villages of Xcacal Guardia represented for Redfield the starting point of a gradient of contemporaneous social types — from tribe through peasant village and small town to city — reflecting the historical stages of Maya people's becoming "modern" and "civilized."

Anthropologists have much criticized Redfield's work on the Yucatan Peninsula for a variety of good reasons, and that work is largely ignored today. He was, however, a recognized pioneer in the study of small communities within complex societies and was among the first seriously to include within the anthropological ken not only the small community or discrete tribe, but the larger, far-flung network of human interconnections of which they were a part.

Yet, in his treatment of the data gathered by Villa in the villages around Xcacal Guardia, Redfield was so concerned with how Mayas were becoming, as he once put it, "part of modern world civilization," that he failed to grasp that they already were, and had long been, a part of the modern world. They were not the small, homogeneous, meaning-filled, untroubled, family-oriented, self-sufficient social isolates of a more pleasant human past that Redfield imagined and wrote about while the world agonized through the Great Depression and stumbled from one world war toward another. The Mayas of Redfield's day, those living around Xcacal Guardia included, were, rather, the disinherited offspring of colonial empires and part-time laborers in the capitalist world economy, as well as citizens of a "community" of nations repeatedly at war within itself. Drawing upon Villa's work as he did, most of Redfield's facts about the Maya of central Quintana Roo were accurate. But his selection, assemblage, and interpretations of them to constitute a portrait of folk society required prodigious feats of imagination and denial, particularly concerning the Mayas' relations with foreigners like himself.

Of the several communities considered in his comparative study, the village of Tuzik was taken to be the most distant from the portal of modern influences represented by the city of Merida. Isolation, Redfield was careful to explain, meant not only lack of contact due to geographi-cal distance from people of another kind living quite different lives. Even when contact might occur, isolation was manifest in the lack of significant communication due to barriers of illiteracy, culture, and habitual patterns of interaction and avoidance. For Tuzik to serve its purpose in Redfield's scholarly lament about the erosion of isolation and the process of becoming "modern," one had to ignore the Mayas' long contact with other portals of outside influence. Only twice in his major work on Yucatan did Redfield mention Belize (once only to cite its annual rainfall). He made little of Mayas' communication with local representatives of the outside world — Villa and Morley among them; that they sought closer relations with foreign powers; that they did, in fact, attempt to negotiate their way into an advantageous posi-tion within a field of competing powers they knew they could not long ignore.

It was the Mayas of another small community in Yucatan, Chan Kom, whom Redfield came to know most directly, actually living among them for a number of weeks. He returned to study that commu-nity again in the mid-1940s, and the book that resulted from his subsequent research — *Chan Kom: A Village That Chose Progress* — is insightful and still worth reading. One gets the impression he liked the Chan Kom Mayas better than those of Quintana Roo, for they were friendly and gripped by enthusiasm for the progress they could achieve through their own hard work together with technical assistance from their government and from foreigners like the Americans at Chichen Itza. Some of them later came to regret this enthusiasm, when the future turned out to be other than they had imagined. But such regrets made them all the more dear to Redfield, who could empathize with their ambivalence:

> [They] have no choice but to go forward with technology, with a declining religious faith and moral conviction, into a dangerous world. They are a people who must and will come to identify their interests with those of people far away, outside the traditional circle of their loyalties and political responsibilities. As such, they should have the sympathy of readers of these pages.[61]

As for the Mayas of central Quintana Roo, it was much more difficult to ask sympathy for them, too. They had already long known the world to be a dangerous place and their interests to be linked "with those of people far away." From the Americans and Europeans they sought not sympathy but guns.

VIII

RUMORS
OF WAR

THE LAST SEVERAL decades have been tranquil ones in central Quintana Roo, as solutions applied to the acute problems of the 1930s succeeded in greatly reducing tensions and fears. One by one settlements around Xcacal Guardia received grants of forest lands arguably adequate for the number of able-bodied workers in each (and, when it was not, they asked for and got more).[1] Government-run cooperatives brought order to the gathering and marketing of chicle in the region; since only they could buy chicle and only their members could sell, the annual invasion of the Mayas' forest by outsiders ceased. Primary schools were established in most of the Maya villages, usually without incident, though for several months federal troops were stationed in Tuzik to help its residents reconcile themselves to cooperating with the new teachers in their midst. Some communities got small health clinics as well.

Felipe Carrillo Puerto, still referred to by Mayas as Santa Cruz, became the seat of a large county encompassing all the villages around Xcacal Guardia (as well as the other former rebel communities to the east and south). The former ghost town has had to expand its limits many times to accommodate so many new residents, and daily it bustles with Mayas from the outlying villages who travel there to buy and sell in the marketplace and stores, petition the government, get drunk or bail someone out of jail, visit friends or find a mate, take a child to boarding school, see the Catholic priest, or catch a bus to some other city.

Other things have changed, as well. Many new settlements have appeared, founded by groups of kinsmen who hived off from the older rebel communities or by Maya-speaking colonists from Yucatan. By now there is no forest thereabouts to which one village or another does not lay claim. Some villages of Villa's day have disappeared, including Sergeant Chaac's Chunkulche and Captain Cituk's Xmaben, the latter abandoned when its well failed in the 1940s. Others have endured and grown quite large: Tuzik has more than quadrupled, and Señor has grown even more. Most villages have donned a new appearance, abandoning the wild layout of forest hamlets in favor of an urban look—surveyed grids of streets, house lots, and a central plaza surrounded by houses of stone and mortar, rather than wattle and daub.

Each settlement now elects officials to rule in matters civil and agrarian—a village delegate of the county president and a commissar of the agrarian community constituted by federal law—and though early on these posts were typically occupied by Maya officers, by now the latter have ceded to others all claim to the exercise of such authority. There are still officers, companies, and Maya priests as in Villa's day; guard service is performed, people get baptized and married in the shrine village, masses are said by Maya priests, and festivals are staged in Xcacal Guardia. But today's officers exert only moral influence, at best, over subordinates, who increasingly decline to devote time and effort to such unproductive rituals away from home.

Making a living now takes most of everyone's time. They farm, gather chicle (though not nearly so much), and hunt as they did decades ago. But to that basic round of productive activities have been added new forms of apiculture, irrigated gardening, lumbering, and wage laboring—in the village, in the county seat, on roads throughout the region, or at tourist resorts that have sprung up along the coast. Cancun is the best-known of those. Everyone is hustling these days to make ends meet, while sending their children to primary and maybe secondary schools, perhaps even a few to college, hoping they can make better lives than their parents have had. (It is almost impossible to find anyone today who will admit to having ever opposed the founding of schools in their villages.)

When I arrived in Quintana Roo in 1978 to study the changes in Maya lives that several decades of peace had surely wrought, I found Maya officers and common people alike declaring the present the time of freedom whose coming was foretold by the prophet Florentino Cituk. The past, they said, was a time of slavery. They refer not only to the time of servile laboring on the estates of Yucatan from which distant predecessors freed themselves through rebellion and flight, but also to that time when Maya officers imposed a stern law upon their own people, meting out corporal punishment or death (as Zuluub was said to have done) to lawbreakers, insubordinates, witches and political rivals; when teachers were not allowed into the villages because the officers would not permit it; and when fear and force, rather than free will and piety (so they now say) ensured universal service under Maya military-religious authorities. I found the "time of slavery" in present usage had come to include those very same years when Maya officers sought aid from Sylvanus Morley and his kind so as to continue governing their people in the manner to which they were accustomed.

Though freedom is now said to prevail, there is still talk of war, especially the War of the Castes, in dramatic and detailed stories of the trauma of flight, hunger, disease, battle, the great cruelty of the enemy, and the cruelty of their own kind as well. Mayas can speak at length of the ingenuity of the first rebels and fugitives, who did not know how to make war but who, once forced to do so and at great cost to themselves, learned how. And they speak of divine intervention, of battlefield miracles worked by True God on their behalf. Women told these stories to their children, grandchildren, and godchildren, some of whom grew up to become the public men, the "important men," of present-day Maya communities.

When speaking of the past war, these men express both pride in the achievements of their predecessors and horror at so much slaughter and suffering. For the Mayas still living in once-rebel territory, that distant war remains an immediate historical reality — an essential part of their identity and their ideas about how the world about them acquired its present form. It is so immediate, in fact, that it is scarcely *historical* — not past, that is, just temporarily subsided; not forever concluded, but to resume once again after the hiatus of the present.

Though now is the time of freedom, there is talk of war still to come. "There will be the becoming of another. As war arose in the past, thus will war arise again." Mayas around Xcacal Guardia say that True God told them this, in obvious allusion to the contents of the Divine Commandments. Rumors of war abound — among both officers and common people, men and women, the old and the young, most of whom suppose that war is not much further off than the year 2000 and that it is inevitable. A minority argue it is neither imminent nor inevitable, but admit that matters of war and peace are issues of their time.

As it came before, war will come once again. In the course of my travels I have found such talk extends far beyond the villages surrounding Xcacal Guardia, beyond the heartland of once-rebel territory, to Maya towns and villages elsewhere on the Peninsula of Yucatan. But as

Mayas on the peninsula have had varied experiences with past wars, so do their imagined future wars look different. While in the 1920s and '30s Maya officers of Xcacal Guardia plotted holy war against a government they considered alien and evil, Mayas in the north were already construing battle in quite different terms. After the Mexican Revolution, the socialist government of Yucatan actively proselytized among a rural Maya populace that it hoped would form a bulwark against conservative reaction. Every day Mayas were harangued in their own language about socialism and the Great Depression.

Opponents of socialism charged that such revolutionary propaganda drew upon "racial" themes, and in fact when Felipe Carrillo Puerto was the leader of the socialist party and governor of Yucatan (he was assassinated in 1923), he did seem to link himself and his party to aspects of Maya oral history and the heroes of past Maya rebellions. As he toured the countryside and "told the people they should have the land of the dzulob [i.e., white men, foreigners, rich people, etc.], and promised them clocks, and tools, and wire, and schools, and music," some Mayas said that perhaps *he* was the expected king who had long lived hidden underground at the ruins of Chichen Itza. Finally, when in the early 1920s they took up arms against their rival neighbors and political enemies Maya socialists told themselves that "God will not allow anything bad to happen to us because we are workers," and they entered battle shouting, "Long live the Supreme Socialist Government of the Nation and of the State! Long live liberty of the downtrodden workers!"[2]

In the northern villages and towns where such slogans were once heard, one can hear talk today of war to come, talk of how the rich people, who were expelled during the Mexican Revolution and the socialist regime in Yucatan, still prosper from the labor of the Maya, and of how they will soon try to return, seizing the land and forcing Mayas back into slavery. The new slavery will not be exactly like that before. The "rich ones" have studied the matter, Mayas say, and have found ways to conceal their true designs. Some Mayas protest they will not passively accept the reinstitution of slavery, whatever its form, and they count themselves many thousands ready to fight, with the crudest of weapons if need be (and certainly with God's help, they add), for even as "with sticks it began, so with sticks it will end."

To these Mayas of Yucatan future war looks to be class war, a war between the workers and those who would deny them the means of livelihood and the vote. To Mayas in Quintana Roo who are descendants of Caste War rebels and fugitives, the war to come is not so much a class war as a race war—not the workers slaying the rich, but rather Mayas slaying their traditional, categorical enemies, the non-Maya usurpers. When speaking of their past war, they say that war arose from slavery, from the moral perversions of the Catholic clergy, and from hunger. In their oral histories, coerced and unpaid labor is the defining feature of slavery. Their descriptions of the workaday life of the slave vary little from one telling to the next, always dwelling upon the long hours of work and precious few hours of sleep; days, invariably begun before sunrise, of extracting from leaves of henequen the fiber for twine, rope, and even cloth; tasks that followed—water carried to irrigate the master's plantings, hours then spent in cornfields, evening hours spent sewing clothes by candlelight; whippings administered for the failure to complete one's work.

Debt, Mayas tell you, was the device of their enslavement. Though they labored hard to produce food and fibers and to elaborate from them articles for consumption and exchange, the products of such labor belonged to the ǰúul, the "white man, rich man, foreigner." Anything the slave consumed in the course of merely staying alive appeared as a debt in the written registers of the estate, and the debt, unavoidably accumulated, bound one to such laboring forever. So, for example, though they then farmed much as they do today,

> ... the thing was,
> ... everything you planted like that, if you wanted to
>   eat it, it couldn't be eaten just like that.
> You would tell your master how much.
> You want to eat a couple of yucca roots, you eat them,
>   it's the same story. "Go ahead, boy, eat them! Eat them!
>   Eat them!"
> He grabs his booklet. *Harat, harat,* he scribbles it down,
>   the corresponding price. There's no way out for you.
> You are a slave.
> If you want to eat squash or anything, you tell your master.
>   "Eat it, boy!" He won't tell you not to eat it. "Eat
>   it!"
> He grabs his booklet. *Harat, harat,* he's scribbling it
>   down.
> There's no day you'll get out of it.
> You are a slave.

Added to such hardships were the alleged outrages of the Catholic priests, who are said to have taken young Maya women, ostensibly to deliver them into the service of True God, but in fact to exploit them as concubines. The priests eventually slew them, it is said today, to conceal the evidence of the offenses apparent in their distended wombs.

And people speak of the hunger of those times. "Hunger made the war occur," is a ubiquitous refrain. "It didn't just happen. If you are full, you will not go to war. Hunger did it, for people were hungry when it happened. People were hungry." It is as though when speaking of the epoch of slavery one cannot possibly say "hunger" too many times. They say that war arose from anger and desperation born of that hunger and exploitation. By reference to such anger, descendants of Caste War rebels excuse the terrible deeds of their predecessors — countless homicides; the slaying of innocent men and women, and defenseless children, too; the cannibalizing of fallen enemy soldiers; the burning of towns and villages and destruction of great churches. By invoking that ancient anger people suggest what *they* might be capable of (what might even be required of them), under other circumstances in a time not so far off.

But the present, they say, is a time of freedom. For Mayas living in the northern reaches of the peninsula, freedom seems to reside in having land to farm and a vote to cast. They reckon these are what keep them out of bondage. For Mayas to the south, far from the large plantations and with little experience of electoral politics, the imagining of freedom takes quite a different form, the key to which is found in their talk of "opened roads" and "closed roads." In that vein the turn-of-the-century prophet Florentino Cituk reputedly pronounced:

> Today stone to stone we walk, on hidden roads we walk.
> But there will be, says he, says True God,
> there will be the opening of all roads.
> We will eat together with the foreigner.
>   We will eat together with our enemy.
> We will converse with him.
> There will come the time
> when white roads cross in Noh Cah Santa Cruz.

Lieutenant Zuluub exhorted Sylvanus Morley: "All the roads, they are all closed by the Mexicans. Therefore I say to you, may there be your opening of the roads for us." And in stories those Mayas still tell today, Sylvanus Morley speaks in similar terms: "Now the roads are closed," he is said to have once said, "[but] there will be the opening of the roads, in the Final Days." The present and future condition of the "roads" is a matter of interested and disputed comment these days, and to declare them "opened" or "closed" is social commentary of sweeping proportions.

What these Mayas mean by all this begins with the most literal interpretation of the phrase "the roads are opened": there will be routes of safe travel through the dense green mass of the forest, whether well-worn paths, dirt roads, or paved highways, along which people can move for various purposes. Though in the early nineteenth century the eastern forest of the Yucatan Peninsula was crisscrossed by measured and charted paths and roads (each league marked by a cross), those routes virtually disappeared during the War of the Castes. As one observer of that war's later years noted:

> The population of Chan Santa Cruz is chiefly confined to the strip of territory between lake Bacalar and Ascension bay, for the fierce and long wars have resulted in an ever-increasing concentration of population on the part of the eastern Indians and also on that of their enemies, in consequence of which uninhabited tracts of land lie between the two factions, in which the former roads have been rapidly overgrown and rendered impassable by the luxuriant forest vegetation.

The reopening of those roads should be taken as an ominous sign of impending calamity, that observer went on to note, for "even though Indians can use these overgrown roads in case of need in single file, the Santa Cruz Indians will always be obliged to open new roads for incursions on a larger scale, which will serve to warn the inhabitants of the threatened district well in advance."[3]

Rebel Mayas maintained roads for internal travel and troop movements, most notably one between Santa Cruz and Bacalar. It was eight feet wide and, like those of an earlier time, its entire length was punctuated by sheltered crosses. As for roads to the exterior, it was not a Maya army, but rather an invading Mexican army that opened one at the end of the nineteenth century. After years of usually ill-fated probes into the territory, the rebel Mayas' enemies deployed a new war tactic. Combining snail's-pace invasion with road construction—felling trees, leveling ground, burning bush, stringing telegraph wire, and fighting Indians at the rate of ten miles per month—a Mexican army advanced toward the rebel capital of Santa Cruz until it fell in May 1901. Rebel Mayas withdrew from its path to found the settlements that would later constitute the Xcacal Guardia cluster.[4]

To foreign visitors in the 1930s the roads still seemed closed. Mayas kept the foot trails in the vicinity of settlements narrow and concealed, while routes to the outside world were "rocky, shut in, and lonely," "long closed and almost forgotten." The notable exception was that turn-of-the-century invasion route along which abandoned settlements were being repopulated both by remnants of the local population and by colonists from Yucatan. Not until the late 1950s and 1960s were broad paved highways cut through the heart of this territory, and since then a web of secondary roads has been built so extensive that almost every settlement can now be reached by motor vehicle.[5]

Contemporary Maya allusions to road "closings" and "openings" arise from a history of developments such as those. The allusions extend to changes in the technology of conveyance, as well. Florentino Cituk spoke in that vein:

> *There will come the time*
> *when white roads cross in Noh Cah Santa Cruz, there*
> *will the white roads cross.*
> *There will be the passing of running-fire [motor vehicles].*
> *There will be the passing of bird-fire [airplanes].*
> *There will pass running by wound-around-vines [bicycles]."*
> *He [Cituk] did not say what these things are that he spoke*
> *of thus, but he knew that they would be.*

And in more obscure allusion to telegraphs and telephones, today they say it was also prophesied:

> *There will be tautly planted the roots of the anikab vine*
> *here in my blessed town," he says. Beautiful Lord is*
> *giving his blessing like that*

(*Anikab* is a vine used for lashing and tying together poles, for example. It appears elsewhere in published prophetic texts in a similar context — mention of the stretching of this vine alluding to the stretching of wire between telegraph or telephone poles or, in this case, the laying of underground cables.[6])

To speak of "opened roads" today, then, is to invoke an image suggesting free movement and communication of peoples, starkly contrasted to the "closed roads" of the epoch of slavery ("there is no day you will get out of it") and to the "closed roads" of war, when, people recall, they had to "shut themselves up" in the forest for fear of encountering their enemies.

This Maya invocation of freedom by mention of "opened roads" is more exotic than might first appear. In our perspectives upon progress, roads and the rest of the infrastructure of human communication may be said to contribute to freedom through such intermediate agencies as economic development, free markets, free labor, the free exchange of information and ideas, and so on. For us, "roads" can stand for progress and freedom as means can stand for ends. When in 1875, for example, the first rails were laid for the first railroad in Yucatan, élite celebrants of the event expected that railroads would serve as a "most powerful stimulus to work and production," would reduce the distances separating men and link them all in active, mutual commerce, thus making possible the achievement of one of the "most noble ideas of progress" —"Universal Brotherhood." After the first rails had been blessed by Catholic priests and spikes driven through to root them firmly in Merida's Plaza de la Mejorada, Square of Betterment, one observer declared that

> hearts beat with joy, hope enraptures the soul, and so it seems that in the smiles of merriment lies assurance of a future of peace, freedom, and wealth. So bitterness is forgotten, rancor ends, and looking upon one another with kindness, we defy misfortune and give fraternal embraces with most affectionate effusion of emotion.

"Shine forth the dawn of the great day!" that speaker commanded.[7] It was a day for dreams—the fulfillment of dreams and the sharing of dreams. The dreams of Yucatan's modernizing élite, that is, who amidst an unarmed and servile Maya labor force felt they could well speak of future things as if they were gods. They even called themselves the "Divine Caste" and spoke of fulfilling God's plan for creation, the plan called Progress. For anyone to deny that "all creation marches along the path of progress" seemed to them to "deny God, supposing Him without foresight and without the infinite wisdom with which He is endowed."[8] There in Yucatan, the extension of a vast network of rail lines rapidly brought prosperity unparalleled in the state's history, a prosperity founded upon the production and export of henequen, and the almost total enslavement of the Mayas.

But the Mayas too had dreams occasioned by the coming of the railroad, the dreams of their prophets passed on by word of mouth.

> The talk of the ancient people, the first people of Yucatan. Obscurely they spoke in ancient times. "There will be the seeing of running-fire at the little roads." They, they had no understanding, nor did

they know what the fire was. They said, "When that is seen, the world is ending." Mercy they asked of the lords in the sky and on the earth.

The "old people" had still other visions: they said that the day would come when speech could be heard in ropes, when it would travel thus from Valladolid to Merida. They said the day would come when one could have morning chocolate in Valladolid and lunch in Merida, only five hours later. They said, "There will be leather money." And they said, "As the earth began, thus will it end." When the trains came, some thought the end was near.[9]

On that grand day in Merida in 1875, when speaking of the progress that railroads would bring, some had in mind the subjugation of the rebel Maya to the south. One who spoke for the owners of henequen plantations mused in print that

> the farmers of the south and east will already have need of new lands to work, because they will already have exhausted those they now possess, and it will be necessary to think of wresting from the barbarous Indians the lands that they occupy, and it will be necessary to arrive even unto Chan Santa Cruz, preceded by the locomotive which will be the voice that calls those brothers of ours to peace and progress, to work together in the happiness of the state.[10]

Years later such men were still looking for the peace and progress that railroads would bring to rebel lands. One man in 1885, for example, reported a dream he had while riding back to Merida after having taken the train on its inaugural trip from the henequen depot of Acanceh to the southernmost railhead at Peto, on the very border of rebel territory:

> Great change there is in the land of the uprisen aborigines. With the explosions of saltpeter and the sledge-hammer blows opening wide breaches in the rock for the bed of the double line of rails; with the echo of happy shouts of one ovation after another; with the appearance of ruins reanimated with new settlers who carry rifles among the tools of their work, and, foremost, the most brave resolution in their chests; upon hearing the whistle of the machine which flies along attached to the earth, like the light shadow of a cloud that crosses the heavens, the barbarians who cannot buy the protection of the Britannic Leopard with the daily spoils from our

defenseless settlements will disperse and finally surrender; or they will emigrate to the ancient forests of the banks of the Usumacinta River [far to the southwest].[11]

The rail line that was finally built in rebel territory in the first decade of this century connected the conquered rebel town of Santa Cruz with meager dock facilities on the Caribbean coast at Vigía Chico. To some it represented a "guarantee for the future, an example and vivid expression of what determination and action can attain." In a book intended to serve as "a sure guide for the immigrant and the capitalist," an apologist for the Mexican military regime in the territory speculated that, with further rail development, "this people now defeated and formerly rebellious before the law will give full homage to progress, without knowing it or feeling it, only attracted by the irresistible force of civilization."[12]

It was to be progress of the sort in which foreigners could also share. Already the British were supplying rails for Yucatan's prodigious rail network and Americans the locomotives, box cars, and passenger cars; both bought the henequen transported by railroads.[13] Writing in 1901 to the Assistant Secretary of State, the American Consul to Yucatan, Edward Thompson, reported upon the Mexicans' capture of the rebel Maya town of Santa Cruz in 1901 and went on to observe: "The reconquering of this territory is of importance to the United States for it means the opening up of large tracts of land containing mahogany, cedar, logwood, and sapote. It has been a tantalizing proposition to many Americans but until now the obstacles have been hard to surmount. Those obstacles will soon not exist."[14]

When the first rails were laid in Quintana Roo for the line to the Caribbean coast, the assembled public were exhorted to "Make ourselves soldiers of progress." Soldiers would be needed, indeed, as the still-armed rebels viewed such developments as a hostile invasion, which in fact they were. The scant fifty-seven-kilometer line between Santa Cruz and Vigía Chico, constructed by soldiers and by Mexican political prisoners exiled to hard labor in Quintana Roo, claimed five human lives per rail tie laid—lives lost to starvation, disease, and frequent skirmishing with hostile Mayas. Appropriately it was dubbed the "Alley of Death."[15]

Other plans for railroad development in Quintana Roo never proceeded, and when the federal army quit the territory with the coming of the Mexican Revolution, even the single line to the coast fell into disrepair. General Francisco May ordered rails removed from two

two-kilometer stretches in order to close this route of foreign contact, though it was along those tracks, near the point of one such interruption, that Sylvanus Morley had his first encounter with the Mayas of the region.[16]

In Yucatec Maya discourse, the relation between "opened roads" and imagined freedom is not the relation of means invoking ends that underlay the rhetoric of Yucatan's élite, but rather the invoking of causes by mention of effects. Those who live in that forest well know that paths are opened little by little as people habitually travel to and from the same places (a town, village, hamlet, water hole, lagoon), in the repetitive undertakings of everyday life. Every person passing by breaks a few more twigs or branches, slashes a few more times at undergrowth and tramples it underfoot. A fully opened path in the forest is evidence of many people's having walked along there. In wartime this process — part social, part natural — was a problem for rebel warriors and fugitives, who had to walk in ways that would leave minimal traces and work to conceal the trails they had inadvertently created, while unused paths took only a few seasons to revert to bush and be "lost." So "opened roads" in the literal sense of visible routes of travel are effects of a pattern of human activities that we might call "free intercourse." They do not *bring* freedom of movement and so human interaction but, rather, are the tangible evidence of the existence of such freedom.

The wartime prophet Florentino Cituk is said to have prophesied the opening of roads at a time when they were still frightfully closed. Maya officers in the time of Morley complained their roads were still closed, though not to supernaturally powerful allies like the long-dead Queen Victoria, who they expected would one day visit them: "Impassable roads, inhospitable settlements, and unhealthy climate, and a thousand other difficulties are passed over because they think of Queen Victoria as one of the fairies, beautiful and miraculous, for whom no obstacle can exist in the passage of her golden coach."[17] For ordinary humans, however, the roads were difficult, even dangerous, and Maya officers sought Morley's help in opening them, so that they might visit each other and exchange thoughts, words, gifts, commodities, perhaps even colonists. The opening of roads has been, at times, something to hope and strive for. Even young men today recall how as children, when they heard it said that roads would cut a long, straight swath through the forest, they could hardly believe it possible.[18]

But the roads are there now, and life is markedly different. Times of slavery and war were terrible, and all Mayas consider their passing as very fortunate. Yet they speak of the opening of roads and the coming of freedom as mixed and transitory blessings. Mayas were once chastised by the same divinity who had championed their cause in the war against slave masters, because "you are talking about mixing with the enemy, although you see how the enemy exhausts me, you say that no harm will come to you through them, because I am advising you my children, don't say that, it is what the enemy says. It is what you say because he has money and not what my true Lord says."

At some time after the roads did open, that passage was excised from the "Testament," for it must have been inconvenient to officers dealing with foreigners in subsequent years.[19] But oral warnings persisted, and today many hold them to have been well justified.

> You WILL see: The leader of your communities [General
>   May] will go to the town of Mexico. Then with that,
> people will enter here again. You will see it [happen]. But
>   on its indicated date . . .
> Nineteen twenty it will arise, when he goes again to know
>   Mexico.
> Then will open again another opening in the road. Then
>   they will come in again.
> At FIRST it will be good,
> very loving,
> fine and happy. Together you eat, together you drink,
> good food, good drink you will have.
> Amongst that, you will drink from à single cup.
> Then you will see: They are becoming unhappy with you.
>   Your younger brother will come, or your older brother
>   will come.
> They are becoming unhappy with you.
> Which means they will cease eating. THEY WILL BE LEFT
>   eating just by themselves for two days.
> They will ENJOY THEMSELVES. Forty years they will enjoy
>   their lives. Whatever they want, they will do. You will
>   be RULED OVER here in your land.

Today there is diversity of opinion and some spirited argument among Mayas regarding the freedom in which they live. And there is talk of the return of slavery. None denies that they are now free to work where they will, unlike predecessors bound in servitude upon a henequen plantation. All are aware that corporal punishment of workers has been eradicated. But still, many point out, how free are they *really* if they must work so many more hours and days than was common less than a generation ago and yet have less food? In Morley's day, slash-and-burn corn farmers cultivating the soils of near-virgin forest spent only half a year engaged in all their productive pursuits (farming, hunting, bee keeping, the manufacture of domestic necessities), and with that they managed to provision their households adequately.[20] Productive and income-generating efforts today are necessarily year-long, and still many households fall far short of making ends meet. The labor of once-autonomous farmers and hunters has yielded to a mixed regime of traditional farming and hunting, wage laboring in village and town, directed labor on government-organized agricultural projects, expanded apiculture, gardening, and more. New forms of labor have entailed new forms of organization and discipline, as well as government involvement, all of which spurs talk of a return to forced labor and slavery.

Visions of decline and talk of slavery also reflect changes in the conditions of commerce and consumption. There was a time, Mayas now recall, when they had access to the currencies and commodities of other nations—especially those of the British Commonwealth. Goods were cheap and money in its various forms (gold and silver coins, American dollars, British pounds, Mexican pesos, Peruvian soles) was worth a great deal, so the products of one's labor offered in sale could garner a seemingly fair return in cash and goods. Not so any more. Though the roads are "opened," the markets seem ever more closed and hostile. With consumer prices rising at astounding rates, people today may disagree as to the proximity of slavery's second advent, but all agree that when it comes it will come on the backs, as they say, of commodities.

The Mayas' present-day ambivalence toward their recently achieved freedom arises from their experience of ever-more-demanding work, ever-greater vulnerability to markets they do not control, and increasing dependence upon the beneficence of a government once considered foreign and enemy. It arises also from their own apparent complicity in constructing this way of life as laborers, consumers, and citizens of Mexico. Once unremittingly and, as they construe it, *properly* hostile toward non-Mayas, they acquiesced in speaking with the enemy, trading with him, allowing him to settle in their midst and eventually even to rule them. In time they accepted schools, loans, technical assistance in agriculture, wage employment, missionaries, and civil authority under Mexican law. Meanwhile, they ridiculed and rejected the more recalcitrant of their contemporaries, who argued for continuing divinely ordained resistance against the enemy kind. Most even choose to disguise themselves in the garb of the foreigners, abandoning the distinctive clothing and ornamentation of their predecessors for manufactured clothing sold by itinerant and town merchants.

> *There will come the hour of*
> *your clothing yourselves with the clothes of the foreigner.*
> *It will number three layers, your clothes. . . .*
> *There will be passed by the door of your houses every-*
> *   thing proclaimed*
> *for you to buy.*
> *But just for a short time, not for*
> *all the year. When that has happened like that, it will*
> *   get painful.*
> *It will get somewhat difficult for us.*

Disdainful references to those who abandoned True God in favor of the fleeting benefits of forbidden fraternization with the enemy — expressed through succinct imagery of coveted sweets, coffee, factory clothing, and money — are indirect self-criticisms and belated laments. Thus do Mayas today chastise themselves, their predecessors, and their children for having abandoned True God and relinquished the subsistence-sustaining and war-fighting powers that flowed from His love of His favored and obedient children. "He says thus," one fellow told me regarding a common theme of True God's beneficence:

> *"If you remember, if you trust in me," he says,*
> *"How I will love you!*
> *I will adopt you. . . .*
> *But if," he says,*
> *"If you leave me, if you*
> *do not remember me, then your livelihood you will be left*
> *   without.*
> *Little by little it will be spent.*
> *Nor will you know how I will take it from you," he said.*

Their abandonment of True God was prophesied, they say, in inspired words that spoke of men and women so consumed with their dealings with the foreigners and with the new lives they were crafting that they neglected the patron of their power, health, and fate:

> *There has already arrived the hour of the abandonment*
> *of True God, like that.*

He has already been left behind, he is not even needed.
Because of the freedom, supposedly. Because it was said:
"You will use
freedom for two days.
But just for two days, not for the entire year."

During those "two days" Mayas will have ceased talking with True God, with whom they had been conversing for a very long time. That silence has already come upon them, they say. True God speaks to them no more, and the last divine communications were received, it seems, a decade or more ago.[21] He has been left behind, in part because Maya ears are now so full of the sounds of the foreigners.

Look and you will see
the ladies of the foreigners. You are going to hug the necks
of the foreign ladies.
The foreign lords, you're going to press your heads together
with those of the foreign lords.
My father is not remembered.
Over how many LEAGUES will you make yourselves chil-
dren of the foreign ladies? You are listening to their
words.
My father, you will not hear.

Both sexual and social intercourse are alluded to—and radios, as well.

Do you know why it is said like that?
Today, look at a radio like this one. Look at it.
We are listening to it.
We are listening to it.
Hmm. We are listening to it.
That god there in Xcacal, he is not remembered.
He is finished.
More ready are we to listen to the words of the foreign
lords from far away.
Even from the United States, from Cuba, from wherever
they are heard.

In their dialogues with foreigners Maya officers had once couched notions of justice, fair exchange, divine will, and political alliance in terms of "goodness, love, and propriety." Nowadays injustice, unequal exchange, and political subordination seem to them like nothing so much as "getting fucked" in the social intercourse of daily life. *Top* is the Maya root I translate here as "fuck" or "screw," the Maya term marked like the English ones by vulgarity, violence, and exploitation. (A different Yucatec Maya root, *c̓iis,* refers rather neutrally to the act of coitus.) Yucatec Maya words constructed with the root *top* trip off the tongues of contemporary Mayas—of central Quintana Roo, at least—in as wide a range of usages as is spanned by, for example, the Spanish word *chingar* in certain Mexican circles. These diverse usages share the connotation of exploitation, of getting the better of someone, of "scoring" at someone else's expense. The word *yakunah,* "love," was central to earlier Maya strategies in their interactions with foreigners. The word *top* sums up contemporary assessments of the results of those dealings.

While engaged with the foreign Other in a now perverse intercourse, Mayas repeat rumors that the sale of the divinity itself was prophesied: "It was said, 'It will be sold, the Beautiful Father there is there in Xcacal Guardia.' " No one can know whether it will be the head priest, or one of the other priests, or perhaps a commander who will sell the crucifix, which local Mayas whisper is jewel-studded and fashioned from gold.[22] Nor need they understand "sell" in this prophecy to mean "sell for cash." As likely, they hold, it alludes to high officers' "selling out" to the enemy, neglecting their divinely ordained responsibilities for more lucrative subservience to Mexican authority. It is widely rumored (and is in fact true) that Maya officers today receive stipends from the government.

No one knows how long all this can go on, how bad things can get, with prices rising faster than wages, with agricultural production chronically insufficient to sustain a household, with old patterns of authority and respect crumbling before their eyes, and with the passing of a former consensus as to the nature and predilections of things divine. But it is evident to all, and it is a fundamental premise of these Mayas' historical sense, that even as past war arose from the sufferings of predecessors, so will future war come in the wake of life's present drift toward great hardships. According to one young officer, father already to seven children, war may seem improbable in today's climate of peace and freedom,

> but then God said it will, the war will *come again.*
> *Because,*
> *because merchandise will get so expensive.*

Things were cheap long ago, but it was known they would
    get expensive.
Because corn,
there will come the time when there isn't any once again.
It will be
removed by God, to make us remember him. Because war
    will not just happen *again. Rather, it will happen*
    because of hunger.
There is nothing for you to eat, there is nowhere for you
    to get any food, nowhere for you to earn it.
Well,
there will then . . . This then will cause people
to get together again to go
break into a store or wherever, because before
dying . . .
well, they look for ways to kill, so that they stop feeling
    hunger.

A somewhat older man, also head of a very large household, who knows well the stories of the past, when asked if slavery would come again replied:

Hah! It will. That's what's coming to pass, so it will remain
    so.
Not like it was, perhaps. Its form is different.
Different, but still that's it.
Only its form is different as it is instituted again.
But if it's really instituted, MOTHER, *people will get mad.*
People will get mad again. Oh MAN, *look out! It's going*
    to happen again!
Oh MAN, *how many people will get mad!*
Poor people will get mad.
Those who have the means of livelihood won't get mad.
They won't get mad. Even if things get very expensive,
    they have money.
But those who have no money, they're the ones who'll get mad.
They . . . well . . . When there's no place for them to buy
    their clothes,
they'll increase in number.
Before you know it, another sixty thousand have already
    come together.

177

"Well, we're not going to get fucked! Let's go fuck them!"
Well, here go things getting bad again.
First you get fucked. Well, isn't that how it happened
  long ago?
First they got fucked, because of hunger. Well, because
my late father told me, hunger made the war happen, he
  said. It didn't just happen, he said. If you're full, you
  won't make war, he said.
Hunger did it, supposedly, when it happened long ago.
  Yes, people were hungry.
People were hungry.

Talk of war today among the villages of Xcacal Guardia, Chun Pom, and Chan Cah Veracruz (the three shrine centers of central Quintana Roo) is talk of a war quite different from that envisaged by Cituk, Zuluub, and the other Maya officers in the time of Sylvanus Morley. It is no longer a matter of local war to right local wrongs, to set things straight, to set them back. It is no longer a matter of just expelling the Mexicans from rebel territory in which they are now firmly entrenched. It is not talk of the kind of war that, had international circumstances been different, Morley's nation might well have helped Mayas wage, though surely to the latter's grave misfortune. Rumors of war today are rumors of total war, world war, the war of the end of the world. They are rumors of a war that will sweep away *all* injustice and evil, while ushering in the next creation.

The war that is coming,
God will make it,
in every nation,
all over earth.
Because the war that is coming, [it will be] because of
  hunger.
Hunger will make it, surely.
Because there isn't any justice under the big bureaucrats.
  They are paid by the government but
they . . . if you have money you get a raise.
The poor man, nothing is left to him.
There is no justice.
For that reason, then, the thing will happen, easily.
Blood will be shed again.

The poor man here in Quintana Roo,
surely, look and see: the government
already said
it would help the poor. Well, it has not helped. Not a bit
*   of help has it done.*

*   . . . .*

The government, if it will not raise the pay of the work
*   of the poor . . .*
If it were well raised, or if the United Nations
were to say that the wages of the peasants be raised here
*   in Quintana Roo,*
nothing would happen.
Peaceful [things] are left.
But where the wages of the poor are not raised,
there is war.
In all nations. The Third World War.

Chichen Itza figures prominently in the vision of this future war. A new king will awaken there, along with thousands of resurrected beings of a past creation; the petrified feathered serpent will breathe with life again and wreak havoc on the creatures of this creation. Tulum figures prominently, too, for sometime toward the Final Days an undersea road there will open, allowing English currency and commodities once again to flow in from the east.

The line Mayas draw between future friends and foes, the elect and the damned, the righteous and the evil ones, has also shifted. Morley and his kind were in their day likened to the Englishmen of a still more distant time—as friends and allies in war. Today, some Mayas still think of contemporary America as akin to that England of the past.

There you will get whatever the things you need, there
*   with those who are called English,*
with those who are called Americans, red-red men.
They are my servants,
they are my sacred people.[23]

This they say True God has told them. But others muse aloud that perhaps it is the Russians and the Cubans, instead of the Americans and the Englishmen, to whom they must look for help.

The war to come, they say today, will be preceded by suffering greater than that anyone alive has known. There will be drought, crop failures, epidemics, inflation, as all the forces of nature and society work to inflict pain upon wayward Mayas. Until, at least, they return to the fold under a new authority, a young head priest, charged with fulfilling what they take to be God's plan in history, a consummated holy war against non-Maya oppressors. The rule of the new Maya leader will be harsh, and his anger, severe. Repentant Mayas will gather again to grovel before him in Chun Pom, where, speaking for the divinity, he

> will ask you, "What happened to you?
> What happened to you that you are returning here?
> Did you not leave before?
> Did your sugared food turn bitter? Did it turn bitter, your
>   food, your meals with the foreigner?
> Why do you run from him now?
> How many days [has it been]
> since you left me? You belittled me. You did not think of
>   your need for me.
> You, you already left. Now you are coming again.

There will be punishment and a stern law, so stern that "it is not the tears of your eyes you will shed as you cry, but rather the blood of your heart." But repentant Mayas will be accepted back into the fold and the ranks of a new Maya army.

Mayas today know that in any future war they would be seriously outgunned. They never received the weapons they sought from Morley, and today the disparity in might is very much greater. But, having returned to the divine fold, they reckon, they will benefit from divine intervention once again. Divine action will immobilize warfare's modern technology, and combatants will slay each other with simple sticks and stones. Through miracles, opened roads will be blockaded by trees and rocks, so that government forces cannot get through. Or, in yet another usage of the old figure, "closed roads" will rend "open" in a different sense, and into the gaping chasms the invading soldiers will fall.

IX

MEMORIES
AND MONEY

MAYAS AROUND XCACAL GUARDIA today ask about Dr. Morley and whether it is really true that he is dead. (Morley died in 1948 in Santa Fe, New Mexico.) He is remembered kindly. I heard many times of his attendance at the shrine village festival and of the gifts he brought. Though now half a century past, his coming is recounted in minute detail. In the verbal picture that one witness sketched for me, Morley and his companions are sitting on a bench side by side, each with feet placed together and hands clasped in lap, head cocked to the side and chin dipped to a shoulder, a gesture we recognize as attentive listening but that to Maya eyes seems more like an excellent imitation of a parrot on a perch. The narrative of encounters and dialogues that I have presented draws, in part, upon these vivid and picturesque recollections.

Of course they remember Alfonso Villa, too, but not much is said about him — just that he came with Morley, that he was Morley's subordinate, lived in that house still standing over there, spoke some Maya, left suddenly when his wife took sick, and paid brief visits thereabouts in 1977 and 1978. Otherwise, memories and tales of Morley overshadow recollections and talk of Villa, just as when Maya officers spoke to Villa they were actually talking to, pleading with, persuading, courting Sylvanus Morley through him. Of course few people living today actually ever met or saw Morley, so few can remember him in the personal sense. But all except the youngest people have heard of him and have heard him speak through the storytelling techniques of reenacted conversation so prominent a feature of Maya oral performance.

Morley is made to speak like a prophet: "There will come a time when Americans will live among you," he is reputed to have said. "Mexico will oppose it, but it will come to be." There will come a time when the trees around you are worth money, when people pay cash to buy the wood—that is another of his alleged prophecies. He counseled them, they say, against letting themselves be hoodwinked in that new kind of commerce. "Not tomorrow, nor the day after tomorrow," they say he told them, "but it *will be!*" People cite Morley in this way, and by now they have ample evidence of the truth of the words attributed to him.

The older men who actually walked to Chichen Itza to meet and speak with Morley have still other things to say about him. Morley promised them help, they say. Morley said there would be assistance— not tomorrow, nor the day after tomorrow, perhaps, but there *would be,* someday. They wonder where it is. The old man Paulino Yama of Señor, reciting stories in the 1970s for a North American linguist to tape-record, chose the occasion to address the long-dead Morley one more time:

> Well, now . . . now,
> after you've come, [Dr. Morley,], well, WHAT do you
>   have to say to me?
> All of the people act like they don't have MOUTHS,
> they're like mutes.
> That can't talk at all.
> Ahah, well, I'm going to say this,
> Señor Jefe [Mr. Chief], the time has passed.
> Every time we come, every time we come, every time
>   we come here,
> well, you don't say anything to us.
> We don't say anything either.[1]

Some contemporary talk still resonates with the failure of past dialogues. The men who must have felt the failure most acutely are dead now—Cituk, Zuluub, Itza, Barrera, Yama, and others who made trip after trip to see the "important man" at Chichen Itza or to speak with his representative in Tuzik. Before their deaths, infighting and schism took a heavy toll among them. Though in the mid-1930s Villa could say of the head priest Barrera that "no one dares to touch him, to contradict him, or to criticize him," by 1938 he had been forced into retirement, his effectiveness having vanished with growing infirmity.

Captain Cituk seems to have held power until his death, but he too had severe critics, including Paulino Yama, who is recorded as saying that Cituk (then already deceased) "doesn't have any BRAINS. He doesn't have any UNDERSTANDING." As for Lieutenant Zuluub, after a fiesta-time brawl in mid-1937 he and his subordinates and dependents were driven out of Xcacal Guardia and returned to their former village of Dzula, there to begin their lives yet again as best they could.[2]

The fate of Apolinario Itza was especially tragic. Scribes like him enjoyed authority and prestige in Maya communities, but their authority was tenuous. Since they combined, as Indian scribes often do, command of the esoterica of literacy and the esoterica of shamanism, their prestige was tainted by public fears of their possible malevolence and uncontrolled (because not evidently socially bestowed) knowledge and power. Itza was, according to Villa, a man of "striking personality" and "the most intellectual man" of Xcacal Guardia, but he was also a man at risk.[3] In early 1943 he dreamed of a conspiracy against him. But weeks passed and no attempt was made on his life, so he supposed his enemies would not act after all. Then one morning, as he stepped out of his house in a hamlet called Burning Cenote, young men fired from the edge of the forest, killing him on the spot.

A group of men had plotted Itza's murder with the approval, it seems, of Captain Cituk himself, even though Itza had been raised in the same village as Cituk and had long served as his secretary. Cituk's heart was turned against his subordinate and friend by the whispering of enemies, they say today. The charge against Itza was sorcery: Itza was blamed for the death of the wife of Paulino Yama, whose soul Itza supposedly ate. Death was the proper punishment for such a crime. Yet, while sorcery was the public charge, some also despised Itza, it seems, because of his role in the talks with Morley. It was Itza who drafted most of the officers' letters to Morley over the years and who read Morley's responses to the officers. Itza was also "key informant" for Alfonso Villa. Some officers had angrily and enviously noted Itza's growing importance, and accused him of taking money from Morley, aggrandizing himself through his connections with the Americans, and being responsible, even, for the failure of the talks. In the past, political rivalries among Maya officers had sometimes led to coup or assassination. Itza was one of the last to meet that fate.

Itza may have died because of his proximity to Morley and Villa. So too, some say, did Morley die for his contacts with the officers. They know that Morley is dead, and they whisper that the *juramento* killed him—the crosses that he had received from the hands of Apolinario

Itza, but which he apparently failed properly to respect. Itza died the death of a sorcerer, and Morley had his life "removed" by the *juramento,* a power ambiguously similar to malevolent sorcery itself. For that reason today they speak of these things softly.

Not long after the murder of Apolinario Itza, his eldest son, Santiago, or San, went to find Morley while the rest of the family took refuge in another village. (They say San was to have been slain too, but some among the conspirators argued it would be too great a sin to murder one so young.) He traveled to seek protection and justice for himself and his family, just as Maya officers had once done for their people collectively. (His father's jailed killers were soon to be released after only a few months in prison.) As Itza's son tells it, Morley told him there was nothing to be done right then, "the vine," the connection between them, having already been cut. "Let us see," he supposedly told the young man, "perhaps there will be the turning of another turn. If I die there cannot but be another man whose heart is good, who comes to see you in the Final Days." Even if all the Maya officers die, San says Morley told him, their children will remain. "Tomorrow, the day after tomorrow, you will see him if you have not died. When you see a man with a good heart, do again what you have done! You know how."

Others would come, Itza's son says Morley told him. Americans would come to live among them, but not right away, as "now the roads are closed." "But there will be the opening of the roads, in the Final Days. Therefore, let us separate ourselves for one day, to see what will happen." As a parting act, Morley gave Itza's son a plain white baggage ticket upon which he impressed a red wax seal bearing a Maya hieroglyph. The young man fancied it protection of sorts, thinking the glyph was an emblem of the United States, the possession of which would demonstrate for any concerned his link with Americans. So all these decades he has saved it (along with his photograph of Queen Elizabeth and his Union Jack arm patch) for the time it might finally help to open his roads by serving as passport and visa.

Some men think the time to talk has come again. Still alive is Juan Bautista Poot, among Morley's first visitors at Chichen Itza and a member of most of the commissions sent there. He was a teenager at the time, and over the years following he rose high in the ranks of Maya officialdom to become general. From retirement forced upon him in the mid-1980s, he asked me for the name of Morley's brother. (Morley had a younger brother named Henry.) He says Morley told him that if something should happen, if Morley should die, his brother would have the record of their correspondence and would finish the conversation with them. In any event, he reports that Morley said, "We will speak again another time, another day." He alludes to "that matter" that was discussed with Morley and to the conversation that is not finished. He claims:

> We are not looking for him [Morley's brother] in order
>   to fight with them. No. We, just a conversation
>   with happiness and with our hearts like . . .
> like long ago the predecessors . . . the conversation of
>   the important men at Chichen.
> Well, thus we too.
> It is still possible to converse with them.
> Because it is not for a fight. We, a
> slow conversation,
> hmm, that is what we need to have also.

Poot and I spoke for hours. The disclaimers notwithstanding, it was clear what he wanted. Morley spoke of peace and love; some of the men he spoke with are still talking—albeit in more guarded terms—of love and happiness and war. Even as officers of Morley's day invoked memories of their predecessors' talks with the British, some today invoke their talks with Morley as precedent for that which they still pursue. They want returned to them the letters they sent Morley long ago, so that upon the foundation of such written texts dialogues may resume with other interlocutors, including Morley's kinsmen, the President of the United States, or the "Nations" (as they call the UN). In any event, they say, it is imperative that they talk.

The dialogues between Sylvanus Morley and Maya officers contributed to the progress of a long conversation, one that began well before they first met and that has continued after their final parting. Even now Morley, Villa, Cituk, Zuluub, Itza, and others are made to go on speaking to one another in the reenacted dialogues of latter-day storytellers. In this sense of dialogue—dialogue that transcends momentary face-to-face encounters—Morley, Villa, and their Maya interlocutors may continue conversing on into the next century, as Mayas pass on stories of past storytelling, conversations, oaths, cries, protests, beseeching, warnings, threats, fears, sarcastic remarks, jokes, prayers, dances, rituals, fights, and the numerous other significant events of remembered lives.

Old men among Mayas make Morley and dead officers speak in oral performances witnessed by audiences of fellow villagers and co-religionists gathered after working hours in a village store, in a wattle-and-daub church, in the barracks of the shrine village's sacred precinct, or in myriad other settings. Oral performance is a much cultivated and highly valued talent, and a good story expertly recounted makes a day noteworthy and well spent. The stories about Morley and Maya officers are colorful and exciting, but they may contain truth, as well — lessons for present or future generations of officers and common people. So the stories are labeled, like stories of divine revelations and Caste War battles, as "examples" or "histories," distinguishing them from the more casual, often ribald, accounts of recent happenings in the forest, village, or town.

The veracity and relevance of such "true stories" are subject to public dispute, and some old men have turned dour before the incredulity of the young. During field interviews, for example, I often asked old men to tell me about an itinerant prophet called *'enok* (Enoch) who, they say, visited many Maya villages in the first quarter of this century to preach godliness and warn people of the imminent advent of the Antichrist. One man (FC) who I knew had such a story to tell declined to relate it, telling me, "No, the story of Enoch, that one I don't know."

PS: No?
FC: I don't know it.
PS: No?
FC: No. Because that is a very old story.
PS: An old story.
FC: Well, that one, that is a very old story, that one. It was told to us long ago by my poor mother. But, as we were little, we don't very . . .
     We don't remember.
PS: No?
FC: Hmm.
     Well, you're right about that.
     Enoch passed through. He travels on earth
     but . . . who knows just what year that was now.
PS: Aha.
FC: Long ago.
PS: Long ago.
FC: Long ago.
PS: But she saw him, your mother did?
FC: She, she saw him she said. She knew.
PS: Aha.

FC: But if we had been a little bigger, we'd remember too.

PS: Aha?

FC: We'd have asked.

    Hmm. But today, well, this . . .
    The old man over in Chun On,
    if you go to ask him, that old man in Chun On,
    [*FC lights a cigarette*]
    the great commander San Cen . . .

PS: Uhuh?

FC: He knows.

PS: He knows. He saw him [Enoch] too?

FC: He saw him too.

PS: Aha?

FC: But if you ask him about it, he won't say.

PS: No?

FC: Oh my Lord! That . . .

    He won't say so, because he says like this:
    "No, we know about such things," he says, "but not, it's
    not a story," he says.
    "Because it is mysterious talk [*talam iàan*]," he says.

PS: Mysterious talk.

FC: Mysterious talk, he says.

    From . . . well, from God.

PS: Aha.

FC: "It's not like some story," he says.

    "A story," he says,
    "is for the ears of young and old, for anyone to know.
    Because there are people like this," he says, "who believe
    stories," he says.
    "[And] there are people who won't believe," he says.

PS: They won't believe.

FC: Nope. "Since there are times, they say, the old man . . . just
    because he's an old man he knows many things, many lies
    he knows how to tell, so say the children," he says. Hmm.

PS: Aha.

FC: Well, that's what he's going to say to you.

    "Thus," he says,
    "if a man realizes he needs it [the old knowledge], it's
    good then that he come to know it."

PS: Aha.

FC: "But like the children we know today," he says, "you can't
    talk to them. They won't listen to anything," he says.

PS: Aha.

FC: "So I'm not going to tell them [stories] for them to hear," he says.

"It's only in vain," he says.[4]

The skepticism and apathy of the young toward stories of the past is indicative of a more general crisis in language and intergenerational conversation itself, old men will tell you. They feel that decay in the use of language signals a more general, moral decay that will produce, eventually and soon, apocalyptic consequences for all mankind. San Itza explained it to MA and me at some length:

SI: The, the, ah, the life of the era has very much . . . it has already been very used. It has already reached its limit,

PS: Aha.

SI: It has already reached its limit, it has already been completed. Because it is known how many years there are to life as we know it.

MA: Aha.

SI: When it is completed, it is finished. It is terminated. The hammock has been used. Used, it will . . . it will be used a second time.

PS: Aha.

SI: Meanwhile those who have so used it, well, they won't even see [its second use].
Hm?
Like us.

PS: Aha.

SI: We, if we were told, "Speak with this fellow here,"
who knows sweet words?
Maya language?
He knows, I know, then I've got no problem with him.
If a prayer is named . . .
Because it is said, "Name someone to pray!" you don't just say it, you don't say prayers quickly.
There are many deity names you will bring down to bless.

PS: Aha.

SI: So that they can be received.
Hm? Well, thus will come the hour of judgment.

PS: Aha.

SI: But as we are in this time period,
"Let's go quickly pray" [they say].

"Let's go then!"

"Egotist, let's go quickly pray. Hey, buddy [*gallo*] here I come." Hm. Well, then he's really in a chicken coop.

PS: Aha. [I don't understand.]

SI: Hm? [Do you get it?]

The rooster [*gallo*], is it not found in a chicken coop these days?

PS: Coop, ahh.

SI: Of course.

PS: In a coop it is found.

SI: Of course! [*Laughs.*]

Of course, in a coop it is found.

MA: The big man's words are true.

SI: Of course, in a coop it is found.

Hm?

"Hello there, cousin!"

As though you were the fellow's relative.

PS: Aha?

SI: Hm? Is it not [the word] for the son of your aunt? The daughter of his aunt? His cousin! [*Laughs.*]

PS: His cousin.

SI: Ah, of course, hm?

But today . . . "My girlfriend," he says. But she is the daughter of his father's older brother. Hm?

What's that!

No. It's over.

PS: Yes, over.

MA: It's already spoiled that way.

PS: It's strange.

SI: I reckon their eyes are on the back of their heads [i.e. they've got things backward].

PS: Yes. [*Laughs.*]

SI: [*Long laugh.*]

Hm? It's already ruined that way.

PS: It's already ruined.

SI: Hm. It's already ruined. Long ago it wasn't like this.

PS: Not like that.

SI: Hm. Not like this.

Long ago it wasn't like this.

Despite alienation among old men, they do tell their stories and not simply in pursuit of praise from those who share well-cultivated talents of detailed memory and oral art. Old men still invoke past dialogues anew—whether those they or others had with foreigners, or prophets, or deities—because such talk may yet have consequence and, as they say, completion. Former General Juan Bautista Poot put it this way, here attributing his own words to the prophet Florentino Cituk:

> These, his last words he uttered when he said:
> "Companions,
> my final words I am making for you.
> I, I am going.
> I will deliver an accounting, then, to the right hand of
>   Father God, of what I did good,
> of what I did virtuously, all of these things.
> You all then,
> you will see it then, there,
> in another day.
> You fathers, perhaps your children then will see it,
> all the things I speak about." Are not then his words true?
> The fathers who heard him, they did not see it. We children,
>   we see now, then . . .
> Therefore, a story when it is told, pay attention to what
>   you heard!
> It is not said to you. . . . "I am not saying . . . the story
>   that I tell, [it is] not for today. Later!" Well, that is
>   true too.
> True, it is later that you will see,
> everything, like that. Like even the
> conversations the important men had at Chichen. It was
>   said to them [by Morley],
> "Don Tzep [Concepción Cituk], not today.
> We are conversing,
> but not today—later will you see. Perhaps you will be
>   dead, but you have children or grandchildren. They will
>   be the ones who see."
> Thus it was said to them.
> Hmm, thus it was said. Therefore I know how the conver-
>   sation ends.

How can the conversation end? How would Maya interlocutors know that it was completed? What do they expect to result from their continued acts of speaking about, and above all *to,* foreigners? Once upon a time taciturn, secretive, hostile Maya stepped out of their collective character and revealed things about themselves to foreigners—hidden, sacred, and even embarrassing things. It was part of their rhetoric of negotiation, and an element in a long-term strategy to establish with English-speaking peoples the kind of relationship that would get them weapons, favorable markets in which to buy and sell, and independence from Mexico. In time things changed and hopes for alliance dimmed. But these Mayas continue to reveal things about themselves to us. Even the most dedicated of officers will talk about divine communications, prophecy, ritual, the intrigues of shrine village politics, and other matters intended for their eyes and ears only. They will let foreigners peruse and copy sacred papers, record "old talk" and "mysterious words," witness and sometimes even photograph shrine village ritual. They will let us live and travel among them, and permit us to eavesdrop upon both the ordinary goings-on of everyday life and, if we are patient or sheerly lucky, the more exotic and extraordinary happenings of sacred occasions.

This book had its genesis in such continued openness and in the Mayas' cooperation in our historical, linguistic, and anthropological research. Compelled by circumstances of the day Maya officers tried to engage foreigners in homicidal conspiracies laced with words of history, justice, the sacred, and love. They still engage the foreigner in talk of homicide—in the oral history of their killing of their enemies, in detailed recountings of the primitive technology of homicide (how, for example, to fire-harden a wooden lance that can be driven into the skull of an unwary soldier or merchant, make bullets from shredded bits of telegraph wire, fashion a one-shot cannon from a log, dig pit traps, and the like), and in intimations of future war.

When speaking with foreigners, some Mayas still expect that weapons, war, and union may follow. Every anthropologist, linguist, and historian who has visited, studied, and lived in the region since the time of Morley and Villa has received renewed requests for arms and for help in forging long-sought alliances. Repeated requests made of me seemed *pro forma,* initiated with little conversational preparation and hardly with the expectation of an affirmative response. So, too, it seemed to historian Nelson Reed, who, after years spent on archival research into the Caste War, visited the region in the late 1950s to glean what more he could about the history of the war. Reed heard of prophecies of a future alliance between Englishmen and the Mayas, as when his Maya guide told him:

Don [Juan] Bautista [Vega, of Chun Pom] is a very intelligent man. . . . He has a book, a very big book, written in Maya, which tells everything. Don Bautista can read! In this book it tells of the coming of the airplanes, of the road. People were frightened at these things, but he knew. Are your people the same as the English?

" 'Yes,' " Reed reports having responded, "not wishing to distract him."

The book says that one day the English will give us arms and the people will go to war to throw out the Yucatecans. The sign will be when money disappears from the hands, Mexican money; that will be the balance of the year, the end of the world.

" 'When will this happen?' " Reed asked his guide. " 'Who knows if it will be this year or in a thousand years. It will be the balance of the year.' "[5]

In the shrine village of Chan Cah Veracruz, the head priest made a point of telling Reed they could no longer go to Belize to "buy the things we need." "He was making the common error of confusing Americans with the old benefactors of his people, the English south of the [Rio] Hondo, and I asked what sort of goods he wanted to buy in Belize. 'Carbines,' he said, and the word needed no translation." The head priest pressed further: "The book promised that your people would come and give aid to the Mazehual." "What kind of aid does he need?" Reed asked through his interpreter. "Rifles and men to help drive the Mexicans out. When will this be done? Shall I send a delegation to San Luis to arrange these matters?" (Reed was from St. Louis.) Reed had to explain "that this was no longer possible."

When my words were translated, the other men nodded their heads in agreement, as if the reality was something they had already accepted, but without losing their respect for the priest and their belief in the prophecies, the two areas remaining separate in their minds. I went on to say that the only help we could give would be economic.[6]

Other visitors to the region have more deliberately fueled expectations of arms and alliance in order to keep Mayas talking and, ultimately, to gain access to their sacred secrets and sacred places. The writers Milt Machlin and Bob Marx, sponsored by *Argosy* ("The No. 1 Men's Service Magazine"), hunted for a rumored pre-Hispanic Maya hiero glyphic codex among shrine villages of central Quintana Roo in May 1971. Over a decade before, Marx had apparently gotten lost on a hunting trip along the coast and had wandered into the sacred village of Chun Pom. He was seized and threatened until Juan Bautista Vega took custody of him, related once again to a foreigner his life history, told Marx about ancient Maya manuscripts guarded in the church there, and sent him on his way empty-handed but with curiosity whetted. Machlin and Marx, accompanied by a Maya interpreter from the town of Felipe Carrillo Puerto, returned to the region to search for the rumored antiquities.

They began their search in the shrine village of Chan Cah Veracruz. The shrine's guard was not pleased to see them, fearing the strangers were government spies. Julián, Machlin and Marx's interpreter, told members of the guard that they had come "on behalf of an American magazine and a British newspaper, but somehow this message . . . was lost in translation. What came out, we learned later, is that we were emissaries from Her Majesty the Queen of England."[7]

That misunderstanding had a favorable effect, one that the two visitors then consolidated by handing out gifts—"colored wool, brightly-colored bandannas, combs, balls," as well as Polaroid photographs of the members of the guard. Machlin and Marx were admitted to the shrine village church by the head priest, whom they asked to hold a mass for the Queen of England. What may have been an inadvertent translator's error had become a convenient deception that Machlin and Marx would play to the hilt. The head priest was persuaded by the ruse, and he asked Machlin and Marx to intercede on the Mayas' behalf with Queen Elizabeth, so that she would send them weapons. If they agreed to do that, the visitors would have the mass they asked for. Apparently they did, for a mass was said. "Our hearts beat with excitement!" Machlin and Marx later wrote. "It was our first day in the field, and already we had apparently been able to score an important first!"[8] Inside the church Machlin and Marx got a rare view of the altar, which they scanned for old-looking manuscripts. But there were no books, nor would Mayas allow the visitors to take photographs in there.[9]

They next attempted to find ancient manuscripts at Xcacal Guardia, though first they took the advice of their interpreter and sought the assistance of Paulino Yama of the village of Señor, who had been a regular visitor to Morley and Villa forty years before. "As soon as he saw the British flag on our shirts," they reported, "he came up to Marx. Pointing at the flag and pulling at Marx's blond hair, he croaked excitedly, 'Inglés! Inglés!' [Englishmen! Englishmen!]"

Machlin and Marx's interpreter once again explained (though this time with his employers' knowledge, presumably) that the foreigners were emissaries of the Queen of England. The visitors thereupon were given a formal, armed escort into the sacred precinct of Xcacal Guardia.[10] The interpreter and Paulino Yama spoke with the head priest and persuaded him to allow the visitors into the church. Another mass was said, and again the visitors asked to photograph the shrine's altar, replete with saints' images and crosses. "This time, we hit pay dirt!"[11] "The guard officers allowed them to take pictures; Machlin and Marx then asked about books, and after consultation Maya officers allowed them to inspect and photograph one that was apparently old and valuable, though not the ancient screen-folded hieroglyphic codex, which the explorers had sought. They photographed each page.

After lunch they headed for the shrine village of Chun Pom. Once again they presented themselves as emissaries of the Queen of England, gave the guard gifts, and took snapshots of them which they then passed out to their hosts' delight. But tensions were high at the time in Chun Pom. To prevent construction of a road that was to run directly through the shrine village itself, villagers had recently fired on government surveyors, and punitive response by the Mexican army was expected soon. The visitors got edgy, fearing that if they were caught there they might be taken for British spies come to stir up trouble.[12] After attending mass in the shrine village church they asked for the "old books" that Marx had been told about by Juan Bautista Vega, who had since died. The head priest and shrine village officers consulted in private for an hour, and then informed Machlin and Marx that if they wanted to see the books, they first would have to get Queen Elizabeth to send two crates of rifles. "We argued," they later wrote, "that this was not possible because England and Mexico were at peace and the Queen had to stay neutral." The news greatly angered the head priest, until finally the visitors said they would present Queen Elizabeth with the Mayas' request for arms. They would soon return, they said, with her response.[13]

Machlin and Marx hurriedly left Chun Pom, fearful of both their Maya hosts and Mexican army patrols. In Felipe Carrillo Puerto they informed two missionaries of the explosive situation in Chun Pom; the missionaries then intervened with the local military commander to prevent any precipitate move against the village. Machlin and Marx may have helped prevent a skirmish. Later they would publish their stories and photographs. Meanwhile, Mayas continued to half-expect more royal emissaries and their arms.

Despite rumors of war and the occasional lies of visitors, few present-day Mayas truly expect any imminent aid from the United States. Nor is success in future war thought to hinge significantly upon modern war matériel. Talk of war is now talk of apocalyptic events of divine engineering on a world scale; worldly technologies and secular alliances will matter little in such a conflict.

So again, why do they go on telling stories about Morley and fancying their talk with foreigners to be a continuation of the dialogues with him, directed toward that same time-worn goal of alliance and war? For some officers, I suppose, completing the dialogues with Morley and Villa would be a kind of personal fulfillment to a lifetime of laboring (and speaking) for the public good. Officers today have precious few secular functions and prerogatives, their civil authority long since having passed to elected officials in a Mexican mold. Their subordinates, the "soldiers," are ever less ready to serve them in shrine village affairs, and common people pay them ever less respect in everyday encounters. For them to treat with foreigners about the weighty matters of past conspiracies is to recapture, for a moment, what they now believe was one essence of their sacred, official charge.

In their talk of the past, and more so in their talking with foreigners about past dealings with foreigners, officers today are engaging in a self-constitutive activity. They do something that is *like* what their more powerful and respected, perhaps more genuine, predecessors did. Their talk will end with their deaths, but it will be completed when they assume places alongside revered predecessors in the oral texts of future storytellers.

Other motives are evidently at play here, still other reasons for speaking with the foreigner today and invoking the conversations of the esteemed dead. To the complex of motives that once inspired Maya officers another has been added, one which keeps the homicidal motive from being, in the words of the philosopher Kenneth Burke, "drastically itself."[14] Money, quite simply put, is this new, transforming motive. The quest for arms and allies in service of the collective good once inclined Mayas to reveal things about themselves and their past to foreigners. Today, when Mayas consider responding to our questions, they are guided in part by expectations of short-term, individual, monetary compensation. It is as though the myriad intermediary steps once lying between the things Maya officers were willing to do and the hoped-for results have been elided. Conversational exchanges, correspondence, visiting, and hosting visitors like Morley and Villa were once expected to yield commodities—but not with the immediacy of a simple commercial transaction. Conversational cooperation was not a commodity in itself, offered in barter or for sale in the transient marketplace of casual encounter. Today such talk is in many regards just that—a commodity for sale. And so the divine injunction once excised from the Maya officers' sacred "Testament" rings more true now than ever before:

> You are talking about mixing with the enemy, although you see how the enemy exhausts me, you say that no harm will come to you through them, because I am advising you my children, don't say that, it is what the created enemy says. It is what you say because he has money and not what my true Lord says.

The motive of personal gain was sometimes evident when Mayas of the past spoke with foreigners. Explorers observed that Mayas involved in the chicle trade were more forthcoming with information of geographic, archeological, and historical interest. And Alfonso Villa sometimes suspected that when officers asked him to present gifts to their divinity they actually sought them for their private, personal consumption. In the village of Chunkulche in 1932, Villa noted,

> near my lodging lives the *Teniente* [Lieutenant], an old man, robust and dark in color. During the day he came to visit me several times, choosing to do so when I was alone so that he might with more assurance ask me for gifts for the *Santos* on the altar [of the church in which Villa was lodged]. Naturally he wanted those things which appealed most to himself such as: powder, cartridges, earrings, sugar, and so on, all of which I very courteously and diplomatically refused to give him. At least after some grumbling the *Teniente* was satisfied with fifteen candles, which he carried off to his hut, instead of leaving them on the altar "for fear the cat would eat them," he said, trying thus childishly to hide the hypocrisy of his devotion to the *Santos*. The same thing happens in all the villages. The churches thus become lodging houses, whose hospitality is paid for in candles and other articles, in the name of the *Santo*.[15]

Such occasional self-interested piety notwithstanding, the pecuniary now seems central where it was once subordinate to other more powerful motives. Where once they would have asked, "Why do you wish to know?" now "How much will you pay?" seems to trip more readily from Maya lips.

Mayas today expect compensation for answering our questions, teaching us things, and in most general terms conversing with us. These expectations run the gamut from, at one extreme, prepayment for an interview later to be recorded, through negotiated per-story or per-hour wages when assisting research activities, to more traditional and discreet forms of compensation.

Regarding the latter, for example, I found old people quite adept at making compelling cases for my paying them as charity while telling me long and detailed stories about the Caste War battles, the epoch of slavery, prophets and divine words, and so on. They would interject references to their present-day penury in the high-pitched voice and rising tone of utterance endings that is characteristic of what Mayas call *'óoéiltàan*, "poor talk," i.e., "begging." They did not need to ask explicitly for payment for their time and stories, and the occasional shift of topic from past trials to present hardships is in any case natural and fluid in Maya discourse, for historical "lessons" always potentially pertain to present and expected future conditions. The hardship of the elderly and infirm is all too evident, so that both common decency and conversational etiquette would indicate that money should be given.

Occasionally the monetary motive is explicitly excluded from any exchanges of words and information. Some vigorously reject any suggestion that they might sell their communicative services, and they even refrain from asking for the small favors that almost everyone there asks of a visitor. Rather, they assert as motive enough the pure enjoyment of company and conversation, and the moral rightness of teaching others, even us foreigners, potential enemies, the things that True God intended we all know. Conversation may well lead to eventual reciprocities — "loans" or cash gifts to the family when illness strikes, lifts somewhere in a car, and various other such gestures, minor and substantial — but these are the reciprocities of friendship, not the transactions of the marketplace.

Even here, however, the matter of monetary compensation can weigh heavily upon conversations. All the doings of a foreigner — the comings and goings from a village, visits to the house of this person or that, the use of a camera or tape recorder, even the topics of our conversations in "private" — with incredible rapidity become matters of public rumor and gossip, speculation, commentary, and criticism. And, when Mayas talk among themselves about their conversations with us, notions of labor, commodity, value, wage, and price are as prominent as when they talk about farming, wage laboring, the marketing of agricultural produce, and the purchasing of consumer goods.

Today, Mayas who speak at any length and with any frequency with foreign visitors, who habitually consort with us, are suspected by their neighbors, kinsmen, acquaintances, and others of selling sacred knowledge and sacred papers. Or—just as reprehensibly in the eyes of most— they may be accused of *giving* away commodities that are manifestly valuable, since they attract foreigners to such a faraway place as central Quintana Roo. They have long had suspicions regarding the chicle trade, finding it hard to believe that a natural substance allegedly used only in the manufacture of such a frivolous article as chewing gum would attract so much foreign interest and such a high price. Some suspect that chicle must have another extraordinary use; perhaps it is an element in the alchemy of gold, for example, or a constituent of ubiquitous objects made from rubber and plastic, such as tires, boots, and kitchenware.

So too, they have suspicions about the information they have provided us over the years. What these Mayas have revealed in their stories and conversations, the photographs they let us snap of them in portrait or in ritual, the papers they let us copy or carry away, and the myriad things they otherwise let us witness they now well know went into the manufacture of books, cassette tapes, records, movies, and television programs. They reckon that all of that—not to mention the incredible salaries they figure we earn teaching what we learned from them—has made some of us fantastically rich.

Morley told Maya officers that he had sent Villa among them to gather information for a book, and they cooperated in that research more fully than they ever have since. What they then thought, if anything, about Morley's writing such a book is hard to say. Their exposure to books (and to the marketing of books) was nil. But by now at least one of those who participated in the early conversations with Morley, Juan Bautista Poot, realizes that, as he puts it, because of "Morley's book" his own name is known everywhere and his photo has traveled to the ends of the earth.[16]

Villa's ethnography of the Maya of central Quintana Roo was first published, in English, in 1945. Not until 1978 did a Spanish-language translation appear, and then it was distributed only from a single bookstore in Mexico City. To this day precious few copies have made it to Quintana Roo, and Mayas are only now circulating rumors of its existence. However, other recent books that include photos taken by Frances Rhoads Morley are more readily available, such as the Spanish-language edition of Nelson Reed's history of the Caste War.[17] Few Mayas around Xcacal Guardia can actually read that book, but some of them own copies and by its photos discern that the book tells of "ancient" leaders and their subsided war. These books are very expensive by local standards, and so Mayas conclude that the manufacture and marketing of books is far more lucrative a labor than the slash-and-burn corn farming, forest hunting and gathering, and the kinds of wage-earning employment they are limited to. These Mayas suspect they have been hoodwinked in the commerce of information, photos, and books, *their* livelihood growing ever more precarious and difficult despite having time and again cooperated with the rich foreigners who came to write about them. They suspect us of having conned them (or "screwed them") out of their inheritances.

Some Mayas today consider it foolhardy, even negligent toward their dependents, not to obtain proper compensation for the information they can give us. Abandoning the circuitousness of past courtly forms of dialogue, they adopt instead a salesman's rhetoric, aggrandizing the quality of their wares, casting aspersions upon the wares of competitors, and making their best pitch for a transaction to be consummated not eventually and in the collective interest of "their people," but here and now and in private. Talk of war, deities, history, leadership, and more, talk once offered up in expectation of an ultimate return in the form of commodities of war, has become a commodity offered in return for payment in the currency of contemporary Maya sustenance, which is to say, cash for food, medicine, and other necessities of everyday life.[18]

X

UNFINISHED CONVERSATIONS

THOUGH MONEY now weighs heavily upon Maya encounters with foreigners, circumstances can still engender elaborate rhetoric, ambiguity, and intrigue. The terrain of interaction is as ill-charted today as in Morley's time, the conditions of talk with foreigners having so changed as to make paradigms of past dialogue dubiously relevant in the present. So even as Apolinario Itza fell victim to the vagaries of foreign relations, others who now venture to speak with us cannot know for sure just how it will end for them.

Take San Itza, for example, the eldest son of Apolinario Itza. Now in his early seventies, he lives in a village of no more than two hundred people located fifteen miles by rough, dirt road from the highway that connects Felipe Carrillo Puerto (formerly Santa Cruz) with the city of Valladolid. The community was founded in the late 1940s by families that hived off from Tuzik to settle permanently what had until then been seasonal residences occupied when farming and hunting were being done thereabouts. The various founding families still congregate with their kin within the settlement, so the house San shares with his young, second wife and small children is surrounded by the compounds of his older children, his children's spouses, his grandchildren and great-grandchildren, these wattle-and-daub huts and walled-in yards clustered around the extended-family shrine and set off a distance from the houses and shrines of the other principal extended family of the village.

Though his father was a scribe, San never learned to read or write. But when as a young man he witnessed inept shamans fail to cure his father of a chronic illness, San decided to apprentice himself to a master shaman in Yucatan, one who had recently been called into the territory to redo a village exorcism that a local shaman had botched. He would have to leave home to join the master in Yucatan, though, and since he was still unmarried, his father's approval was required. At first his father opposed the idea, but San recalls responding that there were many roads to travel, and he would choose his own. So San spent two years learning the trade, and today he calls himself a master shaman, one of only two of such rank, he says, now practicing in Quintana Roo.[1] He executes priestly duties in agricultural ceremonies and exorcisms for individuals, houses and house lots, ranches, and settlements, and he is a curer of local renown. When at home he receives a train of the infirm, both from his own village and elsewhere, whom he treats through divination, prayer, and the use of medicinal plants. Because of his expertise in things shamanistic, rumors of witchcraft and sorcery surround him, as they once did his father.

Some say San's late wife was a *way,* a transforming witch, killed while in the form of a black dog, the guise she habitually assumed for nightly sexual assaults against a certain young man in the neighboring village. The man would wake up night after night to find himself completely naked, his penis swollen and raw, so one night, the story goes, he lay in wait and shot the witch-dog as she approached. Transformed witches always make it back home and resume human form before dying, and so too did San's wife die at home. Though he refused to let neighbors view the corpse, her clothes were rumored to be bloodstained. Some say San is a witch, or sorcerer, too. He is rumored, for example, to have killed a man with his curse, an old man whom he knocked down in the midst of a heated argument. The fight ended with the unfortunate fellow seemingly uninjured, but his formerly fine health deteriorated over the next three years and he died, presumably victim of San's malevolent utterances. From the threads of such belabored coincidences are witchcraft accusations woven.[2]

San knows people gossip about him, though he denies any evil works. Rather, he told me, sick people come to him for cures but do not want to pay and instead say such slanderous things. People hate him and fear the papers and books he inherited from his late father, which they wrongly believe contain malevolent formulas. And San thinks he's God, he says they say.

San has political enemies as well. Twenty-five years ago he was made an officer of Xcacal Guardia, and since then he has risen to the post of commander. As the principal officer of his own company (whose members are scattered among several villages) San ranks alongside three other commanders of Xcacal Guardia under a single general and the head priest of the shrine. Or that, at least, is how it was supposed to be. But a few years ago during a crisis of succession to the generalship of Xcacal Guardia, officers and their companies split into two antagonistic camps. Just how the rupture came about is a long and complicated story, with many different versions and competing villains.

Present-day troubles stem, in part, from the application of the agrarian reform half a century ago. When Xcacal Guardia was founded in the 1920s, it was to be a place too sacred for mundane habitation; none was to reside there save the head priest himself, while the companies of surrounding villages helped maintain and guard the shrine, which they could all equally call their own. Then came the refugees of Dzula, Lieutenant Zuluub and his company, who were allowed to build their houses there. Though Zuluub and many of his followers were later expelled, the shrine village thereafter always had a small number of permanent inhabitants.

When Maya officers petitioned for an agrarian grant in the late 1930s, they sought a single, undivided grant encompassing woodlands sufficient for all the villages around Xcacal Guardia, with the shrine village right in the middle. But it did not turn out that way, and Xcacal Guardia was excluded from the huge grant (General Melgar's corrective orders notwithstanding), which today belongs to the large community of Señor. Threatened by encroachment by new settlements of Maya colonists from Yucatan, the few residents of Xcacal Guardia finally petitioned for and received their own small agrarian grant in the early 1960s. No provision was made then, as it should have been, to exclude from that grant the land upon which stood the church and barracks of Xcacal Guardia, nor was there set aside even a small stand of forest from which pilgrims to the shrine could take firewood and building materials for the three great festivals biannually celebrated there. In the eyes of federal law, therefore, the thirty-odd residents of Xcacal Guardia who were beneficiaries of the grant could claim ownership of the shrine itself and forbid pilgrims to make any use of the nearby forests and fields. In times of harmony they would not so treat their co-religionists, of course. But that loophole in the agrarian grant handed to one of the several companies of the Xcacal Guardia group—the company to which the residents of the village happened to belong—became a useful weapon for internal political struggles yet to come.

In the early 1980s the general of Xcacal Guardia asked the county president in Felipe Carrillo Puerto to donate to the Maya church a gasoline-powered mill for grinding the corn consumed in their great festivals, the same kind of mill from which merchants in many villages made tidy profits, grinding every household's daily corn. The donation was made, but somehow the aging general got it into his head that, since it was he who had asked for it, the mill was his personal property, so he felt entitled to keep it at his own home in the village of Yaxley. Outraged, Maya officers protested to county officials and deposed the general, forcing him into overdue retirement. From two candidates among their ranks, a new general, Sixto Balam, was chosen after some tough and astute politicking. Apparently the county president even got into the act, backing the successful candidate for general (and arranging an audience for him with the President of Mexico) in return for the new general's support in mobilizing his people to attend upcoming election-year rallies in the county and state capitals. The county president also donated another corn-grinding mill to the shrine. Company members built a house to shelter it, and officers agreed that the mill would grind festival corn free and the daily corn of the residents of Xcacal Guardia at a much-reduced price. The proceeds earned were to be set aside to cover the costs of maintaining the mill.

However, residents of the shrine village protested having to pay *anything* to have their corn ground. It was, after all, their village in which the mill was sheltered, and, by the way, they were sick and tired of having all these people from other villages come into their forest and use up firewood and building materials for church functions. The fact that the residents of Xcacal Guardia were, for the most part, members of a company whose candidate for general had been rejected had much to do with their disingenuous protests. In any event, faced with growing tensions surrounding the mill and its operations, General Balam ordered it removed to the village of Señor, where it would be stored until needed for shrine village festivals. Outmaneuvered and enraged, the residents of Xcacal Guardia, led by a commander who also lived among them, dismantled the barracks of the new general's faction and named yet another new general—the previously unsuccessful candidate—to whom they now pledged allegiance. (To complicate matters a bit more, it very soon became apparent that the second new general was neither astute nor articulate enough to lead his faction in the difficult political maneuvering ahead, so a third general was appointed to help him out.)

Though San was but one officer among many in the faction headed by General Balam, he and his company members caught the brunt of the wrath of Balam's enemies, who were deprived of the corn mill but left in possession of the shrine. When they struck out against their enemies, dismantling their barracks and carrying the pieces away, San's was the first to come down. Principal among San's political enemies is the commander who resided in Xcacal Guardia, reputedly among the assassins of San's father (a crime for which he was apparently convicted and served about half a year in prison). San says the commander hates him because San obviously knows more prayer than he, but clearly the antagonism between them is more deeply rooted in the personal and political animosities of a previous generation. In any event, present-day divisiveness among officers strikes many as the fulfillment of prophecy and a sign of the approach of very hard times:

> *Thus it is said. Thus it is said. We, we have heard it said:*
> *"There will be the fighting of white herons with fellow*
>   *white herons.*
> *There will be the fighting of black eagles with black eagles.*
> *There will be the fighting of ants with fellow ants."*
> *Thus, thus supposedly it is said.*

Since the destruction of San's barracks in Xcacal Guardia, his faction no longer goes there to worship. They prefer, they say, to avoid the fighting, perhaps bloodshed, that would result, and instead pilgrimage to other shrine centers to fulfill their major religious obligations and recruit political allies. (The county government and a federal agency often provide the requisite transportation for the hundreds sometimes involved. It is a gift they provide in return for political support on other occasions.) So it was at ceremonies in the shrine village of Chun Pom that I met San—a diminutive man, body contorted from spinal and limb irregularities. While partaking of ritual foods in front of the church there, we had a brief conversation about a sacred bread called *gopher,* offered on shamans' altars to the Lord of the Earth for the well-being of plant roots.[3] San broadcast his knowledge of such ritual esoterica and displayed an apparent willingness to talk and teach. He was aware I had been to his village twice already to interview another elderly man there, one who though very old did not really know much "history," claimed San. He invited me to come to speak with him instead.

In the years that followed I visited him occasionally to talk of history, prophecy, ritual, his father, Morley, and the like. I got to know him not only as a high officer and master shaman but also as a demonstrably loving husband and father. Despite the accusations of witchcraft and sorcery and the concerns for my well-being expressed by some of my Maya acquaintances, San seemed a generally pleasant and harmless man.

He is an extraordinary storyteller, too, his "conversation" tending to a mode of overly long but interesting monologue. He even talks to his pet animals, his parrot and a captive coatimundi that he and his wife have named Foreigner (*ꞯúul*), because it thrives on sweet foods like bananas, ground corn, milk, and crackers.

San has been discreet about our conversations, but open and apparently uncalculating in sharing stories and knowledge. Neighbors have inevitably witnessed the comings and goings of foreign visitors to his house, not only me but other Americans, Mexicans, Frenchmen, and Germans, who somehow find their way there in search of the fellow with the "old papers." Neighbors whisper that San is selling Maya manuscripts to us, that he is training people like me in the techniques of malevolent sorcery, and that he is privately and selfishly aggrandizing himself on the basis of his inheritance. As far as I can see he is doing none of these, but such public perceptions have plausibility and a reality all their own. They cannot be ignored with impunity.

One of the manuscripts San considers of great importance is a "History of God," wherein are told how the world will end and what signs will announce the Final Days. San knows what it says even though he is illiterate, because his father used to read aloud from these manuscripts and San has a very good ear and memory. He showed it to me—a small notebook now lacking the deerskin covers it once had, filled with a continuous hand-written text on fifteen leaves of lined paper, each leaf doubled over and the bundle crudely sewn together at the folds, the first two having already fallen out and been stuck somewhere in the middle. I recognized it as the so-called Chilam Balam of Tuzik, one of fourteen or so examples of a colonial-era genre of Yucatec Maya anthologies containing revelatory, calendrical, liturgical, and historical writings. San recalled that his father had loaned it to Alfonso Villa and Morley's interpreter, Pedro Castillo, so that they would "renew" the worn book for him. But they had to return it too soon thereafter—before, San said his father was told, a copy could be made. In fact, a copy was made, and it is now at the Peabody Museum of Archaeology and Ethnology at Harvard University.[4]

San asked that I read aloud from the book. I found a long passage that years before I had translated into English:

> As Saint Paul says:
>> Written in the divine writing
> The Word of God
>> To you arrogant one
> Here on earth.

. . . .

1. And here is the first, beginning day,
  There will be . . . a sign.
The sea will rise
  With the great rolling
To the hills,
  Very high ones.
Certainly it leaves
  Its place.
To the hanging fruit it will rise,
  To walls.
2. And here is the second day,
  There will be a sign.
The second day
  It will descend to its place,
To the very depths,
  It will descend to the depths.
Nor is it seen
  Where it goes
When it goes racing
  Into the mouth of the sea.
3. And here is the third day,
  There will be its sign
For you to see.
  It will arrive a second time
As is the coming of the sun.
  4. And here is the fourth day,
There will be its sign.
  And here are all the things of the sea,
And fish.
  They will gather themselves together
On the surface of the water.
  They are suffering-screaming
And moaning
  On the surface of the water,
Because they are frightened
  By the coming of the Final Day.
5. And here is the fifth day,
  There will be its sign.
Birds will gather themselves together,
  All of them,

And the remainder of the wild animals,
    They will form a single pile.
On top of each other, too,
    Because it is coming,
Their death,
    On the Final Day.
6. And here is the sixth day,
    There will be its sign.
Fire will come out of the wind,
    In the west where the sun sinks,
And in the east where the sun comes out.
    7. And here is the seventh day,
There will be its sign.
    There will be very many comets,
And lightning,
    As though stars are falling.
It is seen,
    There it comes from the sky.
8. And here is the eighth day,
    There will be its sign.
There will be hurricanes.
    Here then wild animals,
All of them,
    Neither are they standing,
Nor are they sitting either,
    And they will all fall
To the earth's surface,
    All of them, also.
9. And here is the ninth day,
    There will be its sign.
Here then stones,
    All of them,
They will measure themselves,
    They are joining themselves together,
all by themselves,
    Big ones,
As well as little ones.
    And they will break apart in square pieces,
and they will put themselves together again,
    By miracle.
10. And here is the tenth day,

There will be its sign.
Here are all trees,
  As well as brush too,
There will descend blood upon them,
  As upon them descends dew.
11. And here is the eleventh day,
  There will be its sign,
Here are all hills,
  And mounds,
And the large constructions
  Of men,
And high forest,
  Will all fall
To the earth's surface.
  12. And here is the twelfth day,
There will be its sign.
  They will gather themselves together, wild animals
All of them,
  In a clearing.
They are perhaps suffering pain,
  The end,
The days,
  Of all wild animals.
13. Here is the thirteenth day,
  There will be its sign.
And here are all the graves,
  They will split open,
All their openings
  All come from the east,
Where the sun comes out,
  And come from the west,
Where the sun sinks.
  Here are the bodies of people,
They will all be the same,
  The opening of the graves,
All the same,
  Because of miracle,
It will come to be seen.
  14. And here is the fourteenth day,
There will be its sign.
  Here are all people,

They hid themselves.
   In caves they are fornicating
With their sin.
   They will come out from caves,
From limestone too.
   If they hid themselves,
They will all come out.
   Nor does it matter that they talk to one another there,
They do not understand,
   If they are different,
Nor are they hearing either.
   This because they are ashamed
When they came out,
   All of them,
Their words,
   Nor are they seeing,
That it happened.
   15. And here is the fifteenth day,
There will be its sign,
   When will descend fire,
Come from the sky,
   As it is renewing itself,
the surface of the earth,
   As it will burn all the world,
In fire,
   In the power of
The fire,
   The pain,
The coming,
   The Final Day,
Our great king,
   My lord,
Jesus Christ,
   He had redeemed us.
He is arriving,
   In the power,
And in the great glory too.
   Amen.[5]

The language is somewhat archaic, and my Maya reading was far from fluid. (Nor is my translation without error, I suspect.) San nodded here and there in recognition of something heard before, but the text was difficult for him as well. In any event, he said, he would not part with this or other such manuscripts for any amount of money, though he would let visitors like myself read them and study them there in his presence. After his death, he said, his young wife can sell them if she needs the money, or pass them on to his sons by the previous marriage— that will be her decision to make.

BON KOH (a pseudonym I will use), who reckons he is about seventy-four, was the son of a lieutenant of Xcacal Guardia in Morley's time (not Zuluub, though). So that he would learn to read and write in Yucatec Maya, Bon's father apprenticed him to Apolinario Itza's older brother back in the 1920s. Bon learned well, and he is today the most important Maya scribe in central Quintana Roo, secretary to the present-day officers of Xcacal Guardia, occasionally to officers of other shrine centers, as well. He too has a small personal archive of Maya manuscripts, which he has written or copied over the years, as well as miscellaneous correspondence in Maya. Foreigners who inquire about such things are eventually directed to see Bon, self-described "Professor of Quintana Roo," "Defender of the Church," and the only wise man thereabouts, the only one with "education"—a Maya education, that is. Though a corn farmer, hunter, logger, and so on, like his fellow villagers, Bon's labor of love is providing contemporary Maya officers with the "orientation" that only he can now provide. And he thrives on audiences of interested foreigners, as well.

Like San, Bon is subject to public scrutiny and criticism. I had heard of him, years before our first meeting, from people who spoke of a scribe caught forging letters from True God to the officers at Xcacal Guardia. Since well before Morley's time, it seems, letters from God would appear once a year or so, addressed "To Whom It May Concern," signed "I Don Our Father Three Persons," and left at the foot of one of the perimeter shrines of Xcacal Guardia. The letters would be discovered by the head priest of the shrine or one of his subordinates, communicated to officers and soldiers, and added to the corpus of sacred writings that each shrine village maintains. After one such letter was found (in the late 1950s, I believe), the handwriting was recognized as Bon's, and fraud was charged. Obviously much more is involved in such a charge of forgery, however, since some of these Mayas understand and accept that their own scribes set genuine divine communications to paper, though presumably under suitable inspiration.[6]

In the village where Bon was said to reside—a small settlement southwest of Xcacal Guardia, near the village of Tabi—I found his younger brother, who claimed not to know where Bon lived those days, saying that his older brother was like a kite floating on the wind, landing now here, now there. Bon had not descended very far away, however, for after some inquiries in Tabi I soon learned that he was staying with a married daughter in the next community. When I went to find him there, Bon was not home, and his daughter told me he had gone to the shrine at Chan Cah Veracruz. After telling her of the difficulty I had in locating him, she said yes, her father's kin and former neighbors hated him because he was always traveling about on official business between the shrine centers of the region, and they envied his knowledge of prayers and Maya writing. Bon was also subject to such public gossip as had branded San a sorcerer, though he is evidently adept at deflecting the worst of such accusations.

A few days later I returned and managed to catch Bon at home. I introduced myself as someone interested in the history of the region, and in particular in the visit of Sylvanus Morley to Xcacal Guardia. Surely, I suggested, Bon had met Morley and could tell me things about that visit? (As it turned out, he had not known Morley.) Our first conversation (or more accurately, Bon's first somewhat intoxicated monologue, for which I was sole audience) ranged through such topics as the long drought that had farmers of the region then worrying about crop failure, to hunger, poor wages, and Mayas' dissatisfaction with the limited assistance the government was providing them. Bon talked of Caste War battles, sang a couple of "ancient" war songs, and spoke of war to come. God shed his blood to redeem them, he noted; so too will they shed blood until the blood of people of many nations mingles in ankle-deep puddles in the plaza of Santa Cruz. Before that, four kings will appear, one in each of the shrine centers of Xcacal Guardia, Chun Pom, Chan Cah Veracruz, and Tulum. They will be young men who are great Caste War generals resurrected or, perhaps better put, reincarnate. One will recognize them because they will know the histories of the Caste War in such detail as to leave no doubt that they actually *lived* those days.

The Russians had already provided weapons to one of the other shrine centers, Bon told me; Russia and Cuba, it had been said, would help the Mayas. But the United States could help prevent the war that was coming, he said. Right now God was in the sky watching, just waiting to see what would happen. While talking he pulled out of a crumpled plastic bag some manuscripts, including a small notebook—

old-looking, with leaves falling out—in which he claimed was recorded the history of the war, how it started, how it concluded, and how the world would end. Bon had written in it over the years, using a fountain pen and ink he made from charcoal. It was faded but still legible, and Bon remarked that its renewal was long overdue. He called it the Book of Quintana Roo, and said it contained many important things, matters that might be of importance, even, to the president of my country. Would it be possible for me to arrange an audience with the president, for Bon to explain how things are in Quintana Roo? Perhaps Bon could get the aid, he suggested, that would prevent the coming war.

I said nothing in response, and leafed through the manuscript he had put in my hands. It contained a miscellany of texts, mostly common prayers in Maya and Spanish; texts of two short "war songs" that Bon had sung for me; historical annotations regarding one General Vitorini, who had died, Bon explained, fighting at Chunyaxche in 1910; various notations of the dates of Bon's attendance at shrine village events; and other graphic and cryptic entries. There was nothing, so far as I could see, of the lengthy history that Bon claimed it contained.

I asked Bon if I could tape-record this "orientation" he was providing. "How much will you pay me?" was his instant retort. I must have looked surprised, and said I did not know. He would know better what the "orientation" was worth. Ten thousand pesos, he suggested. I said I thought that was expensive. He replied that it was cheap, considering that I would make millions from the information he was giving me. That wasn't so, I said, and we both laughed. Bon explained that he had rare skills and he should be able to make a living with them without having to work like any other farmer. Didn't I make a living from my knowledge of reading and writing, he asked rhetorically?

Bon's wife chimed in to say that many have come seeking him and, having gotten what they want, quickly departed again, leaving Bon no better off than before. All right, I replied. I would pay him for an interview, but we would not conduct it that day (since Bon had been drinking). Rather, I would return eight days from Sunday, pay him the money he asked, and record an interview with him.

When the time came, both Bon, who was wearing a tourist cap with "Chichen Itza" emblazoned on the front, and his wife were furtive, asking me not to tell "them," the neighbors and folks back in the other village, what we did that day. After the interview I raised with Bon the possibility of my copying the manuscript in his possession. Though clearly of recent vintage, and not what Bon claimed it to be, his book *is* of the Chilam Balam genre—an anthology, that is, of historical and prophetic texts and prayers—and its documentation might have some scholarly value, I thought. Bon said yes and immediately suggested I give him a new notebook in which to hand-copy the entire manuscript. I had it in mind (perhaps even said I wanted) to photograph it, and considered Bon's suggestion a stall. So I showed him a photograph of one page of the Chilam Balam of Tuzik, which I had obtained from the Peabody Museum. If this document was of interest to him, I suggested, then let's swap—you let me copy yours so that it will find a place of similar safekeeping in my country, and I will obtain copies of this other manuscript for you. Bon was very interested in acquiring other Maya manuscripts that I might come across. But as for copying his, well, his book would be of little value without him, surely unable as we were to read or understand it (and as regards certain passages he was quite right). No, he must come back to the United States with the book.

During our first conversation, Bon asked who had given me his name. How did I know to come looking for him? I said various people had, so well known is he in the region, mentioning San among them. That was a mistake. San was a good friend of his, Bon said, and the reference was a solid one. After our interview he asked if I would take him to see San; he had wanted to visit him for some time, but didn't have the means to travel to San's village, which was so far off the highway. What, I asked, was he going to see him for? Business, Bon said. He had some business with San.

We went the next day, with Bon's wife, too. San was not home when we arrived, and his young wife claimed her husband had gone to his apiaries some two leagues away. She did not know when San would return. Bon explained he had come to help me read San's papers, since they were important papers and I could not read them myself. Here was the first inkling I had that Bon was a true schemer, though he was inattentive to flaws in his plans as they developed in the course of execution. He and I had already spent hours conversing in Maya, but he did not grasp the implications of my fluency for the plot he was now hatching. I could fully understand what he was saying to San's wife and was annoyed that he had not even cleared his concoction with me before offering it up. But I said nothing. Unfortunate it was, San's wife repeated, that she did not know when her husband would return. Better not to wait for him.

We'll wait, Bon decided; he and his wife, meanwhile, left to visit other acquaintances in the village while I stayed behind in San's house.

"Why did you bring *them* here?" San's wife asked me, once the others had left the house. Her husband had gone to check his beehives, but they were not far away, just beyond the edge of the village. He'd be back any minute!

She said, Bon is wily and ambitious (*muy político*). He's been saying for over a year now that he's going to come to the village, but only because he wants her husband's papers to copy them and sell to the *gringos* in Tulum or Cancun. That is what he does, and he makes a lot of money doing it. Suppose he does that with her husband's papers, sells them to others? Then you will have come to learn about them for naught. Everyone will have them. San won't charge for knowledge, as Bon does, she noted, as though it were a flaw in her husband's character.

I explained that Bon had not told me of the purpose of his visit, only that he had to see San, and I had assumed his intentions were proper.

What if, San's wife suggested, you go and tell Bon that San has gone to check on his beehives, which have suffered from ant infestations, and that he's not coming back until he finds the ant colony and fumigates? Then surely San will not return until nightfall. Do you think he'd believe that?

I said I thought so, let's see.

Bon and his wife fell for it. We left (just as San arrived at his house, I later learned), and on the way back down the highway to his village he asked that I pull off into Xcacal Guardia—he had some pressing business with the commander who lived there. It was on the way, and though again I should have been more wary, I agreed.

We found the commander at his home on the edge of the village's sacred precinct, which still looks much as it did in Morley's day, though the church and its now parallel public meeting house have since been renewed, as well as the surrounding barracks. The commander and I had met several times before and talked briefly each time, though Bon could not have known that. The "pressing business" Bon had was to tell the commander that I had come all the way from the United States to seek out Bon, the most-noted scribe in the entire region, because of things he knew that in the United States were considered of the greatest importance, and that I had brought along a fragment of an ancient document (the photograph of a page of the Chilam Balam of Tuzik) for him to decipher, and that I wanted him to return with me to further serve in the United States. Bon rapidly explained that he had told me that was not possible, so many and important were Bon's duties there in Xcacal Guardia, Chun Pom, and the other shrine centers of Quintana Roo. Though astounded, I remained quiet, not then wanting openly to contradict and so embarrass him.

The scheming Bon could fabricate an intricate story and weave webs of intrigue more rapidly than anyone else I have ever met. But this time they were of little avail. The commander cut him off several times, and, finally, definitively. *He* had something *he* wanted to raise, and Bon's business was clearly secondary. It was not that the commander was uninterested in the possibilities of alliances with foreigners, I had learned before. (I had denied or evaded earlier requests for guns and ammunition, and as a result our conversations had always been brief and awkward.) But today he wanted to talk about recent divisions among the officers of Xcacal Guardia. And he had a paper for Bon to read. A *gringo* (Americans, Englishmen, Frenchmen, Germans are all *gringos* to the Mayas) had given it to him in Tulum, asserting it contained ancient Maya writing. Bon was now to read it and see if that was so. Bon took the paper and started reading aloud:

Jesus, Mary, in the beautiful name of Our Lord True God the Father, and in the beautiful name of Our Lord True God the Son, and in the beautiful name of True God the Holy Spirit, Amen Jesus. Thus then the holy hour there is the counting of the month of June of 1888 years, truly the necessity of my giving my beautiful commandments.

He stopped at the word *'almahtàan,* "commandments," and all knew immediately what this document was — the "Santo Almahthan," the "Divine Commandments," the "Testament," "The History of God," or what North Americans and Europeans know as "The Proclamation of Juan de la Cruz," the most treasured and secret of these Mayas' sacred manuscripts. Versions are kept in all the shrine villages of Quintana Roo and are read aloud, by Bon himself, on now rare occasions to select assemblies of the faithful.[7] It is not supposed to circulate in the unguarded public domain, and certainly not to fall into the hands of foreigners.

Many foreign visitors have written about Mayas' reluctance to talk about the "Testament." One was falsely told in Xcacal Guardia that they no longer had "the sermon." Another found that his Maya assistant would not relate its contents for recording unless sure no one else was present. On another occasion a researcher recorded the text recited from memory by the scribe of Chun Pom, Juan Bautista Vega, who posted sentries outside his hut "to watch for hostile 'Guardia' [guard] members."[8] That researcher noted, regarding the "Testament" in Chun Pom, that from the hostility shown to any outsiders who try to inquire about it, the perpetual watch that is kept by an armed guard around the temple where it supposedly resides, and the difficulty we had in convincing Juan Vega [the scribe in Chun Pom], even in what might be called the decadent state of the cult now, to relate it from his memory, it appears to be understood by them as some sort of sacred appearance.[9]

As for me, of all the "secrets" Maya interlocutors ever divulged to me, the only one they ever explicitly insisted I keep secret was that it was they who told me about the existence of this manuscript—much less, of course, its contents.[10] And now here it was, obviously out circulating in the hands of foreigners and tourists!

Officers of Chun Pom had accused those of Xcacal Guardia of having leaked the "Testament" to the foreigners. The Xcacal Guardia officers had denied the charge, saying that if the document had been leaked it was not *their* doing; and besides, there was no proof that the "Testament" was in foreign hands. Now here was incontrovertible proof, and in an instant Bon and the commander hit upon the likely culprit. Was it not San who was in charge of the shrine-village guard one day four or five years before, when some Americans had visited it? There were rumors that the Americans were allowed, for a price, to see and copy the "Testament." Surely this paper now in the commander's possession was the product of that sellout.[11]

From where I was sitting in the commander's dimly lit hut I could see that was not so—not precisely so, at least. What Bon had just read aloud was the "Testament" all right, but it was not the version photographed in Xcacal Guardia by the Americans Machlin and Marx in 1971 and subsequently published in facsimile in *Argosy* magazine. Nor was it any of those versions published by Leticia Reina or Victoria Bricker from documents unearthed from military and civil archives of Mexico, where they had been deposited after capture during nineteenth-century raids on Maya villages of Quintana Roo. Nor was it the Xcacal Guardia version that Apolinario Itza had allowed Sylvanus Morley to copy and which Villa published in English translation in 1945. Nor was it that oral version recorded by Charlotte Zimmerman in Chun Pom, recited to her by the then aged scribe Juan Bautista Vega. Rather, what Bon had just read aloud I could see came from a book published by Santiago Pacheco Cruz in 1960; his version of the manuscript had been obtained by a schoolteacher in Chun Pom in the early 1950s, I believe.[12]

I kept silent about my knowledge of the document's provenance, as

I had always kept silent concerning the multiple versions of the "Testament" that had fallen into foreign hands. We retired for the moment to the church. Bon and his wife removed their sandals, lit candles, which were then placed on the candle rack before the church's altar, and knelt down to pray. Meanwhile, the head priest and half a dozen other men doing guard service in the shrine village were called over from nearby barracks. Back on his feet, Bon read aloud from the document the commander had brought to his attention. They were upset. The commander and scribe said San had certainly done it; a million pesos had been paid, a son of the late Captain Cituk said.

Bon also mentioned my having brought an important paper (the fragment of the Chilam Balam of Tuzik). I explained to these men that I had come across such documents in an archive where they were deposited by the late Dr. Morley, and that I had come to learn who among them today might be authorized to receive them, should their return be deemed desirable. Some of the men recognized me as the American who had lived in Tuzik so long (while doing fieldwork between 1978 and 1980). But they were little interested in all of that. It was the "Testament" that now concerned them.

They seemed to agree that punishment was in order. They must plan a punishment. Other things to that effect were quickly uttered in the momentary confusion of several agitated men speaking at once. Bon, taking notice of my continued presence, halted the discussion and suggested this was something they should deal with later.

I have no doubt that homicide was what they contemplated. When I warned San about this later, he was neither surprised nor greatly moved. They were his enemies, he already knew that. Some of them had assassinated his father over forty years ago, and once again their rancor was fueled by sacred papers, sacred talk, and officers' intercourse with foreigners.

We left Xcacal Guardia to see Bon's older brother in the next village, and this time the commander from Xcacal Guardia joined us. Bon's brother was general of the Xcacal Guardia group (or, better said, one of several generals after the succession crisis that split the group). Bon and the commander entered the general's masonry house, offering formulaic protestations of respect and requests for the general's blessing. I followed behind them, they taking up seats at the general's feet, I being offered the hammock a bit further away. Even reclining in his hammock, resting with a stomach ache, the general was a commanding and eloquent, yet good-humored presence.

Once again the first matter Bon raised was the document I had shown him, and there followed my by now often-repeated story of an archive in my country where other such papers once belonging to Dr. Morley were preserved. The general was interested; he said yes, Apolinario Itza had given some papers to Morley, but the officers had kept that information to themselves—they did not speak a word of this to the common people. I offered to return copies of the papers if they were still of any use to the officers, to which the general said they were very much needed and I should send them to his brother Bon. Then on to other business, the accusation against San. The commander spoke this time, relating for the general how a tourist in Tulum had given him a paper that he realized, when Bon read it, was the "Testament." Mention was made of a million pesos paid, and San was blamed. . . .

Though the general agreed with them on how the "Testament" fell into foreign hands, he seemed unmoved and remained smiling. He had other things to discuss with his two subordinates, speaking for a while over Bon's continuing accusations before his younger brother and the commander dropped the matter. They went on to talk of local politics, as I listened from the hammock a few feet away.

Meanwhile, the general's wife pulled out some of his official, festive clothing to show me—a long-sleeved pleated blouse with little buttons sewed down the middle in two long rows, the buttons set so close that they touched, and a pair of baggy white pants with embroidered cuffs. This was the distinctive, festive garb of the Mayas of Quintana Roo, like that worn in Morley's time by which he was said to recognize the wearer as a man from the south. Some women still know how to make such exceptional garments, now worn only by elderly officials on ceremonial occasions. Prophecy has it that one day such old-style clothes will again become common, as the rebels come out of hiding and, so to speak, show their true identities. The general's wife asked if I wouldn't like to buy her husband's blouse and pants.

In the car on our way out of the general's village, the commander spoke to me again of their need for help. He had done that every time I saw him, though because our encounters were so infrequent I suspected he forgot what he had told me or asked for before. He usually asked for a cauldron or some other gift for the shrine village church, at least, and then, as he did this time, further aid, usually unspecified but just as well understood. This time he went on to speak of his dislike of the Mexicans, the difficulty of their present circumstances, and so on. "Could not the President of the United States be informed of our predicament?" he asked. "And might not some aid then be given?" In fact, his questions were constructed more as declarative statements to which no direct response was necessary, it seemed to me. I said I could give the shrine village a cauldron. As for the other aid, I chose to remain silent and just drive on.

WHILE OFFICERS of Xcacal Guardia were fighting and scheming against one another, tearing down barracks, denouncing their colleagues, and rallying hundreds of followers to their actively hostile factions, a miracle occurred in the village of Dzula, home of the late Lieutenant Evaristo Zuluub. In June 1985 there appeared what some called a "king," others, a "god," still others, a "god-king." Word of his coming spread rapidly throughout central Quintana Roo.

When I heard about it in the villages around Xcacal Guardia, the story then was that several young boys of Dzula had gone to gather firewood in the forest thereabouts. They foraged amidst the recently felled and rough-hewn trees on which adults from the village had labored and which soon would be collected, sold, and exported to serve as railroad ties in some distant part of Mexico. (In recent years the production of railroad ties has supplanted the gathering of chicle as a principal means by which those corn farmers earn some cash.)

The boys had already gathered and bundled the kindling and wood to burn on their family hearths, hoisted the heavy loads upon their small backs, and started for home when a thin, high-pitched voice was heard to say: "So you're going. Well, take me to your village, too." The trees and grass seemed to sway in the still air, and the boys were startled. "So you're going. Well, take me, too. My older brother gave himself to the enemy, but I decided to stay among the *masewal* [the once-rebel Maya]," the voice again said. The boys could not discern where the voice came from or who was speaking to them. The hair stood up on the backs of their necks. "Children, what do you come to do hereabouts? I will come back with you. If you adopt me, I will adopt you."

Frightened but curious, two of the boys put down their loads and searched the bush. Before long they found, set between two stones and half buried in the soil, a stone figure of some kind of being, presumably him who had just spoken to them. One of the boys picked it up, perched it on his load of firewood, and took it home, where he set it down on a cluttered table.

The boy's parents were home, but they noticed nothing. His mother called him to eat beside the hearth in an adjacent hut, to which he replied that he was not hungry. She called again, and again he said he was not hungry and did not want to eat. The mother complained to the boy's father, who was resting in a hammock a few feet away in the family's main hut. "The boy doesn't want to eat; what's the matter with him?" she reportedly asked. The boy's father was a shaman, used to divining the hidden causes of human maladies, though it was probably as an ordinary parent that he quizzed his son about where and with whom he had gone. The boy told of having gathered firewood and gave the names of his companions; he said nothing of the voice of the god-king. Thinking little of his son's lack of appetite, the man suggested to his wife: "Perhaps it's because you scolded him before sending him to fetch firewood." In any event, the boy was sent out to buy Coca-Cola at a corner store.

Meanwhile, now alone with the father, the god-king spoke again: "From San Antonio I have come. My older brother gave himself to the enemy, but I decided to stay with the *masewal*. I was just there by that tree and asked to be brought to this place. But I'm not a plaything! If you adopt me, I will adopt you." The father was startled, even as his son returned from his short errand. "Was that you just then?" he asked the boy. "No," the son responded. "Why, did you hear something?" The father repeated what the mysterious voice had said. "Oh," the son replied, "that must be the god I brought back." (Children can be so nonchalant about the fantastic.) So the boy's father learned of the god-king's appearance, and soon the strange new member of their family asked to have a church built for him. The family's meager hut—they were among the poorest of families in the village—was quickly turned into a chapel, and as word spread among kin and neighbors, fellow villagers, and beyond, worshipers came daily to view the image, hear the boy's story (now officially related by the father), and pray before the new god-king.

A few weeks passed before I began hearing such stories around Xcacal Guardia, and by then there were already several different versions about what the god-king had said and about punitive miracles he had performed against skeptics and unbelievers. As for the reference to San Antonio, San Itza, whose version of events I have just related, reckoned it had dual significance. First, the god-king had appeared on the name day of the saint—June 13; second, it was, as San had it claiming, the younger sibling of a pair of divine images once sheltered at the now-abandoned wartime shrine center of San Antonio Muyil, northeast of Xcacal Guardia near the vast pre-Hispanic ruins of Coba. About thirty-five years ago Mayas from the village of Xcan, east of Valladolid in Yucatan, had ventured south to retrieve the neglected divinities; but only one was found and taken back north. The other was lost, presumably having retreated underground to venture forth in another time, much as the other fantastic subordinates of the Maya king will do in the Final Days.

The troubled summer of 1985 was a very good time for his return. The rainy season, upon whose regularity forest farming entirely depends, had started auspiciously enough toward the beginning of the previous May. But the rains ceased prematurely, leaving every farmer's field languishing in various stages of feeble growth. By July talk was that there would be no harvest at all that year. Few households had any corn left from the previous year's poor crop, and its price at the government warehouse, the only place one could find corn to buy, was already very high. Hunger was on people's minds. The drought was surely divine punishment, probably inflicted because of the squabbles of Maya officers, though perhaps also sent as a brief preview and reminder of the coming of Final Days now seemingly only fifteen years away. One fellow in Tuzik told me that perhaps they would have to do as had their ancient predecessors, from the time before Christ: take a girl child, stretch her out on her back, tear out her heart, offer it to God, and throw the body into the great sinkhole (*cenote*) at Chichen Itza. I assumed, of course, he was joking, but lacking were the smile and laugh that would have made that obvious.

As collective anxieties increased with each new sunny day, to make things worse the funding for various government-sponsored agricultural and forest projects was also drying up, and payrolls for the Maya workers on those projects could not be met. Some took to seizing the government's trucks and jeeps to hold as hostage until some money again flowed their way. Meanwhile, a serious dispute also erupted between residents of the shrine center of Chan Cah Veracruz and loggers operating from the neighboring town of Felipe Carrillo Puerto. Villagers were angered over the latter's timbering in a part of the forest thought to have been granted to the shrine center through the agrarian reform many years before. So they blocked roads and stopped trucks from removing timber thereabouts, until federal soldiers were sent to the shrine center to help the trucks get through again. They were met by village women in a tense standoff that sent tremors throughout the region, though violence was ultimately avoided and the dispute was resolved, temporarily at least. For many the incident was all too indicative of further troubles yet to come.

I do not know whether the god-king in Dzula has had much more to say by now. Beleaguered Mayas obviously hoped that he would have *something* useful to say or some positive miracles to perform. By the time I visited his small chapel a month after his appearance, a large church was already under construction a few yards away. It was completed a year later in time for the first anniversary of the god-king's coming. The day before that anniversary the stone image—only vaguely anthropomorphic, less than three feet tall, and looking very paunchy swaddled in doll's clothing—was escorted in great ceremony from the small chapel to the new church before hundreds of kneeling worshipers united in Maya prayer.

Pilgrims had been coming from as far away as Yucatan, and many had helped to build the church, in which the god-king would reside until the Final Days. The county president had even donated construction materials as his way of getting into the act. But, since its appearance a year before, interest among the villages of Xcacal Guardia had already waned, for despite their early attentiveness, the officers did not welcome the prospect of a new, rival shrine center, with its own roster of officials, complicating their already too intricate political lives. While they graciously accepted the divinity of this new being in their midst, they subtly suggested his worship was the business of the people of Dzula (and perhaps of the group of villages around Chan Cah Veracruz, to which that village "belonged"), not the affair of Mayas everywhere.

Just what role the new god-king assumes in the contemporary Maya pantheon and political hierarchy we will have to wait and see, and I do plan to return again soon to hear what new stories are being told. Meanwhile, there will be other apparitions, sacred things revealed in dreams, tours of heaven and hell by pious Mayas on deathbeds, miracles, letters from True God, and other divine communications and new prophets in the months and years to come. Of that we can be sure. That Maya lives will grow increasingly difficult seems unfortunately safe to say, as well. Political instability, national economic crisis, climatological and ecological changes affecting the kind of livelihood they may garner from the forest in which they live, all guarantee that those Mayas will continue to find ample reason to believe that the days of the world as they know it are drawing to a close. What kind of active responses the wedding of continuing divine contacts and worsening crisis will engender among Mayas is impossible to predict. It is something that I, or some of my colleagues, will return to study, I fully expect, thus continuing the anthropological work and intercultural dialogues begun by Villa, Redfield, and Morley half a century ago. As for what role we and other future "foreigners" will have to play as those Mayas negotiate the next few, seemingly perilous, decades of their history, none of us can say.

Notes

ABBREVIATIONS

Archives and Manuscript Collections

APS   American Philosophical Society Library, Philadelphia

CIW   Historical Files, Carnegie Institution of Washington, Washington, D.C.

CIW-PM Carnegie Institution of Washington Collection, Archives, Peabody Museum of Archaeology and Ethnology, Harvard University

NA   National Archives and Record Service, Washington, D.C.

PM   Archives, Peabody Museum of Archaeology and Ethnology, Harvard University

PRO   Public Records Office, London

RRP   The Robert Redfield Papers, The Joseph Regenstein Library, University of Chicago

SRA   Archivo de la Secretaría de la Reforma Agraria, Mexico City

TL   Tozzer Library, Harvard University

TU   Latin American Library, Tulane University

Frequently Cited Manuscripts of Alfonso Villa Rojas

DEg   "Diario etnográfico," 1935–36, RRP

DEl   "Diario etnológico de un viaje a Quintana Roo, 1932," RRP

DG   "Quintana Roo: Datos Generales," 1932, RRP

FN   "Field Notes. Quintana Roo Trip, December, 1932," CIW-PM

N   "Notes Regarding Third Trip to Quintana Roo, February, 1933," RRP

NP   "Notas preliminares," 1932, RRP

INTRODUCTION

1. See, for example, Helms and Loveland, 1976.
2. See, for example, Asad, 1973.
3. For a much-expanded critique of modern anthropology, see Wolf, 1982.
4. Conrad, 1898, 35.
5. See the "Statement on Ethics. Principles of Professional Responsibility. Adopted by the Council of the American Anthropological Association, May 1971," reprinted in various places, including Rynkiewich and Spradley, 1976, 183–86.
6. Maurice Bloch's brief mention of "long conversations" and anthropological field research got me thinking along such lines (Bloch, 1977).

I. SPEAKING WITH THE ENEMY

1. Many of the historical and prophetic texts translated from Maya and quoted in this book, such as the prophecy attributed to Florentino Cituk, derive from field interviews I conducted on the Yucatan Peninsula between 1978 and 1986.

   The prophet Florentino Cituk is a prominent figure in the oral history of contemporary Mayas of Quintana Roo. In written records his life has left scant trace, though from them a few details can be gleaned. It seems that in 1914 several of Cituk's subordinates went to make purchases in the town of Chichimila, Yucatan, and while there came to the attention of the military commander of Valladolid. The commander informed them that the governor of Yucatan had abolished slavery, and he asked them to carry a message back to "General" Cituk inviting him to come to meet the governor. Assurances were given that he and his companions would be "well treated and given gifts" (*Revista de Yucatán,* October 30, 1914, 6). Cituk never went, it seems, though officers from the shrine village of San Antonio Muyil, to the north of Chun Pom, did accept the offer and had their audience with the governor in the state capital, Merida.

   When mentioned in other published sources, Cituk is said to have received refugees from an abortive revolt in the Yucatecan city of Valladolid in 1910 (González, 1970, 27); to have ruled the entire territory as general before the time of Francisco May (Pacheco, 1962, 71); and to have been "leader of Chun Pom" (Zimmerman, 1963, 55 n.17). A chicle-marketing cooperative has apparently been named after him (Bartolomé and Barabas, 1977, 109).

   In present-day oral history of the region, Cituk is said to have come from a village named Actun or Yo'actun, and to have moved to nearby Chun Pom upon assumption of the office of Patron of the Cross (i.e., head priest, not general); his law was strong and his words and thoughts were beautiful and true. God gave him the power to interpret "night writing" ('akabčíib), though people do not contradict themselves when they say he was illiterate. There was a book, they say, a "history," in which was inscribed the future of mankind. Zimmerman and Centina de Duarte offer related versions of the miraculous appearance of a book near Chun Pom, though those stories seem to refer to a manuscript more akin to that which scholars call the Proclamation of Juan de la Cruz than to the book about which Nelson Reed was informed, in which the coming of airplanes and roads was foretold (Zimmerman, 1963, 71; Centina de Duarte, 1943; Reed, 1964, 275).

Cituk's daughter and son-in-law told me he died in the second of the two epidemics. There is some confusion in both written and oral sources concerning the identities of the pathogens at work in the epidemics, though the most likely seem as reported above — that the first was smallpox and the second influenza, a local outbreak of the great influenza pandemic of 1918 that killed millions around the world (cf. Villa, 1945, 30; Mason, 1927, xi; Périgny, 1908, 69; Reed, 1964, 251; Sapper, 1904, 627-28; Frans Blom, Field Diary of the Grey Memorial Expedition [typescript copy], July 27, 1928, TU; Cook and Borah, 1974, 2:151, 153).

2. Quoted from Bricker, 1981, 188. The revelatory experiences and the reorganization of rebel Maya military and religious authority that they reflected have been dubbed by outsiders the Cult of the Talking Crosses, and one can find ample discussions of that religious movement in books by Nelson Reed (1964) and Victoria Bricker (1981). At least some divine communications were set down on paper, and multiple versions have been recovered from state archives and published (Bricker, 1981, 185-207; Reina, 1980, 406-10), or copied from manuscripts still in Maya hands (Bricker, 1981, 185-218; Pacheco, 1960, 167-73). Such manuscripts are referred to in Western scholarly literature as "Proclamations of Juan de la Cruz." To my knowledge the revelations of Florentino Cituk were never written down.

3. Bricker, 1981, 189.

4. Ibid., 200.

5. Arnold and Frost, 1909, 162; Sánchez and Toscano, 1919, 229; Case, 1911, 212. Authorities and merchants in British Honduras recorded some information about military and political developments in the territory, as did some members of the Mexican and Yucatecan expeditions against the rebel Maya.

6. Stephens, 1843, 2:335, 331.

7. Ibid., 2:468. Later advances in correlating the Maya and Christian calendar and in deciphering hieroglyphic dates reduced estimates of Chichen Itza's antiquity by as much as several centuries.

8. Dimensions from Morley, 1925, 71.

9. Stephens, 1843, 2:292.

10. Ibid., 2:280-89.

11. Charnay, 1862, 347; Maler, 1944, 33.

12. Charnay, 1862, 348; Augustus Le Plongeon, letter of January 27, 1876, published in Salisbury, 1877; Maler, 1944.

13. Charnay, 1862, 339.

14. Thompson, 1932, 176. In the late nineteenth century travel from northern points of departure to the ruins of Coba was particularly risky. Charnay was planning to visit Coba in 1886 when Indian attacks against a frontier town spawned fears of a new rebel offensive, drawing off troops he needed to escort his subsequently canceled expedition (Charnay, [1887] 1978, 24). On his way back from a visit to Coba (ca. 1890s), E. H. Thompson fell victim to a trailside booby trap that nearly cost him his leg and even his life (Thompson, 1932, 175-78). When Teobert Maler visited Coba in 1891, accompanied by a dozen

well-armed men, he observed no signs of the rebel Mayas but nonetheless reasoned that the proximity of rebel Maya settlements made more than a couple of days' work there too dangerous. He declined to explore two distant pyramids visible from the lagoon of Coba, as travel to them entailed risk of a rebel attack from the rear that would cut off his route of return to Yucatan (Maler, 1944, 10–11). Finally, the American linguist Alfred Tozzer decided against overland travel from Chichen Itza to Coba and Tulum in 1903: "To reach that place [Tulum] is out of the question and even to go as far as Coba is rather doubtful policy. The sublevado [rebel] Indians are up in arms again and there is no knowing when and where they will turn up" (Alfred Tozzer, Field Diaries, January 19, 1903, TL).

15. Among such fictions I am inclined to count the tale told by Augustus Le Plongeon, who lived at and investigated the ruins of Chichen Itza in the 1870s. He claimed to have been visited there one day by a rebel Maya patrol whose members took him to be, at Le Plongeon's instigation, a disenchanted flesh-and-blood being akin to those whose carved images were so plentiful at that sacred and mysterious place (Desmond and Messenger, 1988, 39–40). That rebel Mayas might mistake him for an ancient forebear come to life amidst those ruins is possible, but too difficult to accept is Le Plongeon's claim that these alleged rebels went unarmed — except for their machetes — while on patrol in disputed territory, and that their belief in his extraordinary nature occasioned only a falling to the knees, a kissing of the hand, and a bit of curious banter before the patrol moved on to continue its mission. Either Le Plongeon fabricated the incident to spice up his book on the Mayas, or he mistook a group of local Mayas for the rebels he rightly feared.

Edward H. Thompson and/or those writing about him fashioned such fictions, as well. So we can read that, tired of waiting for a long-expected rebel attack on his hacienda at Chichen Itza, he traveled south to meet the enemy on their own ground, only to find the rebels, as he is reputed to have said, "a peaceful, friendly lot of ignorant Indians," who wished to make him chief of their tribe (Willard, 1926, 17–18). Nowhere in his own publications did Thompson mention any such encounter with rebel Mayas. By his own account, in 1894 he at one point had "a large warparty of these ferocious Indians" hot on his trail after an exploratory trip to Chichankanab Lagoon, on the periphery of rebel territory. He eluded capture by riding hard, and once out of danger he "left a large pile of *tortillas* near our camp for them to eat when they came up later, for one must be polite and pleasant under all circumstances" (Thompson, 1932, 136).

16. Sapper, 1904, 632. Sapper speculated that "this reputation and the slight commercial relations of the independent Mayas are probably the principal reasons why scientific travelers so seldom visit these regions." French Count Maurice de Périgny, when exploring Quintana Roo in late 1906 under the sponsorship of the French Ministry of Public Education and the Société de Géographie, found pacified Mayas similarly obliging enough to provide guides and porters for his archeological research in the southernmost reaches of the territory (Périgny, 1908). For travel further north, however, he accompanied Mexican soldiers and proceeded from one military outpost to the next until reaching the town of Santa Cruz, which by then had been under Mexican

military occupation for several years (Lemoine, 1906, 485). Finally the archeologist Raymond Merwin of the Peabody Museum Expedition of 1912 thought better of extending his investigations much north of Bacalar because of the threat believed posed by the still-hostile Mayas around Santa Cruz (Raymond Merwin, "The Ruins of the Southern Part of the Peninsula of Yucatan, with Special Reference to Their Place in the Maya Area" [unpublished ms., ca. 1913, TL], 6–7).

17. Miller, 1889, 23, 27.
18. Ibid., 26.
19. See, for example, Morley, 1917a, 191; Morley, Brainerd, and Sharer, 1983, 357–61.
20. Stephens, 1843, 2:405–406, 408.
21. Lothrop, 1924, 3; Le Plongeon, 1886, 65–66.
22. Lapointe, 1983, 94, 98, 135, 146.
23. Holmes, 1895, 75.
24. See Le Plongeon, 1886, 65–66; Thompson, 1888, 249; Howe, 1911, 539–40.
25. Howe, 1911, 548.
26. Ibid., 549–50.
27. Lothrop, 1924, 41; Morley, Brainerd, and Sharer, 1983, 595, 601; Gann, 1924, 106–107.
28. Sylvanus Morley quoted in Hewett, 1936, 161–62.
29. *Santa Fe New Mexican,* July 24, 1913, 3.
30. Morley, 1917a, 192–94; 1917b, 338. Morley failed to find stela #1, having read about it in Stephens's well-known book but unaware that Howe and Parmelee had buried it after their frustrated attempt to remove it.
31. *Santa Fe New Mexican,* July 24, 1913, 3.
32. Morley, 1917a, 202; see also, Morley 1917b, 338–39. The Peabody Museum Expedition of 1913–14, consisting of Raymond Merwin and C. W. Bishop, was apparently prevented from visiting Tulum by Mexican authorities in Santa Cruz de Bravo, though the expedition did explore other, more remote, sites along the Caribbean coast of Quintana Roo from Cancun to Ascension Bay (Morley, 1917a, 192; Jens Yde, "Architectural Remains Along the Coast of Quintana Roo; a Report of the Peabody Museum Expedition, 1913–1914, compiled from the field notes of Raymond E. Merwin" [unpublished ms., 1941], TL).
33. Catherwood, 1844, 23, re: plate 23, "Castle, At Tuloom"; Howe, 1911, 549; Mason, 1927, 89; Gann, 1924, 106, 133. Later explorations generated still more such fictions. In 1918 Sylvanus Morley, John Held, Thomas Gann, and others explored Tulum and other sites along the Caribbean coast of the Yucatan Peninsula. At one point Morley and Held traveled inland to the all-but-abandoned town of Santa Cruz. Gann wrote a short but vivid account of their arrival in Santa Cruz, describing how he and the others "hunted up the single Indian family" there. "None of them could understand a word of any language but Maya. Our wants, however, were easily indicated — food, plenty of it, and right away" (Gann, 1924, 34). Gann may well have been thinking about food at that time, but he was doing it miles from Santa Cruz, which, Morley indicated in his diaries, Gann did not then enter (Sylvanus Morley, Diaries, February 10, 1918, in Lister and Lister, 1970, 72).

34. Prince William, 1922, 105–107.
35. Lothrop, 1924, 174, 24.
36. Mason, 1927, 211–12.
37. Mason, 1927, 195–96, 293; Villa, 1945, 154. Another version of this story can be found in Bartolomé and Barabas, 1977, 61–63. The story seems to allude to the fate of early sixteenth-century Spanish castaways Gerónimo de Aguilar and Gonzalo de Guerrero, among the as-yet-unconquered Mayas along the east coast of Yucatan. Both were enslaved by Maya lords, while Guerrero, Spanish chroniclers reported, eventually married a Maya "princess" and became a renowned captain in Maya wars. Aguilar, on the other hand, was retrieved by the expedition led by Hernán Cortés, then on his way to begin the conquest of Mexico. Aguilar subsequently played a critical role in the conquest as one of Cortés's interpreters.
38. Mason, 1927, 214; Adrian, 1924, 236. I have consulted an unpublished English translation of Adrian's article, one prepared by N. C. Leites in January 1937, RRP, 49/12.
39. Compare photos facing p. 108 of Prince William, 1922 and that of Canul on p. 114 of Gann, 1928.
40. Gann, 1928, 114–15. When he visited Gann at the Tulum ruins, Canul brought "a cotton handkerchief, wrapped up carefully in a clean cloth, which he evidently regarded as his most cherished possession, and produced with great pride. Upon it was printed, in crude colours, a picture of King George and Queen Mary. It had been purchased in Corozal, and brought in as a gift by one of his men." Canul wanted Gann to photograph him and his wife standing side by side holding the cloth in front of them, Canul gripping the side of King George, his wife gripping that of Queen Mary. However, Canul's wife would have none of that, so the photo that was taken shows Gann standing in her place (Gann, 1928, 115–16).
41. Alfred Kidder wrote that in his lectures Morley often referred to Mayas as "the Greeks of the New World," a comparison inspired by the elegance of their sculpture, painting, and architecture (Kidder, 1959, 782; Morley, 1913, 63).
42. Adrian, 1924, 235, 237.
43. Sylvanus Morley, Diaries, February 12, 13, 15, 20, and 21, 1922, APS; Adrian, 1924, 236. Thanks to the good offices of those chicle contractors, the German geographer-botanist H. Adrian received local Mayas' permission and assistance to cross out of the boundaries of the concession to explore the overland route from Boca Paila, through Chun Pom, Chun On, Yokdzonot to Chichimila and Valladolid between August 30 and September 15, 1922. He traveled in the company of Mayas from Chun Pom, notably including Juan Bautista Vega.
44. Morley, 1913, 63, 65. The principal source for biographical information regarding Sylvanus Morley is Brunhouse, 1971. Many would now bestow upon the ruins of Tikal in Guatemala the honor of "greatest" center of the ancient Maya world.
45. Regarding the state of knowledge about the ancient Maya in the years about which I write: Morley, 1915 and Morley, 1913.
46. Brunhouse, 1971, 3–13; Morley, 1913, 64.

II. RECONNAISSANCE UNDER COVER

1. Morley took Santa Cruz to be a colonial-era town of Spanish construction, though he was aware of the wartime Cult of the Talking Crosses that was once centered there (Sylvanus Morley, Diaries, February 9 and 10, 1918, in Lister and Lister, 1970, 68–73).

2. Moisés Saenz, quoted in the entry for March 23, 1932, of Alfonso Villa's "Diario etnológico de un viaje a Quintana Roo, 1932," RRP 48/4. (Hereafter cited as Villa, DEl.)

3. Ávila, 1974, 33–52.

4. Villa, DEl, March 24, 1932; Alfonso Villa, "Quintana Roo. Datos generales," p. 7, RRP 48/4. (Hereafter cited as Villa, DG.) In this unpublished manuscript Villa provides a brief summary of the findings of his 1932 reconnaissance. According to oral history in contemporary Quintana Roo, former rebels from Santa Cruz, led by one Tomás Pat, had settled near Kanxoc in a village called Xocen.

5. Ávila, 1974, 76; and from the recollection of people whom I interviewed in that region.

6. Some contemporary Maya prayers include repetitions of deity names and supplications directed not only in the traditional four directions of Maya cosmology, but also to the multiple shrine centers of rebel Maya sacred geography. While in everyday ritual practice and discourse Xcacal Guardia is a shrine center or sacred town (*santo kah*), it is never mentioned in such prayers, which instead invoke the holy places of Santo Cah Noh Cah Santa Cruz Balam Nah, Santo Cah Chun Pom, Santo Cah Chan Cah Veracruz, Santo Cah Tulum Cah, Santo Cah Xocen Cah (in Yucatan), and Santo Cah San Antonio (in Yucatan, also). Native exegesis of the omission of Xcacal Guardia asserts it is represented by mention of Noh Cah Santa Cruz Balam Nah, to which the most holy crosses of Xcacal Guardia will one day properly return.

7. Shattuck, 1933, 179.

8. Frans Blom, Field Diary of the Grey Memorial Expedition (typescript copy), July 29 and 30, 1928, TU.

9. Ricketson and Kidder, 1930, 200. Kidder wrote that the mound appeared 30 miles due east of the mapped position of "Lake Chichan Hanab" (i.e., Chichankanab Lagoon). The most detailed and accurate maps for that region today place the village of Xcacal Guardia 32 miles due east of the lake, and there are prominent pre-Hispanic ruins in several locations thereabouts (Secretaría de Programación y Presupuesto, Carta Topográfica 1:250,000, Felipe Carrillo Puerto E16-1).

10. Redfield to Villa, November 23, 1931, and Villa to Redfield, December 15, 1931, and March 1, 1932, RRP 50/2 and 3. Villages visited in late March and early April included Xpichil, Xiatil, Dzula, Yo'actun, Sahcabchen, Chanchen, San Ignacio (Mixtequilla), Komchen, Chunbalche, Yokdzonot, Yaxche, Xhazil, San Pedro, Kopchen, Petcacab, Pom, Chunhuas, Tzucun, Chunkulche, Señor, Tuzik, another Yokdzonot, and another Yaxche. Other settlements visited included Santa Cruz as well as Yucatecan-settled communities between rebel territory and the state of Yucatan.

11. Villa, DEl, March 16, 1932.
12. Ibid., April 2, 1932.
13. Ibid., March 18, 1932.
14. Ibid., March 29, 1932.
15. Sapper, 1904, 629. Most chicle from Quintana Roo found its way to North American manufacturers via re-export from British Honduras (Hoar, 1924, 7).
16. See Ibid., 1924, 5.
17. Villa, 1939, 235.
18. Villa, DEl, March 24, 1932.
19. Ibid., April 1, 1932.
20. Ibid., April 2, 1932; Alfonso Villa, "Notas preliminares," p. 1, RRP 49/2. (Hereafter cited as Villa, NP.) These are the first few pages of the Spanish original of Alfonso Villa, "Field Notes. Alfonso Villa. Quintana Roo Trip, December, 1932. Preliminary Notes," CIW-PM. (Hereafter cited as Villa, FN.)
21. Villa, NP, 2; Redfield, 1941.
22. Villa to Redfield, April 10 and 22, 1932, RRP 50/3; Villa, NP, pp. 1–3 and December 14, 1932; Redfield to Villa, September 4, 1932, RRP 50/3.
23. Villa, FN, December 13, 1932.
24. Ibid., December 10–12, 1932; Villa to Redfield, "Lista de Gastos," RRP 50/3.
25. Ibid., December 18 and 14, 1932.
26. Ibid., December 31, 1932.
27. Villa, NP, pp. 4–5.
28. Villa, FN, December 17 and 30, 1932.
29. Ibid., December 31, 1932.
30. Ibid., December 12, 1932 and January 3, 1933.
31. Ibid., December 19, 1932.
32. Alfonso Villa, "Notes Regarding Third Trip to Quintana Roo, February, 1933," pp. 2–3, RRP 49/3. (Hereafter cited as Villa, N.)
33. Villa, FN, December 14, 1932.
34. Ibid., December 21 and 31, 1932.
35. Ibid., December 17, 1932.
36. Ibid., January 6, 1933; Villa, NP, p. 5.

III. ILLUSIONS OF ALLIANCE

1. This may, in fact, have been what foreigners told Mayas, for note what Robert Redfield wrote by way of introduction to his article "The Maya and Modern Civilization": "The name 'Maya' is so generally associated with ancient ruins and the mystery of a departed people that, before setting forth certain research plans of the Carnegie Institution of Washington, it should perhaps be stated that the Mayas are not extinct" (1933, 16).
2. See Villa, 1945, 96, and Burns, 1977, 267–68. Some Mayas at that time apparently also called Americans čakpo'ol, "red heads" (Adrian, 1924, 247).
3. Villa, DEl, March 14 and 15, 1932; Escalona, 1940; Larsen, 1964.
4. In a mid-nineteenth-century letter to the Governor of Yucatan, rebel Mayas made reference to their divine patron's having descended into the world at

"Chichen," presumably Chichen Itza (Bricker, 1981, 215). A similar letter is said to have stated that the rebels aimed to "put themselves in agreement with a ruler who was to be found in the ruins of Chichen" (Baqueiro, 1879, 391). The only manuscripts of the Chilam Balam genre so far located in central Quintana Roo make mention neither of the Itzas nor of Chichen Itza. Regarding the Chilam Balam of Tuzik, Villa observed, "Today, the text of this manuscript has no esoteric or political significance for the natives of X-cacal. Its present possessor, the Secretary Yum 'Pol' [Apolinario Itza], could tell me only that it is a 'very old paper written by God' " (1945, 73). Finally, regarding the archway at the hacienda of Chichen Itza, see Thompson, 1932, 249-50.

5. See, for example, Villa, 1945, 55.
6. Morley to Redfield, February 6, 1935, RRP 22/11.
7. Villa, 1945, 96, 164.
8. Ibid., 161.
9. Ibid., 96. The figures referred to are those of the so-called "diving god," which adorn Structure 16 and which scholars have interpreted as representations of the Venus deity and/or bee god (Morley, Brainerd, and Sharer, 1983, 359). Concerning the čak winkob, see Maya tales published in Redfield and Villa, 1934, 331, and Villa, 1945, 154.
10. Officers to Morley, November 18, 1934, CIW–PM. Unless otherwise indicated, when these letters are cited I refer to the original versions—i.e., the officers' handwritten Maya or Morley's handwritten English.

    The letters exchanged between Sylvanus Morley and Maya officers of Xcacal Guardia are contained in a file entitled "Correspondence between S. G. Morley and Various Maya Indian Chiefs from Xcacal to [sic] the Territory of Quintana Roo, Mexico, and Various Associated Villages, from November 1934 to June 2, 1936." Included in that file are English (sometimes Spanish) translations of the Maya letters. For reasons made clear in this book it was necessary to retranslate the letters, and unless otherwise indicated the fragments quoted are my translations from the Maya. I initially worked with Xerox copies of the original Maya letters and of the carbon copies of Morley's letters to the Maya officers made available to me by Dr. Grant Jones, to whom I am indebted.
11. Alfonso Villa, Census, CIW–PM. This is an English-language compilation of the household censuses conducted by Villa in the villages around Xcacal Guardia during September 1935.
12. Villa, 1945, 48-49; Alfonso Villa, Census, CIW–PM.
13. Alfonso Villa, "Diario etnográfico," February 12, 1936, RRP 49/6-7. This is the field diary of Villa's 1935-36 research based in the village of Tuzik, Quintana Roo. (Hereafter cited as Villa, DEg.) In the same collection is an English translation of the entire diary. That translation is sometimes faulty, and unless otherwise indicated quotations are from my retranslation of the Spanish original. Villa, DG, p. 6; Villa, FN, December 30, 1932; Frans Blom, Field Diary of the Grey Memorial Expedition, July 29, 1928, TU.
14. Villa, 1945, 48-49, 161.
15. Morley's translations were prepared by Pedro Castillo of Dzitas, Yucatan, Edilberto Ceme of Chan Kom, Yucatan, and on at least one occasion, by Morley's godson, Isidro Criollo (Morley to Officers, March 22, 1929 [sic, i.e.,

1939], CIW–PM). Pedro Castillo, who grew up in Pencuyut, a town in western Yucatan, was a former Catholic seminarian and a schoolmaster fluent in Yucatec Maya, Spanish, and English (Larsen, 1964, 22; Willard, 1941, 39, 103). Evidently Castillo did his translations hurriedly, taking no more time to render Morley's English into Maya, Morley once observed, "than it had taken me to write it in English" (Sylvanus Morley, Diaries, March 14, 1935, CIW–PM). As for Ceme, he was fluent in Yucatec Maya and most likely Spanish as well, but was probably much less literate than Castillo (Villa, 1945, vii; Redfield and Villa, 1934, 17). More than an occasional translator for Morley, Ceme was Villa's guide and assistant during travels in Quintana Roo, and Villa felt he "contributed substantially in mitigating the difficulties encountered in my travels through the forest" (1945, vii).

16. In 1928 Maya general Francisco May arrived at agreements with the head of federal military operations in the territory and the Governor of Quintana Roo, which among other things expressly forbade the flying of flags other than that of the Mexican Republic. It was, the accords stipulated, the only thing that the federal and territorial governments would "punish severely" as an act of treason (Ávila, 1974, 115). One officer from Xcacal Guardia, Pantaleón May, attended those meetings with Governor Siurob (González, 1977, 76–77). Contemporary officers of Xcacal Guardia say that General May once received a British flag from Englishmen at Corozal in British Honduras, though, based upon his conversations with the Governor of British Honduras in 1918, Morley had understood that it was General May's *brother* who the year before headed a delegation that went seeking the British flag and a British protectorate over Santa Cruz (Sylvanus Morley [Merida, Yucatan] to 'Taro,' March 31 and April 29, 1918, Box 1101, Entry 98 [Intelligence Division, Naval Attaché Reports, 1886–1939), Record Group 38 [General Records of the Chief of Naval Operations], NA). When Mexicans heard of this, the Maya version of the story goes, they enticed the general to take a trip to Mexico City, where he was feted and from which he returned to raise the Mexican flag over Santa Cruz. The anecdote suggests that the officers' request for a flag back in the 1930s was in part, at least, a gesture against General May himself. Some Mayas of central Quintana Roo did get hold of British flags and flew them in their localities anyway (Pacheco, 1947, 145–46). And in 1957 a group of Mayas from the Santa Cruz region traveled to Belize to see the visiting Princess Margaret, "reiterating to her their unbreakable loyalty, since she was 'the sister of Her Majesty' " (Villa, 1962, 227).

17. Officers to Morley, May 3, 1935, CIW–PM; see also Villa, 1945, 49.

18. Bricker, 1981, 192n.

19. Ibid., 191–92.

20. Baqueiro, 1879, 389; Villa, 1945, 161.

21. Morley's English translation of Officers to Morley, November 18, 1934, CIW–PM.

22. Morley to Redfield, February 6, 1935, RRP 22/11; typed version of Maya translation of Morley to Officers, November 21, 1934, CIW–PM.

23. Morley to Kidder quoted in Redfield to Villa, November 28, 1934, RRP 50/5.

24. Officers to Morley, February 9, 1935, CIW–PM.

25. Morley's English translation of Officers to Morley, February 9, 1935, CIW–PM.
26. Morley to Redfield, February 6 and 19, 1935, RRP 22/11.
27. Ibid., February 19, 1935, RRP 22/11.
28. Letters exchanged between Morley and the Maya officers include: Cituk et al. to Morley, November 18, 1934; Morley to Cituk et al., November 21, 1934; Cituk et al. to Morley, February 9, 1935; Barrera et al. to Morley May 3 to 9, 1935 (four parts, one part is missing); Cituk et al. to Morley, June 13, 1935; Morley to Cituk, July 2, 1935; Huuh to Morley, September 20, 1935 (two parts); Zuluub to Morley, September 20, 1935 (seven parts); Morley to Cituk et al., October 11 and 23, 1935; Barrera et al. to Morley, November 25, 1935 (three parts); Morley to Barrera et al., December 6, 1935; Barrera and Zuluub to Morley, June 2, 1936; Barrera et al. to Morley, June 5, 1936; Itza to Morley, August 15, 1936; Morley to Officers, January 28, 1938; Morley to Cituk et al., March 22, 1929 (surely 1939). The texts of the extant letters suggest that the set is complete for the years 1934 to 1936, except for one missing part to the correspondence of May 3 to 9, 1935. The Peabody Museum file includes envelopes of the Maya officers' correspondence, an English translation of part of the Chilam Balam of Tuzik, and a letter from Pedro Castillo to Morley, as well.
29. Officers to Morley, May 3, 1935, CIW–PM.
30. Morley's Spanish translation of Officers to Morley, May 3, 1935, CIW–PM.
31. Redfield to Morley, February 14, 1935, RRP 22/11.
32. Villa, FN, December 15, 1932; Villa, 1945, 44; Villa, DEl, April 2, 1932.
33. Villa, DEg, September 1 and 3, 1935.
34. Villa to Redfield, September 6–10, 1935, RRP 50/6; Villa, DEg, September 5, 1935.
35. Villa, DEg, September 3, 6, and 9, 1935; Villa to Redfield, September 6, 1935, RRP 50/6.
36. Villa, DEg, September 5, 1935.
37. Villa, DEg, September 10, 1935; Villa to Redfield, September 6–10, 1935, RRP 50/6.
38. Typed version of the Maya translation of Morley to Cituk, July 2, 1935. This letter is one of three I found in Quintana Roo among the remains of the personal archive of the late scribe Apolinario Itza. I have not located an English original or any copies of the Maya version among the papers of Morley's estate now deposited in various locations in the United States. Only the first page of an obviously multi-page letter was found in Quintana Roo. And it is possible that the date I read as July 2 was actually to be read July 20.
39. Villa to Redfield, September 6–10, 1935, RRP 50/6.
40. Villa, FN, December 22, 1932.
41. Villa to Redfield, September 6–10, 1935, RRP 50/6; Villa, DEg, September 6, 1935.
42. Villa, DEg, September 10, 1935.
43. Ibid.; Villa to Redfield, September 6–10, 1935, RRP 50/6.
44. Villa, DEg, September 10, 1935.
45. Ibid., September 11, 1935.
46. Ibid., October 7, 1935; Morley to Redfield, October 13, 1935, and Redfield to Villa, October 5, 1935, RRP 22/11 and 50/6.

47. Villa to Redfield, September 6–10, 1935; Redfield to Villa, October 5, 1935, and Morley to Redfield, October 13, 1935, RRP 50/6 and 22/11; see also Morley to Merriam, October 13, 1935, CIW.

IV. ZULUUB'S PLEA

1. Villa, DEl, March 18, 1932.
2. For Zuluub's reported version of events, see Larsen, 1964, 38–39. Several other published sources touch at least briefly upon the burning of Dzula, including Villa, 1945, 33; González, 1977, 80–81; and Pacheco 1934, 17, 78–79.
3. Zuluub to Morley, September 20, 1935, CIW-PM. All of Zuluub's words quoted in this chapter have been drawn from this letter; the translations are my own.
4. Villa, Census, CIW-PM; Villa, 1945, 48.
5. Villa, 1945, 66, 68. See also Sapper, 1904, 629; Hoar, 1924, 5; Gann, 1918, 18. One large foreign concern, the Compañía Colonizadora, could during the first decade of this century work only fifteen square miles of its four-thousand-square-mile government concession, owing to the actions of "hostile Indians" (Arnold and Frost, 1909, 158–59).
6. Villa, 1945, 62.
7. Concerning General May and the chicle business, see, for example, Villa, 1945, 31–32; Reed, 1964, 251–54; Basauri, 1930, 21.
8. Ávila, 1974, 53–54.
9. Villa, 1945, 32.
10. Huuh to Villa, September 20, 1935, CIW-PM.
11. Concerning the destruction of cornfields and food stores during the war, see Ancona, 1889, 4:139, 197, 243, 258, 273–74. The plunder of Maya farms was, according to Ancona, a major obstacle to British-mediated negotiations between rebel Maya and the government of Yucatan during November 1849 (1889, 4:273). As for the situation in 1909, see Arnold and Frost, 1909, 159.
12. Villa, DEg, September 10, 1935. See also Morley to Merriam, December 9, 1935, CIW.
13. Villa to Redfield, December 12, 1935, RRP 50/6.

V. ROYAL TREATMENT

1. Morley to Officers, October 11 and 23, 1935, CIW-PM; Morley to Merriam, December 9, 1935, CIW.
2. Villa, 1945, 23, 72; Villa, DEg, November 5, 1935.
3. Officers to Morley, November 25, 1935, CIW-PM.
4. Villa, DEg, December 5, 1935; Morley to Merriam, December 9, 1935, CIW.
5. Morley to Merriam, December 9, 1935, CIW; Villa, DEg, November 6 and December 5, 1935.
6. Villa, DEg, December 5, 1935; Morley to Merriam, December 9, 1935, CIW.
7. Villa, DEg, December 5, 1935.
8. Palacios, 1935; Morley, 1927, 233; as well as the annual reports of the Chichen Itza project published in the yearbook of the Carnegie Institution from 1924 on.

9. See, for example, Morley, 1913, 79–80.
10. Kidder, 1930, 99; Norman, 1843, 109.
11. Kidder, 1930, 99.
12. Regarding tales of a Maya king and creatures of past epochs, there are many published references and versions. Concerning the ancient race, see Burns, 1983, 74–78; Villa, 1945, 153–54; Redfield and Villa, 1934, 331, 336. Concerning beings underground, sometimes called the Itza, see Maler, 1944, 8; Villa, 1945, 153; Redfield and Villa, 1934, 331; Bartolomé and Barabas, 1977, 61–63; Gann, 1926, 93. A Caste War proclamation directed by rebel leaders to Maya villagers apparently made reference to a "governor at the ruins of Chichen" who would help them in their struggle (Baqueiro, 1879, 391). On feathered serpents there, see Redfield and Villa, 1934, 335. At least two versions of the king tales relate his coming to the appearance of benevolent foreigners, variously identified as "red men," "those who can read the ancient writings (i.e., hieroglyphics)," "tall people with eyes like the eyes of bees" (Villa, 1945, 154; Redfield and Villa, 1934, 331–32). Some versions report that the king lives at Coba, rather than Chichen Itza (Villa, 1945, 153; Maler, 1944, 8; Redfield, 1933, 23).
13. Villa, DEg, December 6, 1935.
14. Ibid.; Villa, 1945, vi; Morley to Officers, December 6, 1935, CIW-PM; see also Brunhouse, 1971, 262–64.
15. Villa, DEg, December 6, 1935.
16. Morley to Merriam, December 9, 1935, CIW; Villa, DEg, December 6, 1935.
17. Villa, DEg, September 26, and December 8, 1935; Brunhouse, 1971, 264.
18. Morley to Officers, December 6, 1935, CIW-PM.
19. I assume that the initial part of the compound is *homa'an,* which refers to open roads (Barrera, 1980, 230). Morley's translator may have intended to render the English word "peace" with the Maya word *hunolal,* "peace," though Maya officers would have used the Spanish word *paz.* In the original English version of Morley's letter the word "peace" occurs several times and is variously rendered into Maya by *homanolal, tibil be* ("virtuosity," "uprightness"), and *yacunahil* ("love," "brotherly love," etc.).
20. Morley to Merriam, December 9, 1935, CIW.
21. Villa, DEg, January 25, 1936. Villa did not want to leave Tuzik for as many days as it would have taken to travel to Payo Obispo, see General Melgar, and return. So instead he asked Morley to telegraph the general on his behalf (Villa to Redfield, February 2, 1936, RRP 50/7). Morley did so, asking Melgar for "his cooperation in carrying out the Institution's program of scientific research in Quintana Roo, explaining the nature thereof." In response, Melgar sent a telegram to authorities in Santa Cruz instructing them to lend all assistance to the research efforts of Alfonso Villa. He sent a copy of that message, along with "a very cordial telegram," back to Morley at Chichen Itza. Morley in turn telegraphed thanks to Melgar "for his generous and public-spirited cooperation" (Morley to Merriam, February 21, 1936, CIW). Concerning federal soldiers engaged in road building in the region, see Villa, DEg, January 28 and April 12, 1936.
22. Villa, DEg, January 29 and February 10, 1936.
23. To construct the following description of Morley's visit to Xcacal Guardia

I have drawn upon accounts left by Morley, Larsen, and Villa: Morley to Merriam, March 12, 1936, RRP 22/11; Larsen, 1964; Villa, DEg, February 29 to March 5, 1936; Villa, 1945, 125–31. Unfortunately, the three do not agree upon just when certain events occurred during the festival. Villa's account seems the most accurate in that regard — it was, after all, his job to make accurate observations and take good notes, and he was able to write up his recollections a few days sooner than the others, who had to walk all the way back to Chichen Itza. I have followed him most closely, though at points his version of the timing of events does not make sense (i.e., regarding when Morley presented his gifts to the head priest), in which case I have relied on Morley and Larsen. These two accounts are clearly not independent of one another, and I suspect that Larsen's diary entries were influenced by her having typed up Morley's letter to Merriam in which his own recollections were set down. Thus my reconstruction is a composite — corresponding precisely to none of the three available versions — and I cite a particular source here only in the instance of direct quotation.

24. Larsen, 1964, 10.
25. "Informe reglamentario que rinde el C. Delegado del Departamento Agrario en el Territorio de Q. Roo . . . ," no date (though figures are given for a census taken May 5, 1937), File 23:25699 (Tihosuco), SRA; Larsen, 1964, 13.
26. Larsen, 1964, 14–15.
27. Villa, 1945, 43; Villa to Redfield, September 6–10, 1935, RRP 50/6.
28. Villa, 1945, 126.
29. Larsen, 1964, 20.
30. Or so, at least, he appeared to Helga Larsen (1964, 30).
31. Morley to Merriam, March 12, 1936, RRP 22/11.
32. Villa, 1945, 127.
33. Villa, DEg, March 1, 1936; Villa, 1945, 127.
34. Villa, 1945, 123; Larsen, 1964, 31; Morley to Merriam, March 12, 1936, RRP 22/11.
35. That, at least, is what I expect they would have done based upon the many *matan* ceremonies I have witnessed, though Villa and Morley had been left far behind in the procession and did not get a good view of what was occurring in the church.
36. Larsen, 1964, 30.
37. Morley to Merriam, March 12, 1936, RRP 22/11; Larsen, 1964, 32; Villa, DEg, March 2, 1936.
38. Villa, 1945, 131.
39. Larsen, 1964, 36.
40. Morley to Merriam, March 12, 1936, RRP 22/11.
41. Villa, 1945, 131.
42. Larsen, 1964, 32–33, 39–40.
43. Morley to Merriam, March 12, 1936, RRP 22/11.
44. Oral accounts of the preparation and delivery of the *juramento* crosses did not specify the precise date of that event. Nor have I been able to discover whatever happened to the crosses. The story may well be apocryphal.
45. Villa, DEg, April 3, 1936; Villa to Redfield, April 3, 1936, RRP 50/7.
46. Villa, DEg, January 19 and April 25, 1936; Villa to Redfield, April 20, 1936, RRP 50/7.
47. Officers to Morley, June 5, 1936, CIW-PM.

VI. MENACE AND COURTSHIP

1. William Stevenson (Superintendent of British Honduras) to Percy M. Doyle (H.B.M. Minister Plenipotentiary, Mexico), October 7, 1856, 50/362, Foreign Office Section, PRO. I am indebted to Dr. Victoria Bricker, who made available to me her copies of this and other Foreign Office documents cited in this book.

2. Rogers, 1885, 226. The Superintendent of British Honduras, at least, understood how limited were their options. "The Indians have no recognized right to the territory they inhabit. We might easily drive them from the ruins of Bacalar; we might, though the march through the forest would cost us some lives, take Sta. Cruz, indeed any of their posts. But what next? We should only be suppressing a Mexican rebellion, and thus making ourselves responsible to a certain extent for the use which the miserable Yucatecans [sic] authorities would make of power so unexpectedly restored to them. But in the meantime the Indians upwards of 20,000 of whom are reported to be in arms, whose troops march along 30 miles a day in the narrow bush tracks, would be intangible but ubiquitous on the [River] Hondo. Each mahogany raft would have to be fortified, and even the crews of armed vessels would be picked off by unseen marksmen lurking among the mangrove roots over which no civilized soldier could hope to overtake the Indian in his flight. The political and natural difficulties of an Indian war in our frontier appear to me to be of such magnitude that nothing on my part shall be wanting to prevent its occurrence. But savages are not to be soothed by softness, and the best way of preserving the peace of the settlement [i.e., British Honduras] is to show that we hold even it of secondary importance to the maintenance of our rights" (Frederick Seymour to Governor Darling, May 17, 1858, 39/5, Foreign Office Section, PRO).

3. Gann, 1928, 128. Gann went on: "The most we could ultimately get from Canul was, 'Well, if you are brave enough to take the consequences of visiting the church yourselves, I have no "orders" to stop you.' As he said this, there was a nasty cold glint in his eye, and I thought his glance wandered towards the four loaded Winchesters, stacked handily near the door" (1928, 128–29).

4. Typed version of the Maya translation of Morley to Officers, November 21, 1934, CIW–PM.

5. Villa, 1945, 96.

6. Officers to Morley, June 13, 1935, CIW–PM.

7. Ibid., May 3, 1935, CIW–PM.

8. Villa, 1945, 96.

9. Maya translations of Morley to Officers, July 2, October 11 and 23, and December 6, 1935, CIW–PM.

10. Officers to Morley, June 2, 1936, CIW–PM.

11. Ibid., August 15, 1936, CIW–PM.

12. Yucatec Maya has lexical means for more precise reference to kinds of love, including elaborated constructions which in appropriate contexts can denote filial love, servile love, divine love and mercy, lust, narcissism, greed, mutual love, and more. But translators little availed themselves of such resources.

13. Paraphrased from Andrade, 1971, text 6, "El Hombre del Pene Chico," collected ca. 1930.

14. Burke, 1969, 208.
15. Gumperz, 1972, 16; see also, Gumperz, 1982.
16. Burke, 1969, 115.
17. Redfield and Villa, 1934, 97.
18. Andrade, 1977, texts 14, 18, 80; Barrera, 1965; Brasseur de Bourbourg, 1872, 120–21; Edmonson, 1982; Edmonson and Bricker, 1985, 52.
19. On one other occasion Villa was startled to see his long-time Maya friend and assistant kiss his wife goodbye. "Since in my view it was something completely new, I took advantage of the first opportunity to interrogate Edilberto about the reason for this new form of expressing his affection, he responding to me . . . 'Well, as those of us in Chan Kom have already seen the ways of civilized men, we have already begun to kiss our wives and our children. We did not do this before because we were very backward. But today, I do it, the Tamay's, Don "Eus" and I believe even Adolfo' " (Villa to Redfield, September 6–10, 1935, RRP 50/6).
20. Redfield and Villa, 1934, 97.
21. Andrade, 1977, texts 15 n.3 and 18 n.1 and n.4.
22. Burns, 1973, 67–68.
23. One recent study, Holmes, 1978, is a major advance into the realm of these neglected topics. See also Elmendorf, 1972.
24. Baqueiro, 1879, 147.
25. Ibid., 442. The Indian commander's letter is found among the documents of the Yucatan Collection on Microfilm in the University of Alabama Libraries, film Yuc. 1, reel 3 (Bingham, 1972). Only the Spanish translation of José María Tzuc's letter was found there, so I rely on other letters in Yucatec Maya from that period to establish that the Spanish word *amar* reflected an original Yucatec *yakunah,* "love."
26. Baqueiro, 1879, 396, 400.
27. The last page of the letter, which would have had the final words of the closing and the signature of José María Tzuc, appears not to have been microfilmed. I have completed the closing, with the interpolation "my heart" based upon seemingly identical phrases earlier in this text and in other Maya letters.
28. Baqueiro, 1879, 160. In 1849 defenders of Bacalar had accepted a similar offer of surrender and safely left the war zone (Baqueiro, 1879, 149–51).
29. Ibid., 439.
30. Burke, 1969, 110–14.
31. Baqueiro, 1879, 168.
32. Frederick Seymour to Governor Darling, March 13, 1858, 39/5, Foreign Office Section, PRO.
33. On one occasion Villa chided Morley for having given a Maya visitor 24 pesos, noting that "the Indians were going to get accustomed to receiving, for no reason, such sums, later refusing gifts of little value." Villa then told Morley that this one time he would reimburse the expense Morley had incurred in furtherance of Villa's research, but "from now on it was better to flatter such Indians with less costly gifts and [ones] of immediate utility, like sandals, knives, medicines, etc." (Villa to Redfield, October 26, 1935, RRP 50/6).
34. Shattuck, 1933, 175.

35. Villa, 1945, 34; Basauri, 1930, 20. Some reports claimed they also preyed upon the well-provisioned camps of chicle gatherers in order to "augment their incomes," or slew the crew of vessels stranded on their coast the better to "take possession of the ship and its contents" (Villa, 1945, 32; Basauri, 1930, 20; Le Plongeon, 1886, 62–64).
36. Villa, FN, December 30, 1932.
37. Ibid., December 14, 1932.
38. Villa, DEg, January 31 and February 1, 1936.
39. Ibid., January 18, 1936; Villa to Redfield, April 10 and 20, 1936, RRP 50/7. Villa actually wrote "infinite patience and tactics [*táctica*]," but I presume he meant "tact" [*tacto*].
40. Villa was seldom equipped to provide his patients anything more than quinine, aspirin, purgatives, laxatives, boric acid, solutions of permanganate and salicylate, and Argyrol, an antiseptic. He felt that, given the unhygienic conditions of village life, his doctoring was well-nigh in vain (Villa, DEg, especially during 1936; Villa to Redfield, April 20, 1936, RRP 50/7). For the quote regarding his motives for continuing such doctoring, see Villa, DEg, February 13, 1936.
41. Villa to Redfield, March 26, 1936, RRP 50/7.
42. Mason, 1927, 294. Some offered Mayas money to bring them artifacts recovered from such ruins. See, for example, Sylvanus Morley, Diaries, February 15, 1922, APS.
43. Officers to Morley, September 20, 1935, and August 15, 1936, CIW–PM.
44. See, for example, Dumond, 1977.
45. Villa to Redfield, January 18, 1936, RRP 50/7; Villa, DEg, January 15, 1936.
46. Villa, DEg, September 25, 1935, and January 17, 1936.
47. Villa, 1945, vii.
48. Villa, FN, December 17, 1932. The parenthetical interpolation, "to be courted," is Villa's.

VII. BETRAYAL AND RECONCILIATION

1. Villa to Redfield, August 11, 1936, and May 3, 1937, and Morley to Villa, May 1, 1937, RRP 50/7 and 8, and 22/11. Long before, Redfield had alerted Villa to possible difficulties with Mexican authorities over photographing Indians. Customs officials, he said, sometimes considered ethnological photographs "denigrating" and would not permit their removal from the country. Redfield suggested that Villa give the negatives of pictures taken during the 1932 trip to Quintana Roo to friends who could smuggle them out of the country (Redfield to Villa, n.d. but apparently in May 1932, RRP 50/3).
2. Brunhouse, 1971, 115.
3. See, for example, Katz, 1981 and Tuchman, 1958.
4. Orders establishing intelligence operations under William R. Rosenkranz (formerly of the Office of Indian Affairs of the U.S. Department of the Interior) as Naval Vice Consul at Veracruz directed: "The Mexican coast requires a close watch on the oil supply and basing facilities for submarines. A particular watch, including water patrol and inspection, must be had from the point of Campeche to the Chinchorro Bank, including all outlying cays on the Campeche Bank, to guard against the establishment (without our knowledge)

of submarine bases and caches. Close touch with the trend of public opinion and general operations originating from the principal ports, is necessary. Close touch with the patrol forces basing at Key West and with the United States and Allied ships is necessary, when this can be accomplished. The coast line of Mexico from the Rio Grande to British Honduras has been designated as Area No. 1. This area has been divided into twelve districts, with district stations at the following points: Tampico, Tuxpan, Vera Cruz (Chief), Champoton, Campeche, Celestun, Progreso, and Port Morelos [on the coast of Quintana Roo]. Vera Cruz has been designated as the central station for the entire area" (Orders to [Agent] No. 143, July 2, 1917, File 20944-531, Entry 78A [Office of Naval Intelligence Confidential Correspondence, 1913-24], Record Group 38 [General Records of the Chief of Naval Operations], NA). For rumors of German U-boat activity along the coast of the Yucatan Peninsula, see Memorandum, August 3, 1918; M. Churchill (Colonel, General Staff of the Chief of the Military Intelligence Branch, Executive Division) to Roger Wells (Director of Naval Intelligence), n.d.; Report No. 20961, July 20, 1918; and H. Scougall to (?), April 17, 1917; all included in File 20961-583 ("German Sub-bases on Mexican Coast. General"), Box 22, Entry 78A (Office of Naval Intelligence Confidential Correspondence 1913-24), Record Group 38 (General Records of the Chief of Naval Operations), NA.

5. Brunhouse, 1971, 143.

6. Morley had previously reported: "The Santa Cruz [Indians] number between five and ten thousand souls. The head chief is General Francisco Mai [i.e. May] who lives at Chunpup, 25 miles northwest of Vigia Chico. . . . There are two secondary chieftains one at San Antonio Muyil west of Acumal . . . and the other at Chan Santa Cruz north of Bacalar. . . . These Indians have little love for the Mexicans as I have shown — only having left off killing them less than three years ago — but are on the contrary friendly with the people of British Honduras. They go to the colony frequently for trading purposes and indeed summer before last (1917) General Mai sent a delegation to Belize headed by his own brother to ask the Governor of the colony to take the Santa Cruz and their country under the protection of the British flag and to attach it to the British Empire!" (Sylvanus Morley [Merida, Yucatan] to 'Taro,' March 31, 1918, Box 1101, Entry 98 [Intelligence Division, Naval Attaché Reports 1886-1939], Record Group 38 [General Records of the Chief of Naval Operations], NA). In the above quotation I have omitted only the numbers keying place names to a map that accompanied the report.

7. Sylvanus Morley (Merida, Yucatan) to 'Taro,' April 29, 1918, Box 1101, Entry 98 (Intelligence Division, Naval Attaché Reports 1886-1939), Record Group 38 (General Records of the Chief of Naval Operations), NA; Tulchin, 1971, 15-16; Katz, 1981, 515.

8. Aide for Information to Commander of Naval Forces in the Canal Zone and Commandant, Fifteenth Naval District, Balboa, C.Z. to Commandant, Fifteenth Naval District, memo re: "Agents for Area 2," March 14, 1918, File 2115-3 (also quoted in Dorwart, 1979); Henneberger (Aide for Information of the Office of Commander of Naval Forces, Balboa, C.Z.) to Charles Sheldon (c/o Office of Naval Intelligence, Washington, D.C.), June 25, 1918, File 2115-3; L. R. Sargent (Commander of Naval Forces in the Canal Zone) to

Director of Naval Intelligence, "Area No. 2 — Report from Dec. 1, 1917 to March 31, 1918," April 1, 1918, File 2115-7; Sylvanus Morley (San Salvador, El Salvador) to Mr. Wilbur, February 1, 1919, File 2115-7; each of the above from Box 85, Entry 78A (Office of Naval Intelligence Confidential Correspondence 1913-24), Record Group 38 (General Records of the Chief of Naval Operations), NA.

The naval aide quoted in the text continued: "In the case of [Agent] #238 [who was attempting to pass as a mining engineer] questioning brought out the fact that he was in no sense of the word a mining man, nor could he possibly pass for one in Central and South America. . . . Moreover, a mining man can only be used in a mining country, which limits his availability to, in our case, the Western portion of Central America."

9. Franz Boas, "Why German-Americans Blame America" (1916), in Stocking, 1974, 331-35; see also the several essays accompanying Stocking, 1968.

10. Boas quoted in Stocking, 1968, 148.

11. Boas, "Scientists as Spies" (1919), in Stocking, 1974, 336-37.

12. American Anthropological Association, 1920, 93-94. Besides Morley, those who voted to censure Boas and who worked for military intelligence included Herbert J. Spinden and Samuel Lothrop, spies like Morley, and W. G. Farabee and M. H. Saville, who had served as captains in military intelligence (AAA 1919:104; *Who's Who in America* vol. 16, 1930-31, p. 1945.) Stocking's in-depth essay on the episode is persuasive in suggesting that those voting for censure of Boas did so in part for reasons unrelated to the issues of espionage and patriotism (Stocking, 1968, 270-307).

As for Morley, his labors on behalf of U.S. Naval Intelligence continued for at least a short time after the conclusion of hostilities in Europe. In January 1919, Morley, then in El Salvador, was ordered to end his work and return to Washington. He sought permission from his superiors to stay in Central America, offering to "continue to make reports to them [i.e., Naval Intelligence] until I return to the United States, whenever that would be, just as though I were still on active service . . . the only real difference being that I would be drawing my salary and expenses from the Carnegie Institution instead of from our friends in Washington" (Sylvanus Morley [San Salvador, El Salvador] to Mr. Wilbur, February 1, 1919, File 2115-7, Box 85, Entry 78A [Office of Naval Intelligence Confidential Correspondence 1913-24], Record Group 38 [General Records of the Chief of Naval Operations], NA.) However, Morley was apparently soon discharged from Naval Intelligence, in March, 1919 (Brunhouse, 1971, 113).

13. Adams, 1967, 20; American Anthropological Association, 1967. For further reflections upon anthropological research and espionage, see Beals, 1969.

14. War Diary, U.S.S. *Salem,* August 1-6, 1918, WE-5 — Mexico: Conditions in Mexico, Misc. 1913-17, Subject File 1911-27, Record Group 45 (Naval Records Collection of the Office of Naval Records and Library), NA; Dorwart, 1983, 108; D. J. Kendall (U.S. Special Service Squadron, Peninsula of Yucatan), Intelligence Report Ser. No. 15-1939, June 2, 1939, Box 1101, Entry 98 (Intelligence Division, Naval Attaché Reports, 1886-1939), Record Group 38 (General Records of the Chief of Naval Operations), NA.

15. Kidder, 1930, 98-99.

16. Villa to Redfield, April 20, 1936, and Villa to Morley, May 11 and June 4, 1936, RRP 50/7.
17. Villa to Morley, June 4, 1936, RRP 50/7.
18. Menéndez, 1978, 68–76; Villa, 1945, 34. Application of the agrarian reform in Quintana Roo had begun about the same time as the exchange of visits and letters between Morley and the officers of Xcacal Guardia. In 1929 and again in 1935 villages near the shrine centers of Chun Pom and Chan Cah received their grants, for example (File 23:19058 [Felipe Carrillo Puerto], SRA). Several officers later associated with Xcacal Guardia had attended a similar meeting held in 1929 with the Governor of Quintana Roo, General Siurob. This was before the Xcacal Guardia officers' final break with General May (González, 1977, 76–77).
19. File 23:19058 (Felipe Carrillo Puerto), SRA.
20. Menéndez, 1978, 76. Others also were of the opinion that the economic development of the territory would depend upon its colonization by outsiders, those remnants of the rebel Maya population then occupying the forests being too few (approximately 0.15 people per square mile in central Quintana Roo in 1915, for example [Cook and Borah, 1974, vol. 2:151, 153]) and too recalcitrant to support a development program. Regarding the latter point: "At first glance it seems that the Mayas should be used, trying to civilize them; but upon knowing them, one understands how useless would be such effort: the Maya is more savage than the wild beast, in his ancestral soul has taken root a hatred for the Mexican, whom they [Mayas] kill without mercy. Furthermore, the Maya is degenerate, having no pleasure other than drunkenness" (Sánchez and Toscano 1919, 230). Concerning the subsequent colonization of Quintana Roo, see Bartolomé and Barabas, 1977, 50–54. The 1980 census of the state indicates that 37 percent of the population of central Quintana Roo (the *municipios* of Felipe Carrillo Puerto and José María Morelos) consists of people who were born in other states (Mexico, 1982, 1:51).
21. Villa, DEg, September 16, 1935.
22. Officers to Morley, November 25, 1935, CIW–PM.
23. Villa, DEg, February 13, 1936. Elsewhere Villa noted that to the Most Holy One "they attribute great and incredible powers, being the greatest, that of destroying airplanes and rendering harmless all weapons and means of attack that the *huaches* [Mexican soldiers] may try to use to invade the Sanctuary or dominate its devotees" (Villa, DG, pp. 6–7).
24. Letter of August 22, 1935, File 23:23219 (Xmaben), SRA; Villa, 1945, 44, 95. One resident of San Jose who signed that early petition for federal action became, many years later, a general of the Xcacal Guardia group.
25. Villa, DEg, April 26, 1936.
26. Villa to Redfield, May 26, 1936, RRP 50/7; Villa, DEg, May 17, 1936.
27. Villa, 1979, 53.
28. Villa, DEg, May 24, 1936; Villa to Redfield, May 26, 1936, RRP 50/7. In September 1935 Maya officers indicated they considered as Maya territory everything from the Caribbean coast to a semicircular perimeter connecting Puerto Morelos, Acambalan, Tepich, Dzonotchel, Chichankanab Lagoon, Yokchen, and Payo Obispo (Villa, DEg, September 30, 1935).

29. Villa to Redfield, May 26, 1936, and Villa to Morley, June 4, 1936, RRP 50/7; Villa, DEg, May 26, June 12 and 16, 1936.
30. Villa to Melgar, May 25, 1936, RRP 49/4.
31. Melgar to Villa, June 24, 1936, and Villa to Redfield, July 4, 1936, RRP 50/7; Villa, DEg, July 16, 1936; Villa to Redfield, July 16, 1936, RRP 50/7.
32. Villa, DEg, April 1, 3, and 5, 1936.
33. Ibid., July 4 to 7, 1936.
34. Ibid., July 8, 1936.
35. Villa to Redfield, July 16, 1936, RRP 50/7.
36. Ibid., August 13, 1936, RRP 50/7.
37. Ibid., August 13 and 6, 1936, RRP 50/7.
38. Maya original and English translation of Officers to Morley, August 15, 1936, CIW-PM.
39. Villa to Redfield, August 11, 1936, RRP 50/7.
40. Ibid., August 11, 1936, RRP 50/7.
41. Ibid., September 9, 1936, RRP 50/7; Villa, DEg, August 23, 1936.
42. Villa to Redfield, September 9, 1936, RRP 50/7.
43. Chaac et al. to Melgar, August 23, 1936, File 23:23219 (Xmaben), SRA.
44. Villa to Redfield, October 3, 1936, RRP 50/7.
45. Villa to Melgar, December 4, 1936, RRP 50/7; Dictamen del Departamento Agrario, Comisión Agraria Mixta, November 27, 1936, and Acta Relativa a la Posesión Provicional del Ejido de Xmaben . . . , December 14, 1936, File 23:23219 (Xmaben), SRA; Villa to Redfield, January 31, 1937, RRP 50/8.
46. Villa to Redfield, May 3, 1937, and Morley to Villa, May 1, 1937, RRP 50/8 and 22/11.
47. Villa, letter to the author, July 7, 1987.
48. Document of the Departamento Agrario, Chetumal, Quintana Roo, September 17, 1937, and Acta Relativa a la Elección del Comisariado Ejidal y Consejo de Vigilancia en el Ejido de Xmaben, December 13, 1936, File 23:23219 (Xmaben), SRA; Villa, letter to the author, July 7, 1987; Villa, 1979, 54.
49. Villa to Redfield, June 28, 1937, RRP 50/8.
50. *Diario de Yucatán*, August 19, 1937 (clipping found with Villa to Redfield, August 23, 1937, RRP 50/8).
51. Morley to Redfield, March 20, 1939, and Villa to Redfield, April 3, 1939, RRP 22/11 and 37/10.
52. Kidder 1940, 261.
53. Dame, 1968, 115, 126–27. Morley did not return to central Quintana Roo; but the Protestant missionary did — the way having been first shown to him by one of the same Mayas who had taken that route to visit Morley in the mid-1930s. As for Morley, he had at least one more encounter with people from the villages around Xcacal Guardia, this time a group from Señor that sought him out at his new residence near Merida in February 1941, bringing complaints about chicle contractors and appeals for relief. Morley advised them to go to the office in Merida of the Governor of Quintana Roo (Sylvanus Morley, Diaries, February 16, 1941, APS).
54. Villa, 1945, vi–vii, 96.
55. Redfield, 1941, 53, 57.

56. Villa to Redfield, December 4 and May 26, 1936, RRP 50/7. Morley's biographer was the first to go beyond what little Villa himself had written regarding his and Morley's complex relations with the officers of Xcacal Guardia (Brunhouse, 1971, 261–69).
57. Hayden White's *Tropics of Discourse: Essays in Cultural Criticism* (1978) has prompted me to examine Villa's and Redfield's respective interpretations of history, while Marcus and Fischer (1986), Clifford and Marcus (1986), and Clifford (1988) have encouraged application of White's insights beyond texts predominantly historical, into the genre of ethnography.
58. Villa, 1945, 20–35.
59. Ibid., 34.
60. Redfield, 1947, 295–301.
61. Ibid., 1950, 178.

VIII. RUMORS OF WAR

1. General Melgar's last-minute orders notwithstanding, Xcacal Guardia (and Tuzik) remained cut out of the *ejido* of Xmaben created in 1937 and finally surveyed, marked, and charted in the late 1950s (Document, December 3, 1957, File 23:23219 [Xmaben], SRA).
2. Redfield and Villa, 1934, 331; Ceme, 1934, 222; Redfield, 1933, 16; Joseph, 1982, 117, 222–23.
3. Sapper, 1904, 628. See also Miller, 1889, 26; Lapointe, 1983, 134.
4. Miller, 1889, 26; Reed, 1964, 239–40; Villa, 1945, 28–29.
5. Villa, 1945, 42; Villa, 1977, 888–90.
6. See, for example, Andrade, 1977, 1009b, text 87.
7. *Revista de Mérida,* April 4, 1875, 2–3.
8. Ibid., 2.
9. Alfred Tozzer, "Modern Maya texts with Spanish translation and grammatical notes, collected near Valladolid, Yucatan," 1901, PM, pp. 149, 151, 165.
10. *Revista de Mérida,* April 1, 1875, 2.
11. *Revista de Mérida,* November 11, 1881, 3.
12. Trentini, 1906, preface, 10.
13. Louis Ayme (U.S. Consul, Merida, Yucatan) to W. Hunter (Second Assistant Secretary of State, Washington, D.C.), "Report: Yucatan; Its productions, climate, monuments, people, customs & commerce," March 10, 1882, Record Group 59 T29 (U.S. Department of State, Despatches from United States Consuls in Merida, 1843–1906), NA (Microfilm, Yale University Library). See also E. H. Thompson (U.S. Consul, Merida, Yucatan) to George Rives (Assistant Secretary of State, Washington, D.C.), February 15, 1888, same record group as above.
14. E. H. Thompson to the Assistant Secretary of State, Washington, D.C., June 1, 1901, Record Group 59 T29 (U.S. Department of State, Despatches from United States Consuls in Merida, 1843–1906), NA (microfilm, Yale University Library).
15. *Revista de Mérida,* September 19, 1900, 2; Turner, 1911, 147. Yet another source says it was locally believed to have cost one life per rail tie, with some 500 to 600 rail ties required for each kilometer of track (Escalona, 1940, 220, 222).
16. Escalona, 1940, 223; Sylvanus Morley, Diaries, February 11, 1918, in Lister

and Lister, 1970, 74–75. Rail lines in the south and north were constructed connecting inland points of agricultural and logging operations with coastal docks (Reed 1964, 244 ff.). For example, a fifty-mile rail line in southern Quintana Roo extended from the Rio Hondo inland and was used to remove felled timber to a riverine logging camp owned by the Mengel Company, the largest manufacturer of wooden shipping boxes in the United States, with affiliated logging subsidiaries in North America, Africa, and Central America (Sánchez and Toscano, 1919, 206, 209; Périgny, 1908, 68). The narrow-gauge line was most likely constructed by British loggers.

17. Villa, FN, December 22, 1932.
18. Villa noted that Mayas of Xcacal Guardia at first opposed the construction of a highway that would cut through that cluster of villages in the early 1960s. However, "when they discovered that they could earn 40 pesos a day as laborers [in road construction], their attitudes changed" (1977, 889).
19. The passage is present in the version of the Xcacal Guardia manuscript copied and translated by Alfonso Villa Rojas in the mid-1930s (Villa, 1945, 164). It is absent in Victoria Bricker's transcription and translation of that manuscript as it was when photographed at Xcacal Guardia in the 1970s (Bricker, 1981, 207). It was likely excised during the process of renewing the manuscript by copying, since Bricker noted the pagination of the Xcacal Guardia manuscript published by Villa differed from that published by Machlin and Marx (Ibid., 338, n.38).
20. Villa, 1945, 77.
21. Zimmerman reported having been told that the divinity ceased to speak back in 1885 (1963, 58 n.28).
22. Apparently some years back the head priest of the shrine center of Chan Cah Veracruz was implicated in the theft and pawning of jewelry that belonged to the divinities of that locale. Much of it, Zimmerman reported, was gold (Zimmerman, 1965, 155 n.38). I was told the priest, Norberto Yeh, went mad and killed himself.
23. Burns, 1983, 85.

IX. MEMORIES AND MONEY

1. Burns, 1983, 80.
2. Villa, 1945, 94; Burns, 1983, 79. Allan Burns, the linguist who interviewed Yama, noted that "the narrator complains that Sylvanus Morley did not seem to understand the requests of the Maya and put them off with polite greetings when they wanted to talk about arms and assistance with the continuing struggle." Yama apparently blamed Cituk for this failure of communication:

HELLO, DR. SYLVANUS MORLEY,
> *we came to talk to you in person here*
> *at "Chhe'en Kuha" [Chichen Itza]*
> *so you can give us some* ADVICE, *some* SATISFACTION.
> *We've already talked with you,* MISTER, *with satisfaction.*
> *You've been asking us,* "WHAT HAPPENED TO US?
> *What has been done to us?"*

WE'RE SO POOR, MISTER, *SO* INNOCENT, *SO* CLOSED.
We don't know what to say.
That important Captain Cituk
that spoke to you
doesn't have any BRAINS.
He doesn't have any UNDERSTANDING.
He just talked even though people told him what he
should have said.

3. Villa, 1945, 74, plate 6c.
4. I did visit the commander San Cen, whose wife is a daughter of the late prophet Florentino Cituk. Though he related tales of Enoch's travels in the region, he was otherwise every bit as taciturn as FC said he would be.
5. Reed, 1964, 275.
6. Ibid., 277–80.
7. Machlin and Marx, 1971, 24.
8. Ibid., 25.
9. Ibid.
10. Ibid., 27.
11. Ibid.
12. Ibid., 27–28.
13. Ibid., 28.
14. Burke, 1969, 6.
15. Villa, FN, December 29, 1932.
16. His photo and those of various contemporaries have become ubiquitous in the literature of Maya studies and in the more popular writings of travelers. Poot's can be found in Morley (1938, 1946, and in subsequent books by Morley, including Spanish-language editions of his classic work, *The Ancient Maya*), Bartolomé and Barabas (1977), Reed (1964, 1971), and adorning the dust jacket of Jones (1977). I even once saw an enlargement of his portrait serving as a poster decoration in a tourist shop in Merida, Yucatan. When Villa visited Poot in 1977, Poot told him no photos, please, so tired was he of having visitors come to take his picture only to leave again immediately (Villa, 1977, 896). Poot is usually identified where his photos appear, but it is really his classic Maya profile and the earring he once wore that make his photo so popular for reproduction. Other Maya officers have been similarly immortalized— Evaristo Zuluub, Concepción Cituk, Apolinario Itza, and Paulino Yama (whose photograph adorns the dust jacket of Burns 1983)—among other prominent Maya individuals.
17. Reed, 1971.
18. Zimmerman has made note of what she called the "avid materialism" of the Mayas she knew in the early 1960s. She wrote of the decline of religious fervor in Chun Pom and Xcacal Guardia: "It is secularism, the materialistic desire to possess money and goods—stealing sacred jewelry, offering to sell religious or any other secrets for money, and other things of this sort—which has filled the void left by the breakdown of the Cult" (1965, 156 n.39).

X. UNFINISHED CONVERSATIONS

1. Villa noted that in the villages around Xcacal Guardia in the 1930s there were only two practicing shamans, who it seemed knew their trade much less thoroughly than did their counterparts in Yucatan (Villa, 1945, 74–75). The word for shaman in Yucatec Maya is *hmen*. The terms San uses to describe himself are *'ahk̀iin bobat* or *'ahk̀iin čomak*.

2. Villa reported hearing a story that attributed the death of a fifty-three-year-old woman in Tuzik (who died of a vaginal infection, he says) to her mother's having cursed her twenty years earlier (1945, 135–36).

3. On gophers and Yucatec Maya shamanism see Rätsch and Probst, 1985.

4. Also at Harvard University one finds an unsigned and untitled manuscript that is an English translation of the Chilam Balam of Tuzik, the work of Morley's translator, Pedro Castillo. A second set of photographic prints from the negatives at the Peabody Museum are with the Ralph Roys Papers, University of Washington Archives (Ventur, 1978, 40), and portions of the Chilam Balam of Tuzik have been published and translated (Barrera and Rendón, 1948; Stross, 1983; Sullivan, 1983, Appendix A).

   A reporter for a major Mexican newspaper went to Quintana Roo looking for the book in the early 1970s, having read about it in Villa's ethnography. He was directed to speak to Paulino Yama of Señor; "unfortunately," wrote the journalist, "the possessor of the manuscript, Mr. Pol Itza, died some time ago and according to Pablo Yaama [sic], nobody knows where the document is" (Alejandro Ortiz Reza, "En busca del documento 'Chilam Balam de Tuzik,'" *Excélsior*, October 16, 1971, 4).

5. Sullivan, 1983, Appendix A.

6. See, for example, Villa, 1945, 74, 161.

7. Victoria Bricker asked about the "Testament" when in the shrine center of Chan Cah Veracruz. She was told they did not have their own copy but, instead, went to Xcacal Guardia to hear it read every two years (1977, 255). Bricker also reported having seen the manuscript kept at Xcacal Guardia in 1971 (1981, 338 n.38). Zimmerman reported that a manuscript, also called *santo 'almahtàan* was read annually in Chun Pom, though that text differs radically from the Xcacal Guardia version, as well as from those versions recovered during the nineteenth century in Santa Cruz (Zimmerman, 1963, 70; Pacheco, 1960, 167–73; tape recording of Juan Bautista Vega reciting the *santo 'almahtàan* from memory, recorded ca. 1960 by Charlotte Zimmerman). Burns's report that the document read aloud at assemblies in the shrine village of Xcacal Guardia is a Chilam Balam–type manuscript is surely mistaken (Burns, 1977, 261; 1980, 312).

8. Zimmerman, 1963, 70; Burns, 1973, 24; Charlotte Zimmerman, letter to the author, August 21, 1985.

9. Zimmerman, 1963, 71.

10. Inquiries about the location and precise material of the most miraculous and sacred crosses are similarly unwelcome. Some outsiders have believed the crosses to be made of gold and jewel-studded (e.g., Burns 1977, 260), while Mayas dedicated to guarding them tell of prophecies of their future theft or

sale. Meanwhile, the Tulum divinity has been moved to Xcacal Guardia because so few men still performed guard service in Tulum and, some say, because of the influx of tourists (González, 1970, 40). Regarding this Maya sensitivity to inquiries about the crosses, see also Heyden, 1967, 238–39.

11. Machlin and Marx were the ones allowed to copy the "Testament." Unfortunately, that does look like San in the photograph accompanying Machlin and Marx's article (1971:24).

12. Pacheco Cruz, 1960, 167–73, published in Spanish translation by Bartolomé and Barabas, 1977, 125–27.

References

Adams, Richard. 1967. "Ethics and the Social Anthropologist in Latin America." *American Behavioral Scientist*, 10, 10:16-21.

Adrian, H. 1924. "Einiges über die Maya-Indianer von Quintana Roo." *Zeitschrift der Gesellschaft für Erdkunde zu Berlin*, 5-7:235-47.

American Anthropological Association (AAA). 1919. "Report of the Secretary, Anthropology at the Baltimore Meeting." *American Anthropologist*, 21, 1:104-105.

American Anthropological Association (AAA). 1920. "Council Meeting, December 30, 4:45 p.m." *American Anthropologist* 22, 1:93-94.

———. 1967. "Statement on Problems of Anthropological Research and Ethics by the Fellows of the American Anthropological Association, 1967." *American Anthropologist*, 69:3/4:381-82.

Ancona, Eligio. 1889. *Historia de Yucatán desde la época más remota hasta nuestros días*, vol. 4, 2nd ed. Barcelona: Manuel Heredia Argüelles.

Andrade, Manuel. 1971. "Yucatec (Maya) Texts. Recorded by Manuel Andrade (1931-33), transcribed and translated by Refugio Vermont-Sales (1963-71)." Microfilm Collection of Manuscripts in Cultural Anthropology, Series 19. Chicago: University of Chicago Library.

———. [1931] 1977. "Yucatec Maya Stories." Microfilm Collection of Manuscripts in Cultural Anthropology, Series 49. Chicago: University of Chicago Library.

Arnold, Channing, and Frost, Frederic. 1909. *The American Egypt. A Record of Travel in Yucatan*. London: Doubleday, Page & Co.

Asad, Talal, ed. 1973. *Anthropology and the Colonial Encounter*. New York: Humanities Press.

Ávila Zapata, Felipe Nery. 1974. *El General May, último jefe de las tribus mayas*. Merida: Ediciones del Gobierno de Yucatán.

Baqueiro, Serapio. 1879. *Ensayo histórico sobre las revoluciones de Yucatán desde el año de 1840 hasta 1864*, vol. 2. Merida: Manuel Heredia Argüelles.

Barrera Vásquez, Alfredo, ed. 1965. *El libro de los cantares de Dzitbalché*. Mexico City: Instituto Nacional de Antropología e Historia.

————. dir. 1980. *Diccionario Maya Cordemex*. Merida: Ediciones Cordemex.

————, and Rendón, Silvia. 1948. *El libro de los libros de Chilam Balam*. Mexico City: Fondo de Cultura Económica.

Bartolomé, Miguel, and Barabas, Alicia. 1977. *La resistencia maya: relaciones interétnicas en el oriente de la península de Yucatán*. Colección Científica, Etnología, No. 53. Mexico City: Instituto Nacional de Antropología e Historia.

Basauri, Carlos. 1930. "Los indios mayas de Quintana Roo." *Quetzalcoatl (Órgano de la Sociedad de Antropología y Etnografía de México),* 1:3:20–29.

Beals, Ralph. 1969. *Politics of Social Science Research: An Inquiry into the Ethics and Responsibilities of Social Scientists*. Chicago: Aldine.

Bingham, Marie Ballew. 1972. *A Catalog of the Yucatán Collection on Microfilm in the University of Alabama Libraries*. University, Alabama: University of Alabama Press.

Bloch, Maurice. 1977. "The Past and the Present in the Present." *Man,* 12,2:278–92.

Brasseur de Bourbourg, C. E. 1872. *Dictionnaire, grammaire et chrestomathie de la langue maya précédés d'une étude sur le système graphique des indigènes du Yucatan (Mexique)*. Paris: Maisonneuve.

Bricker, Victoria. 1977. "The Caste War of Yucatán: The History of a Myth and the Myth of History." In *Anthropology and History in Yucatán*. Grant Jones, ed. Austin: University of Texas Press.

————. 1981. *The Indian Christ, the Indian King: The Historical Substrate of Maya Myth and Ritual*. Austin: University of Texas Press.

Brunhouse, Robert. 1971. *Sylvanus G. Morley and the World of the Ancient Mayas*. Norman: University of Oklahoma Press.

Burke, Kenneth. 1969. *A Rhetoric of Motives*. Berkeley: University of California Press.

Burns, Allan. 1973. "Pattern in Yucatec Mayan Narrative Performance." Ph.D. dissertation, University of Washington.

————. 1977. "The Caste War in the 1970's: Present-Day Accounts from Village Quintana Roo." In *Anthropology and History in Yucatán*. Grant Jones, ed. Austin: University of Texas Press.

————. 1980. "Interactive Features in Yucatec Mayan Narratives." *Language in Society,* 9:307–19.

————. 1983. *An Epoch of Miracles: Oral Literature of the Yucatec Maya*. Austin: University of Texas Press.

Case, Henry. 1911. *Views on and of Yucatan*. Merida.

Catherwood, Frederick. 1844. *Views of Ancient Monuments in Central America, Chiapas and Yucatan*. London: Bartlett and Welford. (Reproduction published by Barre Publishers, Barre, Massachusetts, 1965.)

Ceme, Eustaquio. 1934. "My Story Since I Was Six Years Old." In *Chan Kom. A Maya Village*. Robert Redfield and Alfonso Villa Rojas. Carnegie Institution of Washington, Publication No. 448. Washington, D.C.

Centina de Duarte, Elisa. 1943. "Yalma Than Cichcelemyum." *"Yikal Maya Than,"* 4,44:91–92. (Reprinted from a newspaper article originally appearing in the *Diario de Yucatán,* ca. January 1930.)

Charnay, Désiré. 1862. "Un Voyage au Yucatan." *Le tour du monde,* 5:337–52.

————. [1887] 1978. *Viaje a Yucatán a fines de 1886*. Merida: Fondo Editorial de

Yucatán. (Translation of Charnay's "Ma Dernière Expedition au Yucatan." *Le tour du monde*, 53:273–320.)

Clifford, James. 1988. *The Predicament of Culture. Twentieth-Century Ethnography, Literature, and Art*. Cambridge: Harvard University Press.

————, and Marcus, George. 1986. *Writing Culture. The Poetics and Politics of Ethnography*. Berkeley: University of California Press.

Conrad, Joseph. 1898. "Karain: A Memory." In *Tales of Unrest*. London: T. Fisher Unwin.

Cook, Sherburne, and Borah, Woodrow. 1974. *Essays in Population History*. Vol. 2, *Mexico and the Caribbean*. Berkeley: University of California Press.

Dame, Lawrence. 1968. *Maya Mission*. Garden City: Doubleday.

Desmond, Lawrence, and Messenger, Phyllis. 1988. *A Dream of Maya. Augustus and Alice Le Plongeon in Nineteenth-Century Yucatan*. Albuquerque: University of New Mexico Press.

Dorwart, Jeffery. 1979. *The Office of Naval Intelligence. The Birth of America's First Intelligence Agency, 1865–1918*. Annapolis: Naval Institute Press.

————. 1983. *Conflict of Duty. The U.S. Navy's Intelligence Dilemma, 1919–1945*. Annapolis: Naval Institute Press.

Dumond, Donald. 1977. "Independent Maya of the Late Nineteenth Century: Chiefdoms and Power Politics." In *Anthropology and History in Yucatán*. Grant Jones, ed. Austin: University of Texas Press.

Edmonson, Munro. 1982. "The Songs of Dzitbalche: a Literary Commentary." *Tlalocan*, 9:173–208.

————, and Bricker, Victoria. 1985. "Yucatec Mayan Literature." In *Supplement to the Handbook of Middle American Indians*. Victoria Bricker, gen. ed. Vol. 3, *Literatures*. Munro Edmonson, vol. ed. Austin: University of Texas Press.

Elmendorf, Mary. 1972. *The Mayan Woman and Change (Chan Kom)*. Cuernavaca: Centro Intercultural de Documentación.

Escalona R., Alberto. 1940. "Las vías de comunicación en Quintana Roo." *Revista Mexicana de Geografía*, 1:207–29.

Gann, Thomas. 1918. *The Maya Indians of Southern Yucatan and Northern British Honduras*. Bureau of American Ethnology Bulletin 64. Smithsonian Institution. Washington, D.C.

————. 1924. *In an Unknown Land*. London: Duckworth.

————. 1926. *Ancient Cities and Modern Tribes: Exploration and Adventure in Maya Lands*. London: Duckworth.

————. 1928. *Maya Cities. A Record of Exploration and Adventure in Middle America*. New York: Scribner.

González Aviles, José. 1970. *Stephens y el pirata Molas. Y otras narraciones y estudios*. Merida.

González Durán, Jorge. 1977. *La zona maya (Los rebeldes de Chan Santa Cruz)*. Felipe Carrillo Puerto, Quintana Roo: Edición del H. Ayuntamiento.

Gumperz, John. 1972. "Introduction." In *Directions in Sociolinguistics. The Ethnography of Communication*. John Gumperz and Dell Hymes, eds. New York: Holt, Rinehart and Winston.

————. 1982. *Discourse Strategies*. Cambridge: Cambridge University Press.

Helms, Mary, and Loveland, Franklin, eds. 1976. *Frontier Adaptations in Lower Central America*. Philadelphia: Institute for the Study of Human Issues.

Hewett, Edgar. 1936. *Ancient Life in Mexico and Central America.* New York: Bobbs-Merrill.

Heyden, Doris. 1967. "Birth of a Deity. The Talking Cross of Tulum." *Tlalocan,* 5:3:235–42.

Hoar, H. M. 1924. "Chicle and Chewing Gum. A Review of Chicle Production and Sources of Supply, and the Chewing Gum Industry and Trade." *U.S. Department of Commerce Trade Information Bulletin No. 197.* Washington, D.C.

Holmes, Barbara. 1978. "Women and Yucatec Kinship." Ph.D. dissertation, Tulane University.

Holmes, William. 1895. *Archeological Studies Among the Ancient Cities of Mexico.* Part 1, *Monuments of Yucatan.* Field Columbian Museum. Publication 8. Anthropological Series, vol. 1, no. 1. Chicago.

Howe, George. 1911. "The Ruins of Tuloom." *American Anthropologist,* 13:539–50.

Jones, Grant. ed. 1977. *Anthropology and History in Yucatán.* Austin: University of Texas Press.

Joseph, Gilbert. 1982. *Revolution from Without: Yucatan, Mexico, and the United States, 1880–1924.* Cambridge: Cambridge University Press.

Katz, Friedrich. 1981. *The Secret War in Mexico: Europe, the United States, and the Mexican Revolution.* Chicago: University of Chicago Press.

Kidder, Alfred. 1930. "Division of Historical Research. The Chichen Itza Project." *Carnegie Institution of Washington Yearbook No. 29, July 1, 1929 — June 30, 1930.* Washington, D.C.

———. 1940. "Division of Historical Research." *Carnegie Institution of Washington Yearbook No. 39, July 1, 1939 — June 30, 1940.* Washington, D.C.

———. 1959. "The Diary of Sylvanus G. Morley." *Proceedings of the American Philosophical Society,* 103:6:778–82.

Lapointe, Marie. 1983. *Los mayas rebeldes de Yucatán.* Zamora, Michoacan: El Colegio de Michoacán.

Larsen, Helga. 1964. "Trip from Chichen-Itzá to Xcacal, Q.R., Mexico." *Ethnos,* 29:5–42.

Lemoine, Frédéric. 1906. "A travers le Peten et le Yucatan, par le comte Maurice de Périgny." *La géographie,* 13:482–85.

Le Plongeon, Alice. 1886. *Here and There in Yucatan. Miscellanies.* New York: J. W. Bouton.

Lister, Robert, and Lister, Florence, eds. 1970. *In Search of Maya Glyphs. From the Archaeological Journals of Sylvanus G. Morley.* Santa Fe: Museum of New Mexico Press.

Lothrop, Samuel. 1924. *Tulum, an Archaeological Study of the East Coast of Yucatan.* Carnegie Institution of Washington, Publication No. 335. Washington, D.C.

Machlin, Milt, and Marx, Bob. 1971. "First Visit to Three Forbidden Cities." *Argosy,* 372:5:18–29.

Maler, Teobert. 1944. "Cobá y Chichén Itzá. Relación de Teobert Maler. Estudio póstumo editado por G. Kutscher." *Ensayos y estudios* (Bonn: Ibero-Amerikanisches Archiv), 6:1/2:1–40.

Marcus, George, and Fischer, Michael. 1986. *Anthropology as Cultural Critique. An Experimental Moment in the Human Sciences.* Chicago: University of Chicago Press.

Mason, Gregory. 1927. *Silver Cities of Yucatan.* New York: Putnam.

Menéndez, Gabriel, ed. [1936] 1978. *Álbum monográfico de Quintana Roo*. 2nd ed. Chetumal, Quintana Roo: Fondo de Fomento Editorial del Gobierno del Estado.

México, Secretaría de Programación y Presupuesto. 1982. *X Censo general de población y vivienda, 1980*. Vol. 23, *Estado de Quintana Roo*. Mexico City.

Miller, William. 1889. "A Journey from British Honduras to Santa Cruz, Yucatan." *Proceedings of the Royal Geographical Society of London*, 11:23–28.

Morley, Sylvanus. 1913. "Archaeological Research at the Ruins of Chichen Itza, Yucatan." In *Reports upon the Present Condition and Future Needs of the Science of Anthropology, Presented by W. H. R. Rivers, A. E. Jenks, and S. G. Morley, at the Request of the Carnegie Institution of Washington, Washington, D.C., Nov. 1, 1913*. Carnegie Institution of Washington, Publication No. 200. Washington, D.C.

————. 1915. *An Introduction to the Study of the Maya Hieroglyphs*. Bureau of American Ethnology Bulletin 57. Smithsonian Institution. Washington, D.C.

————. 1917a. "The Ruins of Tuloom, Yucatan. The Record of a Visit of the Carnegie Institution Central American Expedition, 1916, to an Important but Little Known Ancient Maya City." *American Museum Journal*, 17:3: 190–204.

————. 1917b. "Archaeology." *Carnegie Institution of Washington Yearbook No. 15, 1916*. Washington, D.C.

————. 1925. "Chichen Itzá, an Ancient American Mecca." *National Geographic Magazine*, 47:63–95.

————. 1927. "Archaeology." *Carnegie Institution of Washington Year Book No. 26, July 1, 1926 to June 30, 1927*. Washington, D.C.

————. 1938. "The Maya New Empire." In *Cooperation in Research*. Carnegie Institution of Washington, Publication No. 501. Washington, D.C.

————. 1946. *The Ancient Maya*. Stanford: Stanford University Press.

————, Brainerd, George, and Sharer, Robert. 1983. *The Ancient Maya*. 4th ed. Stanford: Stanford University Press.

Norman, B. M. 1843. *Rambles in Yucatan Including a Visit to the Remarkable Ruins of Chi-Chen, Kabah, Zayi, Uxmal, &c*. New York: J. & H. G. Langley.

Pacheco Cruz, Santiago. 1934. *Estudio etnográfico de los mayas del ex-territorio Quintana Roo; su incorporación a la vida nacional*. Merida.

————. 1947, 2nd ed. 1960. *Usos, costumbres, religión, y supersticiones de los mayas*. Merida.

————. 1962. *Antropología cultural maya; reseña histórica de la vida y costumbres de los mayas de los estados de Yucatán, Campeche, y Quintana Roo*. 2 vols. Merida.

Palacios, Enrique. 1935. *Guía arqueológica de Chichen Itza. Aspectos arquitectónicos, cronológicos y de interpretación*. Mexico City: Secretaría de Educación Pública.

Périgny, Maurice de. 1908. "Yucatan inconnu." *Journal de la Société des Américanistes*, 5:1:67–83.

Rätsch, Christian, and Heinz Jürgen Probst. 1985. " 'Le bàho': Ethnozoologie bei den Maya in Yucatán am Beispiel der Orthogeomys spp." *Indiana*, 10:237–67.

Redfield, Robert. 1933. "The Maya and Modern Civilization." In *The Culture of the Maya*. Carnegie Institution of Washington, Supplemental Publication No. 6. Washington, D.C.

————. 1941. *The Folk Culture of Yucatan*. Chicago: University of Chicago Press.

————. 1947. "The Folk Society." *American Journal of Sociology*, 52:4:293–308.

———. 1950. *A Village That Chose Progress. Chan Kom Revisited.* Chicago: University of Chicago Press.

———, and Alfonso Villa Rojas. 1934. *Chan Kom. A Maya Village.* Carnegie Institution of Washington, Publication No. 448. Washington, D.C.

Reed, Nelson. 1964. *The Caste War of Yucatan.* Stanford: Stanford University Press.

———. 1971. *La Guerra de Castas de Yucatán.* Mexico City: Editorial Era.

Reina, Leticia. 1980. *Las rebeliones campesinas en México. (1819–1906).* Mexico City: Siglo Veintiuno.

Ricketson, Jr., Oliver, and Kidder, Alfred. 1930. "An Archeological Reconnaissance by Air in Central America." *Geographical Review,* 20:2:177–206.

Rogers, E. 1885. "British Honduras: Its Resources and Development." *Journal of the Manchester Geographical Society,* 1:197–227.

Rynkiewich, Michael, and Spradley, James. 1976. *Ethics and Anthropology. Dilemmas in Fieldwork.* New York: Wiley.

Salisbury, Jr., Stephen. 1877. *The Mayas, the Sources of their History. Dr. Le Plongeon in Yucatan, his Account of Discoveries.* Worcester, MA: Charles Hamilton.

Sánchez, Pedro, and Toscano, Salvador. 1919. "Breve reseña de una exploración en Quintana Roo. 1916–1917." *Memorias y revista de la Sociedad Científica "Antonio Alzate,"* 38:5–8:199–247.

Sapper, Karl. 1904. "Independent Indian States of Yucatan." In *Mexican and Central American Antiquities, Calendar Systems and History.* Bureau of American Ethnology Bulletin 28. Smithsonian Institution. Washington, D.C.

Shattuck, George. 1933. *The Peninsula of Yucatan. Medical, Biological, Meteorological and Sociological Studies.* Carnegie Institution of Washington, Publication No. 431. Washington, D.C.

Stephens, John L. 1843. *Incidents of Travel in Yucatan.* New York: Harper & Brothers.

Stocking, Jr., George. 1968. "The Scientific Reaction Against Cultural Anthropology, 1917–1920." In *Race, Culture, and Evolution. Essays in the History of Anthropology.* New York: Free Press.

———, ed. 1974. *The Shaping of American Anthropology, 1883–1911. A Franz Boas Reader.* New York: Basic Books.

Stross, Brian. 1983. "The Language of Zuyua." *American Ethnologist,* 10:1:150–64.

Sullivan, Paul. 1983. "Contemporary Yucatec Maya Apocalyptic Prophecy: The Ethnographic and Historical Context." Ph.D. dissertation, Johns Hopkins University.

Thompson, Edward H. 1888. "Archaeological Research in Yucatan." *Proceedings of the American Antiquarian Society,* vol. 4, October 1885–April 1887. Worcester, MA.

———. 1932. *People of the Serpent. Life and Adventure among the Mayas.* Boston: Houghton Mifflin.

Trentini, Francisco, ed. 1906. *El Florecimiento de México.* Mexico City: Bouligny & Schmidt.

Tuchman, Barbara. 1958. *The Zimmermann Telegram.* New York: Macmillan.

Tulchin, Joseph. 1971. *The Aftermath of War. World War I and U.S. Policy Toward Latin America.* New York: New York University Press.

Turner, John. 1911. *Barbarous Mexico.* Chicago: Charles H. Kerr & Co.

Ventur, Pierre. 1978. *Maya Ethnohistorian: The Ralph L. Roys Papers.* Vanderbilt University Publications in Anthropology No. 22. Nashville.

Villa Rojas, Alfonso. 1939. "Notas sobre la etnografía de los mayas de Quintana Roo." *Revista Mexicana de estudios antropológicos,* 3:3:227–41.

———. 1945. *The Maya of East Central Quintana Roo.* Carnegie Institution of Washington, Publication No. 559. Washington, D.C.

———. 1962. "Notas sobre la distribución y estado actual de la población indígena de la península de Yucatán, México." *América Indígena,* 22:3:209–40.

———. 1977. "El proceso de integración nacional entre los mayas de Quintana Roo." *América Indígena,* 37:4:883–905.

———. 1979. "Fieldwork in the Mayan Region of Mexico." In *Long-Term Field Research in Social Anthropology.* George Foster, Thayer Scudder, Elizabeth Colson, and Robert Kemper, eds. New York: Academic Press.

White, Hayden. 1978. *Tropics of Discourse. Essays in Cultural Criticism.* Baltimore: Johns Hopkins University Press.

Willard, Theodore. 1926. *The City of the Sacred Well, Being a Narrative of the Discoveries and Excavations of Edward Herbert Thompson in the Ancient City of Chi-chen Itza . . .* London: W. Heinemann.

———. 1941. *Kukulcan, the Bearded Conqueror. New Mayan Discoveries.* Hollywood: Murray and Gee.

Prince William of Sweden. 1922. *Between Two Continents: Notes from a Journey in Central America, 1920.* London: Eveleigh, Nash, and Grayson.

Wolf, Eric. 1982. *Europe and the People Without History.* Berkeley: University of California Press.

Zimmerman, Charlotte. 1963. "The Cult of the Holy Cross: an Analysis of Cosmology and Catholicism in Quintana Roo." *History of Religions,* 3:1:50–71.

———. 1965. "The Hermeneutics of the Maya Cult of the Holy Cross." *Numen,* 12:2:139–59.

Index

land grants, 139–43, 145, 147–51, 160, 202,
242 n. 18; of Xmaben, 149–51, 154,
244 n. 1
languages, Maya, xix
Larsen, Helga, 91, 95, 101–3, 236 n. 23
law enforcement, by federal troops, 91, 160,
221; by Maya officers, 161–2
Le Plongeon, Augustus, 226 n. 15
Letger, David, 153
Lindbergh, Charles, 33
linguistics, xix–xx, xxvii
Lothrop, Samuel K., 21, 132, 241 n. 12
love, rhetoric of, 108, 109–12, 118–20, 127,
176
lumbering, 161, 170, 219, 221

Machlin, Milt, 192–4, 216, 248 n. 11
mahogany, 128, 170
male-female interaction, Maya, 119, 120,
127; observations by Villa, 41–2,
112–14, 120, 238 n. 19; romance,
41, 112–13, 114, 238 n. 19
Maler, Teobert, 225–6 n. 14
Margaret, Princess, 232 n. 16
Marx, Bob, 192–4, 216, 248 n. 11
masewal, 45, 47, 219, 220
Mason, Gregory, 21, 23, 31, 107
matan ceremonies, 96–7, 99
materialism, increase in, in conflict with
religious fervor, 196, 198, 246 n. 18
Maudslay, Alfred, 80
May, General Francisco, 30–1, 46, 50, 53,
64, 68–9, 131–2, 137, 139, 147, 149,
151, 170, 172, 224 n. 1, 232 n. 16, 240
n. 6, 242 n. 18
May, Pantaleón, 232 n. 16
Maya civilization: ancient, collapse of, 26–7;
languages, xix
Maya of East Central Quintana Roo, The (Villa),
153–6
Melgar, General Rafael, 87–8, 89, 90, 138–9,
141–3, 145–50, 152, 202, 235 n. 21,
244 n. 1
menacing rhetoric, 106–8
Méndez, Reymundo, 73
Mendoza, Sóstenes, 37
Merida, 3, 8, 12, 33, 40, 146–7, 168–9;
Xcacal Guardia delegation in, 148–9
Merwin, Raymond, 227 nn. 16 and 32
Mexican Exploitation Company, 57,
138

Mexican exploitation of Mayas, see
exploitation
Mexican Revolution, 68, 137, 155, 163,
170
military-religious administration, Xcacal
Guardia of past, 49, 161–2, 195, 225
n. 2
Miller, William, 12–13, 128
Ministry of Education, Mexican, 80
"mixing with the enemy," divine warnings
against, 47, 172, 174, 196
Mixtequilla (village), 229 n. 10
monetary motives, for giving information,
195–9, 212–14, 239 n. 42
Mopan Maya Indians, xviii
Morley, Frances Rhoads, 28, 56, 91, 101,
198
Morley, Henry, 184
Morley, Sylvanus, 25, 28–9, 30, 31, 46, 179,
216, 228 nn. 41 and 44, 229 n. 4; The
Ancient Maya, 246 n. 16; at Chichen
Itza, 25, 26–9, 46–7, 48–50, 53–5, 63,
76, 82, 84, 85, 105, 137, 152–3;
Chilam Balam and "Testament" copied for, 128, 205, 247 n. 4; dialogue
(written and oral) with Mayas, 29,
46–57, 58, 60–3, 64, 66–74, 76,
77–80, 85, 87–105, 108–12, 125,
127–9, 131–2, 137, 138, 140, 142,
146–7, 148, 151, 152, 154, 165, 185,
190, 198, 231 n. 10, 233 n. 28, 235
n. 19, 243 n. 53; espionage activities
of, in World War I, 132–4, 136, 240
n. 12, 241 n. 12; juramento for, 103–4,
105, 183–4, 236 n. 44; memories
of, among today's Maya, 181–5, 195;
mentioned, 155, 158, 162, 171, 178,
180, 191, 193, 211, 217, 218; at
Tulum, 16–17, 18, 22–5, 29, 107,
132, 227 nn. 30 and 33; visit to
Xcacal Guardia, 90, 91–103, 236
nn. 23 and 35; Yucatan protectorate
discussed by, 133; Zuluub's accusations
of subversion against, 131–2, 137,
146, 149; Zuluub's letter to, 66–7,
71–2, 74
Most Holy One, Our Lord Three Persons
icon, 53, 64, 67, 76, 98, 99, 103,
140, 147, 153, 242 n. 23; predicted
"sale" of, 176; see also cross at Santa
Cruz
motor vehicles, prophecies of ("running
fire"), 167, 168–9

Permissions Acknowledgments

Grateful acknowledgment is made to the following
for permission to reprint previously unpublished material:

American Philosophical Society Library and *Carnegie Institution of Washington:* Excerpts from Sylvanus G. Morley, *Diaries (1905–1947),* from manuscript collections, item number 126. Reprinted with permission from the American Philosophical Society Library, Philadelphia and Carnegie Institution of Washington, DC.

Carnegie Institution of Washington, The University of Chicago Library, and *Alfonso Villa Rojas:* Excerpts from letters, diaries, and field notes of Sylvanus G. Morley, Robert Redfield, and Alfonso Villa Rojas from the Historical Files, Carnegie Institution of Washington and The Robert Redfield Papers—Special Collections, The University of Chicago Library. Reprinted with permission.

Latin American Library: Excerpts from the Frans Blom field diary of the John Geddings Grey Memorial Expedition of 1928 from the Rare Book Collection, Latin American Library, Tulane University, New Orleans. Reprinted with permission.

Peabody Museum of Archaeology & Ethnology and *Alfonso Villa Rojas:* Excerpts from Sylvanus G. Morley, *Diaries: Guatemala Trip,* Book 1, Number 89 (1935), and excerpts from Sylvanus G. Morley, *Correspondence between S. G. Morley and various Maya Chiefs (November 1929–June 2, 1936);* excerpts from Alfonso Villa Rojas, *Fieldnotes: Quintana Roo (1932–1933);* and excerpts from Alfred Tozzer, *Maya Texts* (1901), from the Peabody Museum of Archaeology and Ethnology Archives, Harvard University, Cambridge. Reproduced with permission from the Peabody Museum.

Paul Sullivan's English translation of excerpts from the original Maya of *Book of Chilam Balam of Tusik* (copied by S. G. Morley [?]) from the Peabody Museum of Archaeology and Ethnology Archives, Harvard University, Cambridge, MA.

A Note on the Type

The text of this book was set in a digitized version of
Perpetua, a typeface designed by the British artist Eric Gill
(1882-1940) and cut by The Monotype Corporation, London,
in 1928-1930. Perpetua is a contemporary letter of original
design, without any direct historical antecedents. The shapes
of the roman letters basically derive from stonecutting. a
form of lettering in which Gill was eminent. The italic is
essentially an inclined roman. The general effect of the type
face in reading sizes is one of lightness and grace. The larger
display sizes of the type are extremely elegant and form what
is probably the most distinguished series of inscriptional
letters cut in the present century.

Printed and bound by Maple-Vail Book Mfg. Group.

Binghamton, NY

Designed by Anthea Lingeman.